Utopia and Dystopia in the Age of Trump

Utopia and Dystopia in the Age of Trump

Images from Literature and Visual Arts

Edited by Barbara Brodman
and James E. Doan

FAIRLEIGH DICKINSON UNIVERSITY PRESS
Vancouver • Madison • Teaneck • Wroxton

Published by Fairleigh Dickinson University Press
Copublished by The Rowman & Littlefield Publishing Group, Inc.
4501 Forbes Boulevard, Suite 200, Lanham, Maryland 20706
www.rowman.com

6 Tinworth Street, London SE11 5AL

Fairleigh Dickinson University Press gratefully acknowledges the support received for scholarly publishing from the Friends of FDU Press.

British Library Cataloguing in Publication Information Available

Library of Congress Cataloging-in-Publication Data Available

ISBN 978-1-68393-167-6 (cloth : alk. paper)
ISBN 978-1-68393-168-3 (electronic)

™ The paper used in this publication meets the minimum requirements of American National Standard for Information Sciences Permanence of Paper for Printed Library Materials, ANSI/NISO Z39.48-1992.

Printed in the United States of America

Contents

Introduction

Barbara Brodman and James E. Doan

Since 2013, we have engaged in the pleasurable task of editing five collections of essays in which contributors have analyzed some of the world's most enduring myths, legends, and artistic visions, focusing on how those images have been reflected in literature and visual arts. Discussions and interpretations presented in each of our volumes have been both enlightening and, not infrequently, thought-provoking. It seems only fitting that we end our series with discussions of images of utopia and dystopia in the Age of Trump. We pass on to future scholars the task of determining what changes in attitudes and institutions, myths, and legends, the discussions generated by our contributors will have on arts and letters of the future.

Utopia and Dystopia in the Age of Trump begins with Daniel M. R. Abitz's poetically evocative treatment of the theme of Utopia in Henry James' "The Great Good Place." After stating initially that the story contains "distinct homoerotic overtones." Abitz goes on to draw a relationship between queerness and spatio-relational fantasy in James's prose portrait of an all-men's space, the utopia of his dreams. As Abitz points out, the writing of utopia, for James, was his attempt to critique the "horrible times" of his present and to imagine an alternative time and space wherein queerness could flourish. The reading of utopia, for us, can be a mode of critiquing our own horrible times, recognizing their past and present contexts, and the impetus to imagine new alternative modes of relationality and sociality that do not delimit who experiences subjecthood, safety, and flourishing.

Literary works from past centuries are also invoked in Christine Jackson's "Poison in the Ear: Lessons of Literary Alt-Narratives for the Trump Era." In this chapter, Jackson examines parallel storylines in Shakespeare's *Hamlet: Prince of Denmark* and Poe's "The Fall of the House of Usher" with an eye toward gaining a perspective on the confusion in our current national narrative. The "play-within-a-play" construct, Jackson tells us, presents an embedded narrative through which backstage or past events resonate with or undercut present action onstage. When multiple eyewitnesses relate the same story, a "Rashomon" model presents a rich view of empirical experience. An unreliable, deceptive narrator demonstrates a shifting subjectivism that can confuse but also can explore depths of psychological perception. Uses of these same constructed narratives in the 2016 Trump campaign and in the first months of the Trump presidency cast a different sheen on the currency of facts. Through these examples, this study examines the power of alternative narratives to question and obliterate truth.

Jeffrey Barber's "The Search for Sustainability Transitions in Science Fiction Futures" presents an overview of science fiction literature and films that explore and expound upon the theme of sustainability from the mid-twentieth century into the Age of Trump and beyond. In this chapter we move from Mary Shelly's *Frankenstein* (1818) and H. G. Wells' *War of the Worlds* (1897) to the dizzying rise of the Internet, nanotechnology, and complexity theory in post-cyberpunk and New Space Opera; from the early sci-fi film *Forbidden Planet* (1956) to *Soylent Green* (1973), *Blade Runner* (1982), and *Total Recall* (1990), and into the plethora of dystopic science fiction blockbusters of the twenty-first century. Barber takes us on a whirlwind journey in support of his main theme of sustainability, and in the process, his chapter serves as an effective transition to the chapters that follow, in which the authors examine race, gender, and lifestyle issues while expounding upon the viability and impact of the present capitalist/corporatist model.

In "Resurrecting and Adapting *A Wrinkle in Time* in the Age of Trump," Emily A. O'Dell compares and contrasts Madeleine L'Engle's classic novel (1962) with its 2018 film adaption. She emphasizes how the film version of the story was designed to focus attention on social issues that, although very much in existence when L'Engle was writing her book, have been brought to the forefront in the Age of Trump. O'Dell addresses how the twentieth-century young adult novel contains a message that speaks to the modern social and political anxieties surrounding the Trump administration. It compares and contrasts the strategic casting, narrative, and aesthetic choices that have been made to modernize the screen adaptations of the novel, so that it adequately reflects the movement to resist totalitarian regimes in a way that speaks to the modern concerns of many Americans.

With a greater emphasis on socioeconomic issues, Daniel Adleman takes us into the psychotic world of *American Psycho*, the 2000 film adaption of Bret Easton Ellis's 1991 novel of the same name. Described as a "black comedy horror film," *American Psycho* takes us into the obtrusively sexist, racist, classist world of its serial-killer protagonist, Patrick Bateman, who perceives most of those around him as excremental "dirt" and sets out on a mission to violently expel the human "trash" from his personal erotic utopia, a sterile, hypermediatized bubble of privilege. Far from transpiring "no place" (*u-topos*), *American Psycho* narrows its gaze on the rapid gentrification of urban spaces such as Manhattan and, more broadly, the corporate homogenization of turn-of-the-millennium America. In this vein, it should come as no surprise that Bateman's mimetic mentors, his aspirational role models, are Donald Trump and Ronald Reagan.

Todd K. Platts and Kibiriti Majuto's "'Horror Movies Are Already Telling the Story' . . . of Trump's America," expands the discussion of social commentary embedded in horror film to include such "classics" as *31, A Cure for Wellness, Alien: Covenant, Belko Experiment, Get Out, Green Room, It Comes at Night, Split,* and *The Purge: Election Year.* The purpose of this chapter, according to its authors, is both to document "how many saw the rise of Donald Trump in horror films released in 2016 and 2017 and how the genre might respond to a president who seems hell-bent to stoke the flames of racial animus, hasten environmental collapse, dismantle public education, and squelch reputable news coverage." The analysis is guided by several analytic premises: cinematic production provides an illuminating social indicator of the realities of a particular era; films can often take on an anticipatory dimension, wherein they provide visions of a society that goes beyond the present moment to express a world that might be or can be; and because horror is produced to scare, shock, sicken, or otherwise unhinge audiences, the genre can potently articulate deep-rooted fears that a society cannot deal with directly.

"Beautiful and Damned: *Tech Noir*, Neoplatonism, and Existential Crises in *Blade Runner 2049*" by Sue Matheson tracks the trajectory of aesthetics (and ethics) in *Do Androids Dream of Electric Sheep? Blade Runner* and *Blade Runner 2049*. This chapter considers Villeneuve's scathing critique of a modern dystopia in which beauty, no longer a mediator among man, nature, and freedom, expresses a severe cultural psychosis. Although Philip K. Dick's *Do Androids Dream of Electric Sheep?* investigates human anxiety concerning technology as Other, Matheson proposes that Villeneuve's disturbing uses of Beauty and the Sublime and the indebtedness of his vision to Dick's and Scott's wastelands and their presentations of humans and androids as cultural objects question the wisdom of the film industry's attempts to "storm Eden." *Blade Runner 2049* failed at the box office, although its critical responses found its ruined world and repellant material culture (and attendant alienation) rendered beautifully. Perhaps Matheson asks the reader to consider a utopia without beauty in the Age of Trump.

Kate Waites returns us to several of the issues discussed in previous chapters with her "Feminism-Reboot in *Mad Max: Fury Road* and Hulu's *The Handmaid's Tale.*" She points out that, ironically, recently intensified and harshly regressive policies concerning women's/others' rights, as well as rollbacks in environmental protections of the earth and its resources during the Trump administration, have sparked a resurgence of collective feminist action. This she sees as pointing the way to a more hopeful future going forward, agreeing with those who see Donald Trump as bad for women but great for the women's movement. The striking display of feminism in the Women's March on Washington and demonstrations around the world, inclusive of environmental, minority, and immigrant rights, she states, signifies a long overdue and much-needed feminist reboot. Waites suggests that nowhere are the dire consequences of a long-standing and increasingly visible war against women and the environment more evident than in two visual texts that place a spotlight on the consequences of patriarchy's long-standing stranglehold on women and its carelessly utilitarian attitude toward the Earth: George Miller's *Mad Max: Fury Road* (2016) and Hulu's 2017 adaptation and updating of Margaret Atwood's *The Handmaid's Tale*, each of which she presents as viable antidotes to the ills of white-supremacist-capitalist patriarchy.

Raúl Rodríguez-Hernández and Claudia Schaefer's "Architectures of *Ustopia*: CDMX as Setting and Character in Mischa Rozema's Short Film *Sundays*" provides a unique perspective on the themes of utopia and dystopia in modern science fiction film. Dutch director Mischa Rozema's first film, a fourteen-minute sci-fi short funded by Kickstarter to the tune of $51,000, offers a double-edged take on cinema in the twenty-first century and on cutting-edge Internet venues for social commentary. The speculative vision of a post-apocalyptic Mexico City sets a single human life, that of the film's "hero" Ben, amid the nightmarish debris and destruction that a moment before had housed the eternal hope of a throbbing heartbeat. In his philosophical quest to recover "something inside" that has disappeared (i.e., truth, love, trust), Ben recovers memories, though his quest ends in a question rather than an affirmation. *Sundays* presents science fiction set in that ambiguous space—simultaneously a good place and no place—as the perfect society deteriorates into the unfamiliar.

Television, film, and comic books provide the inspiration for the next three chapters. As Elisabetta Di Minico points out in "*X-Men* Saga and the Dystopian 'Otherness': Race, Identity, Repression, and Inclusiveness in the Mutant World," in dystopian realities, "other" comes to be interpreted as "dangerous." Mutants, aliens, women, rebels, and those who don't fit the racial, sexual, religious or sociopolitical standards of power undermine the conservative and patriarchal idea of a static and fixed civil identity. Thus, they must be subdued or erased for the safekeeping of the dominant authority. As Di Minico points out, Donald Trump's presidency has also transformed "otherness" into an element of crisis and trauma. Yearning for civil rights, the *X-Men* universe can be interpreted as an allegory for discrimination and violence against minorities. This chapter analyzes the *X-Men* saga through the study of selected comic-book episodes, and it also includes a section on the acclaimed 2017 series *The Gifted*, which clearly reflects political issues of the Age of Trump as well.

Matthew Paproth's "Hang the DJ: *Black Mirror* in the Age of Trump" evokes the relationship between the dystopia created in the long-running (2011–2017) television series and our current cultural moment. The series explores "the potential pitfalls of our fascination with technology in a range of possible dystopian scenarios;" often prophetic of the Trump administration and Britain's crisis over the Brexit vote. As the series continued, particularly in its fourth season, *Black Mirror* unified its timeline, presenting direct evidence (which its creator, Brooker, has confirmed) that the episodes take place in the same diegetic world. Paproth proposes that this invites a more concrete reading of the world/timeline being presented, which should be read as a response to Trump and Trumpism, allowing Brooker to make a more unified, cohesive argument against it.

The next chapter, Tom Shapira's "Through the Eyes of the Wardens: *Judge Dredd* under the Shadow of Trump," examines the comic-book antihero we love to hate from a new perspective. *Judge Dredd*, released in comic-book form in 1977 and in film in 1995, is set in a twenty-second-century dystopic post-nuclear America where a dictatorial judge system rules over what is left of humanity. In that reality the last US president, a fiery anti-metropolitan populist, admits rumors of electoral manipulation and starts a series of nuclear wars that end with the death of billions and that of democracy—as the citizens accept the rule of the fascistic Justice Department. The election of Donald Trump, and escalation of global tensions that followed, Paproth tells us, provide a sharper focus on the themes of *Judge Dredd* as a whole. In the words of the titular protagonist: "Justice has a price. The price is freedom." This chapter explores how, throughout its forty years of history, *Judge Dredd* has forced its readers to grapple with ideas of liberty against order and how the election and administration of Donald Trump changed the way we read these stories today.

Utopian and dystopian visions of the modern political right are the subject of the last two chapters of this collection. In "Grab 'em by the Seeds: The Regressive Utopianism of Trumpism and Katherine Burdekin's *Swastika Night*," Ryan Farrar discusses the 1985 novel from the perspective of a Hitlerian dystopia in which "ideology, not technology, nourishes the totalitarian nightmare of fascist rule" and "lull[s] people into a discriminatory complacency where the theocracy of maleness keeps them in a psychic trance of aggression." In relation to the Trumpian era, he concludes that Burdekin's nightmare future is a regressive dystopia where fascism desiccates the seeds of female empowerment, technological advancement, and international civility. Her depiction of the unyielding but contradictory perfection of blood and kin within the Nazi empire aids in critically reacting to the Age of Trump where the superficial idealism of his nationalistic fervor is belied by unabashed cronyism, racism, and the pursuit of emoluments.

David L. McNaron's "Diverse New Worlds" focuses on two twentieth-century dystopian novels, Albert Camus' *The Plague* and Jean Raspail's *The Camp of the Saints*. Though both works deal with "plague" in a general sense, they develop different views of the causes, effects, and reactions to the pestilence. McNaron suggests that the two novels speak to our current political predicament, presaging "a mostly cold cultural and political war that shows no signs of abatement or peaceful resolution;" as in Paproth's chapter, a conflict that came to the fore with Brexit and the election of Donald Trump. Juxtaposing *The Plague* with Raspail's *The Camp of the Saints*—as novels that examine human responses to collective threats—enables McNaron to raise these questions: To whom should one extend solidarity, humanity at large or members of one's own tribe, and at what cost? Are there limits to altruism? Is altruism subject to Aristotle's theory of the mean?

Whatever the answer to those questions, and others raised in this volume, one thought rings clear: one person's utopia is another person's dystopia . . . and how these concepts will be defined and presented in the future remains to be seen.

Barbara and Jim

Chapter One

Getting Off

Henry James and Writing Utopia

Daniel M. R. Abitz

In *The Treacherous Years* (1969), Leon Edel writes about James's "The Great Good Place:" "The interest of the story, on its biographical side, is not only in its obvious wish for some surcease from the worldly pressure Henry James was experiencing, but his wish for an exclusive man's world, a monastic Order, a sheltering brotherhood. The tale has in it distinct homoerotic overtones."[1] James's wishes for an all-men's space points to a relationship between queerness and spatio-relational fantasy in his story. In "The Great Good Place," George Dane, world-weary writer, overtaxed by work and his social calendar, finds reprieve from his burdens in the figure of an aspiring young author come to call on him: "The young admiring acolyte," relates Edel, "who comes to the great writer, George Dane, sits beside him, puts his hand on his knee, and gives him at once a 'feeling of delicious ease.'"[2] More than simply "a feeling of delicious ease," Dane finds, upon the young man's touch, the opening of a queer lifeworld where Dane can "get off" from his life.

Much of "The Great Good Place" takes place in this good place, wherein Dane talks with other denizens of the "broad, deep bath of stillness."[3] Although most utopian literature unfolds through a narrative dialogics between a utopian subject explaining the content of their utopia to a visiting outsider, the dialogics at work in "The Great Good Place" resist explicit detail or knowability. Neither Dane nor his interlocutors can *explain* the good place. In fact, they have their own names for it: Dane calls it "The Great Good Place," whereas his "Brother" calls it "The Great Want Met."[4] The two men agree that each name suits the place perfectly, and the good place, multiply nameable, lacks a rigid or delimiting coherence. As such, this good place can be read as a utopian aesthetic representation of Jose Eseteban Muñoz's "queer utopian hermeneutic" as discussed in *Cruising Utopia* (2009). "Such a hermeneutic," writes Muñoz, "would then be *epistemologically and ontologically humble* in that it would not claim the epistemological certitude of a queerness that we simply 'know,' but instead, strain to activate the no-longer-conscious and to extend a glance toward that which is forward-dawning, anticipatory illuminations of the not-yet-conscious."[5] The forms of knowing and being that take place in "The Great Good Place" are humble in that they make no claims on formal knowledge or knowable consciousness. Though more than one hundred years separates these two works of queer utopianism, each bears, in some way, the trace of the other, and putting these two works into conversation with one another can lead to a fruitful consideration of what reading utopian literature written in another century affords modern readers.

Little scholarship exists concerning "The Great Good Place,"[6] written in 1898 and published in the 1900 collection *The Soft Side*, and Edel is the only scholar to reference the story's queerness. James did not have much more to say about "The Great Good Place" than scholars, though he did include the story in his *New York Edition*. About "The Great Good Place," James writes, "There remains 'The Great Good Place' (1900)—to the spirit of which, however it strikes me, any gloss or comment would be a tactless challenge. It embodies a calculated effect, and to plunge into it, I find even for a beguiled glance—a course I indeed recommend—is to have left all else outside. There then my indications must wait."[7] Though brief, James's remarks are tantalizing and invite us to attend to the queerness of his writing. For this chapter, I will use Muñoz's *Cruising Utopia* as my exegetical framework for exfoliating the queer utopianism/utopian queerness that makes "The Great Good Place" a viable example of queer reading/writing/imagination for modern audiences. Specifically, I will use Muñoz's concept of the quotidian moment in queer aesthetics, as related to his queer utopian theory, to read the moments of erotic intimacy between George Dane and the young writer who calls on him. Moments of touch, quotidian moments such as a handshake and a hand on the knee, transport Dane to a queer lifeworld free from the interpellations of an overbearing Symbolic and suffuse this lifeworld with moments of queer relationality. In the good place, Dane relates with other men about its dimensions and joys. Though Dane and his Brother(s) never settle on precise details about the good place's form, the good place offers to Dane the safety to recount his moments of contact and connection with the young man. Thus, this despatialized and detemporalized good place emerges out of Dane's "beguiled supposition" to take on the shape of a queer utopian space in which Dane "can repossess his soul"[8] through an exploration of the queer impulses denied to him in the heterosexual(izing) Symbolic.

Ultimately, my aim is to make the argument that utopianism—and *not* dystopianism—should feature significantly in modern aesthetic, theoretical, and philosophical conversations. To do so, I will conclude with Miguel Abensour's ideas that utopia is, rather than a delimited vision with particular parameters, a rhetorical writing device suited for catastrophic times and meant for the opening up of critical, imaginative, and sociopolitical potentialities. That is, rather than read James' "The Great Good Place" as a prescriptive solution for the violence faced by queer (and nonqueer) people in the Age of Trump, I will read James's story as a discursive exploration of the potential queer future contained within the quotidian interactions between George Dane and the young author and between Dane and his Brother(s) in the good place. By turning to the past to critique the present for the future, I am following in Muñoz's path, hoping to open up for modern readers the imaginative, creative, and critical space of queer utopianism.

QUOTIDIAN MOMENTS AND QUEER UTOPIA

In *Cruising Utopia*, Muñoz writes, "We have never been queer, yet queerness exists for us as an ideality that can be distilled from the past and used to imagine a future."[9] For Muñoz, these distillations of the past toward a queer futurity come from reading a "sense of astonishment in quotidian things"[10] found in queer aesthetics. In the Introduction to *Cruising Utopia*, Muñoz analyzes Frank O'Hara's "Sharing a Coke with You" to demonstrate how texts from the past can be read through what Muñoz calls a "queer utopian hermeneutic."[11] By briefly attending to Muñoz's insightful analysis, I will begin to establish the theoretical framework for this chapter's approach to quotidian moments in queer writing.

O'Hara's "Sharing a Coke with You," Muñoz writes, "tells us of a quotidian act, having a Coke with somebody, that signifies a vast lifeworld of queer relationality, an encrypted sociality, and a utopian potentiality."[12] "Consuming a common commodity with a beloved with whom one shares secret smiles," Muñoz continues, "trumps fantastic moments in the history of art"[13] in the poem. The poem's speaker finds and expresses more pleasure in sharing a Coke with his lover than in traveling through Europe and visiting famous art museums, bringing into constellation the queer quotidian moment with classic art's "straight time."[14] The Coke, in constellation with classic art, becomes a partially aestheticized object, but, as both the speaker and Muñoz demonstrate, it retains a sense of queerness in its commonality, and it is precisely this commonality of the commodity object that affords to the two lovers access to a potential lifeworld of queer relationality and sociality.

In "Sharing a Coke with You," the Coke possesses what Ernst Bloch calls the "anticipatory illumination" of art, a concept Muñoz describes as "a surplus of both affect and meaning within the aesthetic."[15] Muñoz writes, "[t]he anticipatory illumination of certain objects is a kind of potentiality that is open, indeterminate, like the affective contours of hope itself."[16] Inherent to Muñoz's reading, then, are acts of sociality and relationality that are indeterminate, open, and non-foreclosed moments that seek a way through the locked-down and dead straightness of a world still so hostile to queerness. O'Hara's poem points toward what Muñoz, borrowing from Giorgio Agamben, calls "a potentiality . . . a certain mode of nonbeing that is eminent, a thing that is present but not actually existing in the present tense."[17] "Looking at a poem written in the 1960s," writes Muñoz, "I see a certain potentiality, which at that point had not been fully manifested, a relational field where men could love each other outside the institutions of heterosexuality and share a world through the act of drinking a beverage with each other."[18] By approaching the queerness of the amorphous good place in James's "The Great Good Place" in the same way Muñoz reads O'Hara, I am looking for "a mode of being and feeling that was then not quite there but nonetheless an opening."[19] Handshakes or Cokes, shared quotidian moments in queer art from the past, as Muñoz argues and I affirm, can be read to open out into non-foreclosed potentiality and futurity wherein queerness can be imagined and experienced.

THE GREAT GOOD PLACE: THE GREAT WANT MET

"The Great Good Place" begins with George Dane waking up "to a bright new day" with "the face of nature well washed by last night's downpour" but his pile of work "but little reduced."[20] Along with this little reduced pile of work, Dane's room bristles with a "hedge of letters" brought by Dane's servant Brown and a pile of newspapers lying as a "row of . . . bodiless heads . . . like a series of decapitations."[21] As markers of "straight time" through the documentation and cataloguing of events, these newspapers, lying "like a series of decapitations," capture the fatalism of straight time for queerness. These dismembered newspapers deepen the trauma of the opening scene, as journals, periodicals, and a sea of books, along with the work, decapitated newspapers, and letters, fill fully into the contours of Dane's room and create an "old rising tide" that "rose and rose even under a minute's watching."[22] Dane, petrified by this ever rising tide—by "the unashamed admonition"[23] that constituted the parameters of his life—"touched nothing."[24] Dane resists touch, an affective tactility involving a reaching-out toward the materials of his life, instead succumbing to a suffocating life. The Symbolic to which Dane awakens is defined by an irreducible workload that threatens him with dismemberment and drowning. Through this opening scene, James initiates readers into Dane's capitalist Symbolic, a social order built by endless work and fatigue.

Dane's tireless work as an author, however, has helped reify such a Symbolic, and this reification of the logics of capitalist production and consumption is why Dane finds himself chin-deep in the "old rising tide" of requirements. The materials that make up Dane's life are both constructive of and by his success as an author. The sea of books comes from publishers, fellow authors, friends, enemies, and Dane's own bookseller.[25] This relational network—publishers, authors, friends, enemies, booksellers—signals both his success and the rising sea that threatens to drown him. The capitalist logics of Dane's Symbolic also carry the mark of heteropatriachy, as the demands to produce and consume morph into demands to relate and socialize in explicitly heterosexual ways. Brown, Dane's attendant of eighteen years, reminds Dane of a lunch date with Lady Mullet and others, and the number of other women planning to attend lunch swings—in the course of Dane and Brown's conversation—from fifty to four or three. It never becomes clear how many women want to dine with Dane, but Dane makes clear his desire to be elsewhere. Upon reading Lady Mullet's latest missive, Dane tells Brown, "You must do it all yourself. I shan't be there."[26] Brown's response, "You'll go instead—k" is met by Dane's, "I'll go instead!"[27] but the two men do not have the same destination in mind. "Oh, I'm not going to *her*!"[28] injects Dane, signaling a particular woman as distinct from the ambiguous number of other women demanding Dane's attention. Rather than going to *her*, a pronoun tantalizingly italicized by James, Dane chants that he is going to "a happy land—far, far away!"[29] The italicized "*her*" and the "happy land—far, far away" are clearly not the same, and their contrast implies Dane's dissatisfaction with *her*. This dissatisfaction can be read as Dane's ultimate dissatisfaction with the heteropatriarchal Symbolic as represented by a social calendar and intimate relationship from which Dane so desperately hopes to escape.

Fortunately for Dane, another caller awaits him this morning, as Brown reminds him of the young man with whom Dane has agreed to eat breakfast. Dane, with much more of an appetite for this young man's company than either Lady Mullet's or *hers*, assents with vigor to Brown's suggestion that the meeting will be good for Dane. As Brown moves away to answer the doorbell, Dane is struck by "two things": "his having utterly forgotten the connection, the whence, whither, and why of his guest; and his continued disposition not to touch—no, not with the finger. Ah, if he might *never* again touch!"[30] The prospect of meeting this young man evokes from Dane a dual response of forgetfulness and reluctance. Forgetful and reluctant, Dane can be read as existing singularly and without relation to the world. With no memory and no tactility, Dane hopes to withdraw himself entirely from a network of relationality that cannot mean a fulfilled life. Dane does touch again, though, or, rather, is touched: "Yet what happened was but that Dane took his hand from his pocket, held it straight out, and felt it taken. Thus indeed, if he had wanted never again to touch, it was already done."[31] The chapter ends here, with Dane's hand in the young man's. The very next moment, the opening of Chapter II, signals to readers that Dane is no longer in his study. Rather, readers find Dane in "the scene of his new consciousness,"[32] The Great Good Place. Thus, a handshake between two men, a quotidian moment of tactile relationality, opens up for Dane a new consciousness, a new mode of man-man sociality that, in its quotidian queerness, creates the possibility of entering into a new utopic space.

Like the two men sharing a Coke in O'Hara's poem, the quotidian act of shaking hands signifies for Dane "a vast lifeworld of queer relationality, an encrypted sociality, and a utopian potentiality."[33] Though James offers no method of contrivance other than Dane's handshake with the young man, Dane has left his room behind and traveled to the good place. The contours of the good place in which Dane now finds himself are boundless, encoded with alternative affective registers, and perfectly queer. Dane initially describes the good place as "an abyss of negatives, an absence of everything."[34] Dane's description holds together seemingly incompatible images inside an unquantifiable space. This abyssal absence marks, for Dane, the "general charm" of the good place, and it initiates the reader into the good place's boundlessness. As Dane continues to build images of the good place, he continues to offer competing images that do not coalesce neatly into a coherent, sedimented image. Rather, Dane's perception of the good place keeps stretching, blurring geographics with metaphors to create what Muñoz might call a "warm illumination of a horizon imbued with potentiality."[35]

James playfully fuses geographics and metaphors, structuring and destructuring, in Dane's figuring out the good place's spatial dimensions. Dane "a little [pretends] to himself" that, "in Italy, in the old days," he had seen something like the "high, dry loggia"[36] of the good place. The good place, in Dane's eye, calls to mind "some mild Monte Cassino, some Grande Chartreuse . . . but [Dane] knew he had really never anywhere beheld anything at once so calculated and so generous."[37] Dane, in a way that calls to mind the queer aesthetics of O'Hara's "Sharing a Coke with You," recalls or imagines places in Italy and France that cannot capture the slippery architectonics of the good place. The good place is at once familiar and unfamiliar to Dane, possibly knowable yet ultimately unknowable; it expands further than the bounds of Dane's imagination. Throughout the story, Dane returns to attempts to emplace the good place, only to have these attempts uprooted by the very rootlessness of the place. As his Brother reflects that the good place must be "much nearer than one ever suspected," Dane asks, "Somewhere, for instance, down in Surrey?"[38] Later, Dane "[cultivates], however, but vaguely, the question of where he was, finding it near enough the mark to be almost sure that if he was not in Kent he was probably in Hampshire."[39]

"Almost sure" and most assuredly unsure, Dane continues to attempt to map the good place to no avail, and while Dane tries to place the good place onto a map of Europe, he "[picks] out of his dim past a dozen halting similes"[40] to ascribe/describe the structure of the good place. Dane haltingly pictures a "sacred, silent convent," a "bright country-house," a hotel, and a club.[41] "Such images, however, but flickered and went out,"[42] and, like the images of Italian loggias or French and Roman castles, none fully encapsulate the good place. Rather, each metaphor, simile, and image, as a network of possibilities, can be read as expanding the depth and breadth of the good place, as a stretching-out of what the good place might mean for Dane and its other denizens.

This architectural and geographic (in)comprehensibility rolls into sonic and temporal (ir)regularity. "From a distance," Dane hears "the sound of slow, sweet bells" and wonders, "How could they be so far and yet so audible? How could they be so near and yet so faint? How, above all, could they, in such an arrest of life, be, to *time* things, so frequent?"[43] Sound and time, like the very shape of the good place, entangle contrastive elements toward a queer effect. The bells, (n)either near nor far, mark time in the absence of time, and it is this timed timelessness that most affects Dane's happiness: "The very essence of the bliss of Dane's whole change had been precisely that there was nothing now to time."[44] Time, or what I previously called "straight time," means for Dane the deluge of work and social responsibilities that meet him when he first awakens on the opening page of "The Great Good Place." The "presentness," as Muñoz says, of straight time, comprises social responsibilities, work deadlines, and an implied heterosexual intimacy ("*her*") from which Dane hopes to flee. The good place, with its queer temporalities, might be the "'happy land—far, far away!" for which Dane so clearly yearns at the story's beginning. For Muñoz, "[t]he present is not enough. It is impoverished and toxic for queers and other people who do not feel the privilege of majoritarian belonging, normative tastes, and 'rational' expectations."[45] Though Dane, in his multiple successes, seems to very much possess the privilege of belonging, it is a belonging to a social and temporal order out of step with his own desires. Dane laughingly calls this success the "the vulgarest kind"[46] of burden, signaling that, though his life appears successful, it appears so on someone else's terms. Or, restated, Dane must keep up appearances on terms assimilable into a heteropatriarchal Symbolic. With "nothing now to time" in the good place, the incessant ticking of the present finally ceases for Dane, and the good place offers to him a queer space of detemporalization.

The lack of coherent geographics or straight time, or, rather, the presence of queered form and queer temporality, in the good place proceeds from what Muñoz reads as "the surplus that is manifest in the complexity of [queer quotidian] moments of contact."[47] This surplus, for Muñoz, is affective and relational, and it begins in/at the quotidian moment and colors the queer lifeworld that opens out from that moment. In "The Great Good Place," a surplus of non-normative feelings, affects, and relationality imbues both Dane's interactions with the young man that transport him to the good place and Dane's interactions with his Brother(s) in that good place. This very surplus, too, creates the conditions in "The Great Good Place" to "see and feel beyond the quagmire of the present."[48] For Dane, the quagmire of the present means the heterosexual logics of the Symbolic that cannot afford him the opportunity to explore his moments of contact with the young man. Instead, the good place offers Dane these affordances. Dane recounts to his Brother in the good place those very moments of contact with the young man. Dane "sees and feels beyond the quagmire of the present" through a narrative dialogics in the good place that opens up for Dane the potentiality of queer relationships and being.

Dane describes to his Brother the sensuous moment of he and the young man "sitting together on [his] sofa as [they] waited for breakfast."[49] Importantly, this conversation about Dane and the young man can only take place in the good place between Dane and his Brother, free of the heteropatriarchal Symbolic. Dane continues, "He presently laid his hand on my knee—showed me a face that the sudden great light in it had made, for me, indescribably beautiful . . . The mere sight of his face, the sense of his hand on my knee, made me, after a little, feel that he not only knew what I wanted, but was getting nearer to it than I could have got in ten years."[50] James's language sparkles with queer erotic energy, substituting for an epistemologically knowable desire a boundlessly affective scene of homoerotic contact and joy. Dane describes the "poor chap" as "serenading closed windows"[51] for ten years, and Dane's invitation to the young man, "the only response ever dropped into his dark street," brings the young man to Dane's apartment where he sees ("it's embarrassing, but I must tell you") "the very blaze of [Dane's] glory."[52] "And he saw in the blaze of my glory—deluded innocent!—what he had yearned for in vain."[53] Dane's embarrassment, the young man's innocence, the sense of yearning all inform and are informed by the eroticism of the young man touching Dane's knee and the pleasure the two take in this configuration.

Dane describes as queer the erotics at play between himself and the young man: "Then it was—at the mere sight of his back, which was turned to me—that I felt the spell work. I simply sat and watched him with the queerest, deepest, sweetest sense in the world—the sense of an ache that had stopped."[54] Dane's Brother, "amusedly" inquiring further into Dane's story, asks Dane both where and who he was at this moment, to which Dane replies, "Just on the sofa always, leaning back on the cushion and feeling a delicious ease" and "Nobody."[55] Dane describes enjoying a delicious ease anonymously, reclined on the couch, watching the figure of this young man.

Dane's anonymity (being a "Nobody") becomes possible from watching the backside of the young man while also functioning as a necessary state of being for Dane to recollect to his Brother the erotic details of this moment. The passage closes, "As nobody talking with nobody, they sat there together still and watched the sweet wide picture darken into tepid night."[56] The two men in the good place are refigured as two nobodies, two anonymous interlocutors sharing an erotic memory via the narrative dialogics made possible by this queer utopian place.

There seems to be an inherent impossibility of any relationality between two nobodies—a network of connection without polarities—and this impossibility poses a question of the good place: who, exactly, are Dane's fellow denizens? When Dane first comes to the scene of his new consciousness, "he was struck as by the reflection of his own very image in this first interlocutor seated with him" on a bench above "the wide, far-reaching garden."[57] Dane describes his "Brother" as "a man of his own age, tired, distinguished, modest, kind."[58] The two men—the two nobodies—have, apparently, a similar appearance. This mirroring continues, engulfing not just their physical aspect but their speech and thoughts as well. After a comment from his/a Brother about "the great Protestant peoples" needing to "learn how to *get off*," Dane replies, "It's charming, how, when we speak for ourselves, we speak for each other. That was exactly what I said!"[59] Not so coincidentally, this entangling of self, selves, and others in the moment hinges on and springs forth from Dane and this Brother both thinking about getting off.

In response, "The Brother, as if it would do them both good, only desired to draw him out," asks Dane, "What you said—?"[60] This desire to draw Dane out (of the closet) leads to Dane sharing with his Brother that the young man received from Dane "such a load" and that Dane, in return, "got the tip!"[61] This dialogue puts into motion a queer network of relationality between two nobodies. The two nobodies look like Dane, share the Brother's hope that Protestants will one day learn "how to get off," and have coterminous desires for drawing Dane out to both their benefits. In *Cruising Utopia*, Muñoz borrows Jean-Luc Nancy's concept of "being singular plural," a concept that Muñoz says "addresses the way in which the singularity that marks a singular existence is always coterminously plural—which is to say that an entity registers as both particular in its difference but at the same time always relational to other singularities."[62] The queer utopia offered to Dane in the good place—and to readers of "The Great Good Place"—is the queerly utopic position of being singular plural. In "The Great Good Place," being singular plural means capturing the "antirelational and relational" ontology of queerness that Muñoz theorizes in his text. Capturing this queer ontology, it does so through the coterminous possibilities that Dane is relating to—albeit quite similar—Others *or* Dane is merely projecting an image of himself to create the space to explore his connection with and feelings for the young man. More to the point, though, is that these two possibilities, being coterminous, are simultaneous and inseparable. It is unknowable whether the good place contains Dane and Others or just Dane and other Danes, but this unknowability makes it possible that *both* are true, further entangling Self and Other—relationality and anti-relationality, Subjecthood and the Social—in the singular-being-plurality of the good place.

This entanglement of subjectivity and sociality that keeps intact both subjectivity and sociality while generating conditions for their inseparability affords the Great Good Place its most queerly utopian/utopically queer quality: a Symbolic that fulfills the desires it generates and accentuates in/for its subjects. As Ruth Levitas discusses in *The Concept of Utopia* (1990), utopia offers subjects a method for recognizing and critiquing the set of material conditions under which they labor. Levitas explains that the modes of satisfaction and fulfillment (narratives of "the good life") designated by the Symbolic are, for many, unattainable, creating a distance between desire and satisfaction. Utopia, for Levitas, is an opportunity for rethinking these desires and imagining new, alternative modes of desiring toward new, alternative forms of fulfillment, success, and satisfaction. This is similar to Muñoz's sentiments about the present's toxicity for queerness, arguing that the modes of success and the various forms of desires generated by the Symbolic refuse queer fulfillment and satisfaction and queerness as it might one day become. Dane, who flees from the idea of lunching with an unknowable amount of women (and from going to *her*), by-products of the forms of success he's attained in the straight time of his present-tense quagmire, finds a new mode of personal (subjective) and interpersonal (relational) fulfillment in the queer social order of the good place.

Dane can do this precisely because the good place, as Dane's new consciousness/Symbolic, makes good on its promises. "The real exquisite was to be without the complication of an identity," chimes the narrator, "and the greatest boon of all, doubtless, the solid security, the clear confidence one could feel in the keeping of the contract. That was what had been most in the wise mind—the importance of the absolute sense . . . that what was offered was guaranteed."[63] The Great Good Place, then, is a Symbolic that allows for a subjecthood predicated on fulfillment and satisfaction. Dane exists as a subject without an identity, and this lack of identity is explicitly tied to the Symbolic's ability to keep its promises, to allow for the subject to produce/have desires and for the good place to provide (for) them. Importantly, though, Dane's lack of identity here does not mean a lack of subjectivity, just as his subjectivity does not mean a lack of relationality. Rather, the singular-being-plurality of the good place replaces the trauma of identity with the potentiality of subjectivity qua relationality inside of a Symbolic designed for the queer subject's fulfillment.

James's story resists any sort of epistemological or ontological rigidity or finitude that might follow a sense of fulfilment. The textual ambiguities so important to the despatialized and detemporalized contours of the good place and to the queer erotics pervading it are also important in resisting a foreclosure of what (forms of) desires can be had/felt/created in the good place and what modes of fulfillment and satisfaction are available to subjects in it. Although it is true that much of what makes the good place's fulfillment of desires so fulfilling is an entanglement of subjectivity and relationality that seems to highlight those two modes of being as inherent to fulfillment or satisfaction, James offers no further prescription in the text than that. The first words spoken in the good place capture the ambiguity so central to the utopics of James' story. "The thing was to find it out!" remarks nobody.[64] Three of these words are repeated with great frequency in "The Great Good Place": "(the) thing," "it," and "out." Two of these words—"thing" and "it"—revel in their ambiguity, calling to mind Lacan's "Das Ding" ("The Thing") and the proverbial "it" of Foucault's conceptualization of sexuality as the secret always revealing itself.[65] Both "the thing" and "it" are constantly revealed and uncovered by Dane and his Brother(s) in the good place because these nobodies/subjects turn them over and over in their conversations. That "the thing" might be considered Lacan's "Das Ding" reemphasizes the centrality of desire in James's story (and in Muñoz's queer utopian theory). That "the thing" is never revised further than being "the thing" disseminates itself as the part of the Self that is both informed by and yet partially free from the impact of the Symbolic. Its ambiguity and retention of its thing-ness, its lacking any further definition, allows for all subjects/nobodies in the good place to have a "thing" for themselves on their own terms. In pairing the Lacanian " thing" with the Foucauldian "it" while also keeping them separate as this speech act does, I am highlighting how "the thing," our most central reservoir of subjective desire, is and is not a desire attached to sex/sexuality. Thus, the desire that the good place fulfills for Dane is sexual (a network of relations with his Brother focalized on Dane sharing his erotic experiences with the young man) and not sexual (the relief from an overburdened life). The queerness of "The Great Good Place" is, then, an erotics both sexual and non-sexual; it is a suffusion of queer erotics that permeates a potential lifeworld that makes it entirely livable for the queer subject.

THE CATASTROPHE OF STRAIGHT TIME

Queer livability and potentiality are foreclosed upon by the patriarchal straight time that has plagued US history. The United States has been defined by a cavalcade of violent, exclusionary sociopolitical structures that have defined and produced US history since its inception via the colonial extermination of native and indigenous peoples.[66] For the purposes of this chapter, we could call our present catastrophic straight time "The Era of Trump." This era, for so many people, is an extenuation and accentuation of US political pogroms against them, another moment in an endless string of dystopic presents. As such, following Miguel Abensour, following Walter Benjamin, this chapter argues that (straight) times of "catastrophe" are times for utopia. Reading Benjamin, Abensour writes, "[i]n the presence of extreme peril, utopia seemed to him more than ever to be the order of the day. In a time of crisis, the need for rescue seemed infinitely greater, and to respond to that need, it seemed best to first rescue utopia by forcing it free from myth and transforming it into a 'dialectical image.'"[67]

We can read the "The Great Good Place" as a dialectical image through which a utopian hermeneutics can be found. Describing another scene of drowning, Dane tells his Brother, "It made me literally ill—made me feel as I had never felt that if I should once really, for an hour, lose hold of the thing itself, the thing I was trying for, I should never recover it again."[68] Dane's fear of losing "the thing" in the "wild waters" closing around him focalizes his personal crises, but his Brother's response contextualizes this personal crisis in a larger, cultural crisis: "The wild waters, you mean, of our horrible time."[69] This is "precisely" it for Dane, and the collectivity of "our" resonates loudly in the Brother's speech. This places Dane's crisis inside a larger crisis, and it signals that, as James was, in the 1890s faced with what Eve Sedgwick names as "devastating bouts of melancholia" and "scouring depressions" brought about by the "obliterative failure of his ambitions as a playwright,"[70] personal crises of James were situated in the larger, global crises of the 1890s. Though the story offers no explicit detail of what "our horrible times" might mean, these horrible times might point to the aforementioned Spanish-American War and Oscar Wilde's trial that occurred three years prior to James writing "The Great Good Place."

Both the Spanish-American War and Wilde's trial caused James great consternation and distress. As mentioned previously, the Spanish-American War "[was] a heavy burden" to James, and James spent much of his time in 1898 feeling "in a vile unrest . . . wretchedly nervous and overdarkened."[71] Edel traces these similar anxieties through James's response to Wilde's trial and imprisonment. Edel relates that "James characterized [Wilde's trial] as a 'a very squalid tragedy, but still a tragedy,'" and that James, in a letter to his friend Edmund Gosse about Wilde, "scrawled across the back of the envelope" an homage[72] to John Addington Symonds, a mutual friend of James and Gosse's and a "crusading homosexual, eager but unable to proclaim from the housetops the ecstasy he felt in love between men."[73] James helped circulate on Wilde's behalf a petition for his release from solitary confinement while also meeting with a "Member of Parliament . . . who sat on the commission for penal reform"[74] to better learn about Wilde's situation and possible release. These two moments correspond with and contextualize both James's "scouring depressions" and the writing of "The Great Good Place," creating a snapshot of the "horrible times" facing James—and Dane—in the 1890s.

The wild waters of our own horrible times are, like James's and Dane's, made turbulent by, among a litany of items too long to enumerate, international war and domestic criminalization of queerness. At the time of writing this chapter, the United States marches on the precipice of a bloody, inhumane Syrian War, just as Donald Trump is attempting to fulfill his pledge to ban transgender people from the US military, to say nothing of the United States' continued military presence in Afghanistan and the epidemic of queer youth experiencing homelessness. That so little has changed in the intervening century between James writing "The Great Good Place" and this reading of "The Great Good Place" redoubles the necessity for turning to utopian critique and imagination. As the Era of Trump has its call for utopia—Make America Great Again—so must we answer this call by both unveiling such a call as the dystopia it is *and also* imagining utopias that seek to destroy a Symbolic predicated on heterosexist, patriarchal, racist, classist, colonial power structures. That both Trump's rallying cry and James's story share a word is not lost on this chapter; rather, this synchronicity further instantiates the need for imagining and redefining what "great" might mean and for whom it might mean. For Trump and his ilk, "great" refers to a temporal past, a bygone era of white, masculine superiority neatly enfolded into the cultural mythos of the United States as both its true history and its salvific future. For James, "great" signaled a stepping outside of this history and future, a movement toward a queer horizonality made possible through quotidian acts of queer intimacy and queer relationality. The writing of utopia, for James, was his attempt to critique the "horrible times" of his present and to imagine an alternative time and space wherein queerness could flourish. The reading of utopia, for us, can be a mode of critiquing our own horrible times, recognizing their past and present contexts, and the impetus to imagine new alternative modes of relationality and sociality that do not delimit who experiences subjecthood, safety, and flourishing. "Do our contemporaries know how to read utopias . . . ?" asks Abensour.[75] This chapter, in its return to the past toward a queer futurity, answers Abensour's question with Muñoz at heart: Do our contemporaries know how to read utopias? Not yet.

NOTES

1. Leon Edel, *The Treacherous Years* (Philadelphia: J. B. Lippincott Co., 1969), 240. In *Henry James: A Life* (New York: Harper & Row, 1985), Edel again titles this chapter of James's life "The Great Good Place," but this time makes no mention of the story's "homoerotics."
2. Edel, *Treacherous Years*, 240.

3. Henry James, "The Great Good Place," in *The Soft Side* (New York: Books for Libraries Press, 1970), 8.

4. James, "Great," 11. For Barbara Young, this phrase signals James's "regression in the service of the ego," in "'The Great Good Place': Where the Great Want Is Met, Psychoanalytic Reflections on the Short Story by Henry James," *International Journal of Applied Psychoanalytic Studies* 6, no. 1 (2009): 89. James's regression mirrors Young's own "regression to my blissful life with my mother" in her analysis (90). For this chapter, "The Great Want Met" in "The Great Good Place," will be understood in the contexts of an impoverished Symbolic Order that generates material sets of conditions incapable of providing a subject with the requisite materials for success and flourishing.

5. Jose Esteban Muñoz, *Cruising Utopia* (New York: NYU Press, 2009), 28.

6. Mary Ellen Herx, "The Monomyth in 'The Great Good Place,'" *College English* 24, no. 6 (Spring 1963): 439–443; William McMurray, "Reality in James' 'The Great Good Place,'" *Studies in Short Fiction* 14 (1977): 82–83; and J. A. Ward, "Silence, Realism, and 'The Great Good Place,'" *The Henry James Review* 3, no. 2 (Winter 1982): 129–132, comprise eleven total pages of published scholarship on "The Great Good Place." Along with Edel and Young, this marks the entire breadth of scholarship on this story.

7. Henry James, *The New York Edition Henry James*, Vol. XVI (New York: Scribner's Sons, 1909), ix–x. James does not mention the story by name in any of his letters, and his notebooks merely contain a brief, one-sentence idea for the story written in 1892 (*The Complete Notebooks of Henry James*, 68–69).

8. Edel, *The Treacherous Years*, 241.

9. Muñoz, *Cruising Utopia*, 1.

10. Muñoz, *Cruising Utopia*, 5.

11. Muñoz, *Cruising Utopia*, 28.

12. Muñoz, *Cruising Utopia*, 5.

13. Muñoz, *Cruising Utopia*, 6.

14. In his read of O'Hara's poem, Muñoz sees classic art as the aesthetic representation of straight time's linear present-ness in its connections to traditional historical valences of art and time. For this chapter, "straight time" reflects the temporal logics of the heteropatriarchal Symbolic, a self-naturalizing march toward a repetition of heterosexual logics that exclude queerness.

15. Muñoz, *Cruising Utopia*, 3.

16. Muñoz, *Cruising Utopia*, 7.

17. Muñoz, *Cruising Utopia*, 9.

18. Muñoz, *Cruising Utopia*, 9.

19. Muñoz, *Cruising Utopia*, 9.

20. James, "Great," 1.

21. James, "Great," 1. It is also possible that this image of newspapers as "bodiless heads" marks James' anxiety about the Spanish-American War. In *Henry James: A Life*, Edel discusses the impact of the Spanish-American War on James: "The press headlines, the dispatches from the United States, and finally the outbreak of hostilities in April, were a heavy burden to the novelist, for whom any conflict evoked memories of the Civil War" (471).

22. James, "Great," 2.

23. James, "Great," 2.

24. James, "Great," 1.

25. James, "Great," 1.

26. 26, James, "Great," 4.

27. James, "Great," 4.

28. James, "Great," 5.

29. James, "Great," 5.

30. James, "Great," 6.

31. James, "Great," 7.

32. James, "Great," 7.

33. Muñoz, *Cruising Utopia*, 6.

34. James, "Great," 7.

35. Muñoz, *Cruising Utopia*, 1.
36. James, "Great," 8.
37. James, "Great," 9.
38. James, "Great," 10.
39. James, "Great," 18.
40. James, "Great," 18.
41. James, "Great," 18.
42. James, "Great," 18.
43. James, "Great," 9.
44. James, "Great," 9.
45. Muñoz, *Cruising Utopia*, 27.
46. James, "Great," 13.
47. Muñoz, *Cruising Utopia*, 14.
48. Muñoz, *Cruising Utopia*, 1.
49. James, "Great," 16.
50. James, "Great," 16, 17.
51. This phrasing calls to mind Romeo and Juliet or Cyrano and Roxanne.
52. James, "Great," 15.
53. James, "Great," 15.
54. James, "Great," 17.
55. James, "Great," 17.
56. James, "Great," 17.
57. James, "Great," 7. The garden here recalls the garden of More's *Utopia*. "The space of the garden," writes Miguel Abensour, is "the space of conversation *intra muros*, safe from observation and indiscreet listeners," set into contrast with "the space of the court" in *Utopia: From Thomas More to Walter Benjamin* (Minneapolis: Univocal, 2017), 36.
58. James, "Great," 7.
59. James, "Great," 12, emphasis mine.
60. James, "Great," 13.
61. James, "Great," 13. The ecstatic nature of this phallic imagery infused in the narrative dialogics of this scene parallels Muñoz's reading of James Schuyler's "A Photograph" and evokes a sense of abandoning the hampering logics of straight time.
62. Muñoz, *Cruising Utopia*, 10–11.
63. James, "Great," 19–20.
64. James, "Great," 7. Though Dane is next to speak, James places this speech act in between a reference to a Brother and a reference to Dane, and thus it resists an absolute assurance that it was the Brother who spoke it *to* Dane.
65. "Out" is repeatedly affixed to come/coming, as in "coming out," something that happens numerous times in "The Great Good Place."
66. The United States here and now, in 2018, looks much like the United States here and now of Donna Haraway's 1984 essay, "A Manifesto for Cyborgs" in *The Haraway Reader* (New York: Routledge, 2004), defined by convolution of "the tradition of racist, male-dominant capitalism" (8).
67. Abensour, *Utopia*, 9.
68. James, "Great," 14.
69. James, "Great," 14.
70. Eve Kosofsky Sedgwick, *Touching Feeling* (Durham, NC: Duke University Press, 2003), 38.
71. Edel, *Henry James: A Life*, 471.
72. James wrote, "*Quel dommage—mais quell bonheur—que J.A.S. ne soit plus de ce monde*" ["What a pity—and a joy—that J.A.S. is no longer in this world"]; see Edel, *Henry James: A Life*, 437.
73. Edel, *Henry James: A Life*, 437.
74. Edel, *Henry James: A Life*, 439.
75. Abensour, *Utopia*, 19.

Chapter Two

Poison in the Ear

Lessons of Literary Alt-Narratives for the Trump Era

Christine Jackson

Less than a week after Donald Trump's inauguration, presidential advisor Kellyanne Conway first suggested the validity of "alternative facts."[1] During Trump's tenure, the White House has let loose a barrage of assertions obscuring definitions of "fact" and "truth." One notably pungent comment has more recently come from the President's attorney and former mayor of New York City, Rudy Giuliani: "Truth isn't truth."[2] The president himself endorses a double storyline: "What you're seeing and what you're reading is not what's happening."[3] This flurry of messages from the Trump White House has led us to doubt evidence from our own senses. In this situation, what are our options on ways to evaluate truth?

The contradictory and tenuous claims overloading the wi-fi signals of our national discourse have prompted many commentators to label these times "unprecedented."[4] History may provide no traditional certainties for a navigational guide. However, we can turn to literature to analyze intersections of true and false narratives. This essay examines parallel storylines in William Shakespeare's *Hamlet: Prince of Denmark* and Edgar Allan Poe's "The Fall of the House of Usher" with an eye toward gaining a perspective on the confusion in our current national narrative. The literary works highlight characters unsettled over an official story that prompts a search for an obscured truth. Shakespeare and Poe portray characters torn with anxiety over not knowing the difference between reality and illusion. We gather insight by analyzing the ways characters confront challenges to events in the narrative, including accepting the possibility that no clear resolutions may be forthcoming.

A dystopian culture wears many dark colors. Lies muddy the waters of truth. Corruption takes control. Voices of authority ring hollow. Citizens may sense that their leaders' policies pursue wrongheaded values, but they feel powerless to resist. Less than a week after Trump's inauguration, Michiko Kakutani's "Critic's Notebook" column was headlined "Why *1984* is a 2017 Must Read."

George Orwell's dystopian culture mirrors our own, Kakutani states. *1984* recreates a world in which the government insists that "reality is not something objective, external, existing in its own right."[5] In the novel, the people of Oceania are exhausted from frustrations over making a living. They welcome distracting illusions and pay more attention to propaganda and trivial or misleading entertainment than to significant harmful actions from people in power.

Contradiction and counterclaims power most literary narratives. At the heart of those contradictions lie questions about the nature of facts and truth. For this argument, we define "fact" as a premise validated with verifiable evidence widely considered as accurate. "Truth" is the structure resulting from bricks made of facts.

In literature, a central line of events may serve as a façade before storylines or alternative narratives. These narrative devices provide a reader with a textured glimpse of experience. Layers of reality lie behind a story's central assertions. These seemingly insignificant subplots do more than weave colorful twists into a story's fabric. The alternative narratives may emphasize, reflect, or mirror a work's central theme, as well as undermine or counter that theme. Invented, stretched, or false "facts" challenge readers' perceptions. Among the various cause-and-effect lines of events, the question is not, what is the "true" narrative? Instead, character, plot, and narration all work together for an integral story.

French literary critic Gérard Genette provides a useful structural model of narrative.[6] The entire narration emerges from the reader's perception of a triad comprised of story, narrative, and narration. Story comes from specifics of the protagonist, action, and setting. Narrative is the chronological or other sequence of events, such as a reverse, circular, or atemporal progression. Narration involves the process of relaying the story from the narrator. The story's teller may be a prominent or secondary character. The narrator could also be a nonappearing presence in the narrative but with an omniscient or limited authorial voice.

Another key feature to the concept of narrator is the teller's distance from the story. Is the narrator immersed in the story? Apart from it? Genette identifies five specific functions to the narrator. A story's overall validity lies in the teller's "degree of detachment or involvement."[7] Clearly, Genette's model perceives the narrative as a dynamic blend between story and teller. A key evaluation about the fact of the story is a careful scrutiny of the source's vested interest. Genette's model of narrative is invaluable in discussing the embedded narratives and varied accounts in *Hamlet, Prince of Denmark.*

From the outset, an eerie shadow narrative powers this tragedy.[8] Marcellus and Bernardo are officers of the Danish guard who have allegedly viewed a ghost on two occasions. The mere hint of an emanation from the spirit world challenges the actual world they are supposed to protect. A lower layer of death has risen to the surface to spread a dystopian narrative. The likelihood of the story's falsehood is strong. However, the reputations of these two, the narrators, outweigh the threat of the ghost report. That they are friends of Hamlet and have no reason to invent a falsehood lends to their credibility.

As tellers, these men have credibility. They are officers with reasonable distance from the story. They carry their story to Horatio, a reluctant listener to poisonous, superstitious tales. Bernardo takes the lead as narrator, with Marcellus standing by to lend credence to the account. Bernardo cites specifics of place and time to set the scene. The same star appearing this night had also appeared there; the ghost had shown itself as the bell rang around one in the morning. These details make the account real for Horatio. They give the story a weight of truth.

They carry enough objectivity to convince Horatio at least to join them on ghost watch. Still, he remains unconvinced: "Tush, Tush, 'twill not appear" (1, l. 29). Then the apparition itself interrupts the narrative of Bernardo for yet a third appearance. "In the same figure, like the king that's dead" (1.1.41). Horatio now perceives the reality of the spirit's appearance. "Before my God, I might not this believe/Without the sensible and true avouch/Of mine own eyes" (1.1.56).

As a way to fathom this apparition, Horatio remembers history. Before Caesar's death, "the sheeted dead/did squeak and gibber in the Roman streets" (1.1.115–116). When the ghost returns, Horatio resists the terror implied by its presence. Rather, he finds a utilitarian purpose. "Stay, ghost. If thou art privy to thy country's fate/Which, happily, foreshadowing may avoid,/O, speak!" (1.1.133–135). Just as Horatio is about to get his wish for a valuable prediction on the country's possibly disastrous future, the cock crows. This marker of earthly time causes the spirit to fade. Horatio urges the company to bring the tale to Hamlet (1.1.169–170). As a listener with much to gain from this ghost's tale, he will serve as a better narrator of what the ghost has to say.

The process of fact and counterfact regarding the ghost's appearance proceeds in this sequence:

Fact: The dead do not walk the earth. Therefore, the fact is false.

Challenge to the Fact: Credible men have seen the ghost.

> Revised Fact: The ghost appears to others, confirming the validity, not of the original fact, but of the challenge to the fact. The account of Bernardo and Marcellus is confirmed. In this case, the dead indeed walk the earth.

The men are duty bound to inform Hamlet of this phenomenon. Horatio's confirmation of the sighting carries enough credibility for Prince Hamlet to meet with the officers. He cross-examines Marcellus and Bernardo on the specifics. What was the ghost wearing? What armaments did he carry? How did he look? (1.2.226–234).

With these details secure, Hamlet agrees to a ghost watch. When the spirit of his father appears, the spirit draws Hamlet apart from the others and shares his tale. He lures his son into his world with an urgent, heart rending plea: "List, Hamlet, O, list/If thou didst ever thy dear father love—" (1.5.22–23).

Then the ghost's tale seeps into the light. Because the narration of this tale happens on another platform and apart in space from the others, the story takes Hamlet into the truth of a different time, not to mention a differently constructed narrative.

The accepted truth of King Hamlet's death is a lie, the ghost asserts: "It's given out that, sleeping in mine orchard,/A serpent stung me; so the whole ear of Denmark/Is by a forged process of my death/Rankly abused:" (1.5.35–38)

The ghost king's reconstructed narrative feeds into Hamlet's unsettled feelings about his uncle's credibility. "Upon my secure hour thy uncle stole,/ With juice of cursed hebenon [sic] in a vial,/And in the porches of my ears did pour/The leperous distilment;" (1.5.59–64). The revised fact is that Hamlet's uncle committed a crime to gain his position of power. His ascent is based on a falsehood. In essence, it has been "rigged."

Hamlet's discussion with the apparition of his father validates Hamlet's sense that all is not right. It represents the first proof of an alt-narrative beneath Hamlet's world of mourning. The ghost's account confirms Hamlet's suspicions about Claudius and Gertrude. Yes, they married too soon after the death of King Hamlet, but Claudius, at least, was directly responsible for the death. Hamlet feels that those in power are thereby wrongdoing, but he rationally recognizes his vulnerability in wanting the ghost's account to be true. He must test to see if Gertrude's character is tarnished as well. Has she been coopted into this corruption?

A mother-son exchange over facts and truth proceeds this way. A series of remarks suggests Gertrude's willingness to take part in this fraudulence, the world of constructed or "fake news." Hamlet wears colors of grief and mourning. Gertrude encourages him to snap out of his depression. Gertrude glosses over Hamlet's sadness. Failing to give her son empathy, she encourages him to "normalize" death and see it as a part of ongoing life: "Do not forever with thy vailèd lids/Seek for thy noble father in the dust./Thou know'st 'tis common: All that lives must die,/Passing through nature to eternity" (1.2.70–73).

> Fact: Everyone dies. Usually, this fact is not to be disputed. However, the scenes with the ghost king reveal an exception to the universal belief.
>
> Challenge to the Fact: Hamlet says that his father is still alive for him. He wears clothes of mourning to honor his father.
>
> Gertrude Challenges the Challenge: "Why seems to be so particular with you?" (1.2.75). Hamlet comes back with a counterargument on the duality of appearance and reality. "Seems, madam! nay, it is" (1.2.76). His mourning clothes might be at odds with the celebratory tone in the court, but they coincide with his feelings. "But I have that within which passeth show/These but the trappings and the suits of woe" (1.2.85–86). Internal truths match those on the outside.
>
> Revised Fact: As Hamlet's exchange with his father's spirit demonstrates, under special circumstances, the newly dead may return from the grave to deliver messages of critical import.

At this point, Hamlet's world qualifies as a dystopia, a kingdom with corruption in control, where lust and vile ambition rule. With authority questioned, the voice of government loses credibility.

The "play within the play" that Hamlet stages forces the issue. The drama presents an embedded narrative to mirror actual events. The reenactment, which Hamlet calls "The Mousetrap," for obvious reasons, becomes a kind of polygraph by which to measure the guilt of Claudius. Hamlet's hope is that when confronted with the true story, his uncle will not only recognize his own culpability, but others will see his guilt. The front drama plays out the backstory of events in the Elsinore court. The drama's portrait of the crime onstage exposes the fraudulence of the current king and queen ruling Denmark. It serves as a public shaming.

Hamlet arranges for the players to perform two different presentations. The "dumb show," or acting out in gestures, reenacts the words of the ghost as an alt-text—a "fake news" account.

The purpose of Hamlet's play-in-play, "The Murder of Gonzago," is to validate that Hamlet's perceptions of what happened are correct. The play's story challenges the official line of what happened to King Hamlet. This alt-narrative connects with Hamlet's will to challenge a so-called "official" fact and to drain the royals of their power.

In a search for a source to this play within the play, critic Geoffrey Bullough finds many parallels to the actual late sixteenth-century murder of Alfonso Gonzaga, duke in an Italian court.[9] Bullough inventories the many changes and revisions that Shakespeare made in adapting "The Murder of Gonzago" for his own production. "Certainly, by whatever process, the original story is completely transformed in the play as we have it from Shakespeare."[10] However, one feature stays consistent in both the original historical accounts and Shakespeare's adaptation: "The poisoning theme is the cardinal link between the play within the play and the Hamlet story proper."[11] Clearly, Shakespeare wants to emphasize the precious nature of storytelling and listening. The toxic nature of poison is a powerful metaphor. Ingesting poison, whether by mouth or absorbed into the ear, is the obverse of speaking and listening.

By launching a production of the "dumb show," Hamlet gambles that the acting of the play carries a reality greater than the false masks of those in power. The dumb show describes the actual story of the king's death through gesture. Do actions indeed speak more loudly than words? Do gestures have a greater weight of truth over words? The gestures do not tell; they show. The proof is in the showing. The entire *gestalt* of the scene carries a weight of context and ring of the genuine by way of reenactment.

Hamlet directs the narrative's spoken performance. Lucianus, nephew of Gonzago the king, pours poison into his uncle's ear. Hamlet delivers a running prose commentary on the action to the audience. He serves as a translating storyteller to underscore the intersection of two narrative events at the Elsinore court. "He [Lucianus] poisons him i' the garden for his estate . . . you shall see anon how the murderer gets the love of Gonzago's wife" (3.2.272–275). Interestingly, this narration is in prose, suggesting an unofficial storyline not to interfere with the players' action. Soon after, Claudius interrupts the action onstage with his own: "Give me some light. Away!" and he leaves (3.2.280). Hamlet takes the departure of Claudius as proof of his uncle's guilt.

The fact that Claudius calls for light does not suggest a dark deceptive quality to Hamlet's scene. Rather, the false king seeks to escape his current darkness. The point is that the narrative from the ghost king, a most unlikely source, validates Hamlet's sense of how his uncle became ruler of Denmark. The play within the play replaces the official narrative with Hamlet's own.

For telling the truth, Hamlet must die. His death comes from poison, the same weapon that killed his father, except the poison sits on a sword tip. The toxin goes straight to the heart, not into the ear. "Oh, I could tell you—But let it be. Horatio, I am dead, Thou livest; report me and my cause aright/To the unsatisfied" (5.2.310–314). Hamlet ends up dead, his narrating voice silenced. Do the truths that Hamlet proved have to die as well?

Fortinbras, prince of Norway, marches onstage to reassert a royal normalcy and restore a workable authority to events. Horatio promises to tell Hamlet's tale of the fabricated facts that emerged from the depths to become public for a time. Horatio pledges, "let me speak to the yet unknowing world/How these things came about; so shall you hear/Of carnal, bloody and unnatural acts,/ . . . all this can I/truly deliver" (5.2.352–58). And Fortinbras promises to listen. The story clothed in truth persists due the integrity of the tellers. Bulwer-Lytton was correct: The pen *is* mightier than the sword.

The intersection between true and false narratives in Shakespeare's play provides guidance for our national situation after the 2016 election. The fabricated story of the path to power for Claudius, pretender to the throne, parallels the tale of Trump. The official story of Trump's election, like the "insect sting" story promoted by Claudius, stands at odds with what US intelligence documents indicate actually occurred. Starting in 2015, Russia and perhaps people inside the Trump campaign poured poison into the ear of the US electorate. The poison continues to drip.

In the twenty-first-century's tragic tale, Special Counsel Robert Mueller plays the role of Hamlet. In the same way that the Prince of Denmark stages his "dumb show" and the onstage murder of Gonzago, Mueller's investigation recreates events surrounding our 2016 election with financial documents and eyewitness accounts. Under the special counsel's direction, this production may yet bring a shadow narrative of the election into the light. Mueller's report could reveal enough evidence to confirm additional criminal wrongdoing behind the Trump scenes.

The report can serve as a corrective to this unprecedented president. Mueller served as Director of the Federal Bureau of Investigation (2001–2013) and is a multidecorated Marine Corps officer from service during the Viet Nam War.[12] In a sense, his investigation adds a "Here come the Marines" element to the national narrative. So far, the special counsel's office has issued criminal indictments against four Americans who had worked for the Trump campaign.[13]

The full picture of Mueller's investigation has still not been revealed. We have only glimpses in the form of these indictments. Americans eagerly await this story and the counterclaims of fabrications and falsehoods that it will spawn. We have some suspense if this story will be told at all, or if, like Hamlet, Mueller will have to declare, "The rest is silence." Regular tweets from the Oval Office and media reports suggest that the president is eager to shut down the investigation. If the Mueller Report fails to emerge, the modern equivalents of Horatio and Fortinbras, that is, our truth-seeking news media and a discerning US public, must serve as storyteller and listener. The two working together are essential for a complete narrative to make its way into our national record.

In *Hamlet*, once all narratives, false and true, are exposed, the court of Elsinore still stands. To the contrary, the house of Usher contains so many sliding doors and hidden compartments that even the most perceptive reader ends up joining the narrator in a whirlwind of confusion over the story's significance. Usher and the narrator immerse themselves in songs and stories that double back on themselves. Like a haunted house at an amusement park, Poe's "The Fall of the House of Usher" (1839) is filled with mirrored hallways and deceptive passageways.[14]

The Usher family was once prominent, Poe's narrator tells us. They had been patrons of "exalted art" and fine music, distributing a "munificent yet unobtrusive charity."[15] Yet the Usher mansion clearly displays signs of the family's downfall as the narrator approaches. The atmosphere is so gloomy and oppressive that the tale's teller feels overwhelmed by his imaginary fears. He can hardly distinguish between the actual house or one in a dream. "It was a mystery all insoluble."[16] Changes in the narrator's perceptions are central in this story. He arrives at the estate on horseback, riding over "a short causeway."[17] Between a rational, everyday waking world and a nightmare world of madness runs a very narrow road.

The narrator's longtime friend lives in the mansion with his sister Madeline. Like Claudius and Gertrude, Roderick and Madeline Usher connect in a corrupt atmosphere tainted with incest. Despite past respectability, they now represent a nightmarish picture of power in decay.

That portrait of Roderick and Madeline inside the story's narrative frame draws the attention of most critics. D. H. Lawrence advances an interpretation of how the mad pursuit of love leads the Usher siblings to their demise. "The brother and sister loved each other passionately and exclusively. . . . They would love, they would merge, they would be as one thing. So they dragged each other down into death."[18] Lawrence throws himself into this interpretation with fervor. He says, "It is lurid and melodramatic, but it is true."

Lawrence's emphasis on the motif of self-destructive codependence fits other short works by Poe, "Ligeia" and "William Wilson," among others. However, this focus on the Ushers fails to give much credence to the "I" of this tale, the narrator who manages to survive. As Genette's model of narrative emphasizes, the storyteller plays an integral role in shaping narrative.

This story's teller is shocked by his friend's deathly appearance. Roderick's sister Madeline shows up once, a ghostly creature passing through a remote hallway and then vanishing. She is as ill as Roderick, even more. The narrator reacts to this fleeting glimpse of the sister "with an utter astonishment not unmingled with dread."[19] He struggles with this oppressive "stupor" and cannot reason his way out of the mood. Only a look at a weeping Roderick distracts him.

At the narrator's urging, Usher presents a musical presentation. The selection is "The Haunted Palace." Accompanying himself on a kind of guitar, Usher warbles about a fertile valley once governed by a powerful king, thought, in a "radiant palace."

This palace may as well be castle at Elsinore under Claudius and Gertrude. As in *Hamlet*, governing principles have disappeared. In their stead, demonic silhouettes of lunacy dance before the garish windows. Stanza VI shows that the once resplendent palace stands as a ruined container for nightmarish phantasms: "And travellers now within that valley,/Through the redlitten windows, see/Vast forms that move fantastically/To a discordant melody."[20] Insanity and loss of reason have taken control. Usher barely perceives this disconnect between the warring sides of his consciousness. Usher's performance relays to the narrator "for the first time, a full consciousness of Usher, of the tottering of his lofty reason upon her throne."[21] Terror overwhelms both the singer and his listener.

In addition to music as a distraction, the two read together from books in the mansion's moldy library. Usher's literary tastes are hardly conducive to calming an agitated mind. The antiquarian volumes are about pseudo-sciences, like palm reading and geomancy. These books present false fronts as stabilizing guides. In actuality, they only promote more disorientation. Poe scholar Thomas Mabbott analyzes Poe's choice of these existing titles, noting that the volumes are more than placeholders on the shelf. They "give us a greater insight into the neurasthenic's [Roderick Usher's] character."[22] Even the narrator feels how the one book on vigils for the dead can draw a reader toward lunacy: "I could not help thinking of the wild ritual of this work and its probable influence upon the hypochondriac."[23] The irrational stories represent tempting open windows for a stumbling psyche such as Roderick's. Poe surprises us with the twist that another one ready to hurtle through a window is the narrator.

When Roderick comes up with his plan to preserve the now-dead Madeline in a vault under the house, the narrator follows Usher down the rabbit hole. Our guiding "I" overexplains that Usher has reason to keep Madeline away from the prying eyes of the evil doctors. Besides, the cemetery is too far away. Usher's unhinged perception of events has drawn the narrator in.

After the two men lay Madeline in the tomb, the narrator continues to call upon his weakening sense of reason. He cannot sleep. He blames his anxiety on the room's somber furniture and the wind blowing the heavy curtains. Another wave of anxiety grips him as terror "sat upon my very heart an incubus of utterly causeless alarm." He decides to get dressed and forget sleeping. Soon after, a gentle knock at his door signals Usher's entrance to his room. Usher fixates on an unearthly vision of the grounds outside "glowing in the unnatural light of a faintly luminous and distinctly visible gaseous exhalation which hung about and enshrouded the mansion."[24] A whirlwind enters the room and completely disorients the two, tossing them with "impetuous fury." The clouds press upon the house and spin with "life-like velocity." The alarmed narrator tries to pull Usher from the horrible sight: "'You must not—you shall not behold this!' said I, shuddering. . . ."[25] His own equilibrium is nearly gone.

To distract his friend, the narrator yet again returns to his role as storyteller. He offers to read from the nearest book at hand, the "Mad Trist" by Sir Launcelot Canning. The narrator mentions the story's traditional pedigree several times, although according to Mabbott and most scholars, "Mad Trist" is original with Poe. The story's title underscores its thematic value in the overall story. Storyteller, tale, and listener unite in a secret meeting with insanity, a "mad tryst."

Usher perks up to listen to this "well known" tale. Ethelred is the story's very drunk hero. Wearing a clanking suit of armor, he staggers through the woods and intends to take shelter at a hermit's hut. Hearing no one inside, Ethelred opts for brute force and breaks in the door. The original Ethelred was a failed British monarch from the tenth century, a name meaning "the unready."[26]

At this point, the narrator stops reading. He hears vague sounds of splintering wood from somewhere inside the mansion, but he attributes the noises to his immersion in the tale: "my excited fancy had deceived me."[27] He goes back to the story.

Once inside the hut, Ethelred encounters a fire-breathing dragon guarding a treasure. A royal shield hangs on the wall behind the dragon. Without fanfare, Ethelred slays the monster with his mace. The shield clangs to the floor, and Ethelred claims the shield and treasure in an empty victory.

By this time, Usher is rocking and swaying in an apparent fit. More grating and grinding noises ensue. The narrator again tries to gather the remaining shreds of his own rationality. The strange noises come from howling storm winds outside and "rattling of the sashes of the casements."[28] However, the narrator is as lost as Usher. When Usher screams, "*Madman! I tell you that she now stands without the door!*" the narrator views the image of a decayed, decrepit Madeline.[29] The label of "madman" refers not to Usher himself, but to the storyteller, the narrator. Madeline is the human representation of the teller's alternative narrative, the story behind the scenes, the truth that was almost buried but returned. She appears outside the door at the climactic moment of the "Mad Trist," a half-dead corpse with blood-streaked white robes. She personifies a story written in blood.

> Fact: The dead do not walk the earth.
>
> Challenge: *Madman! I tell you that she now stands without the door!*
>
> Revised Fact: The dead return to claim those who killed them.

As in "The Haunted Palace," the narrator's reading of Ethelred contains the entire "The Fall of the House of Usher" in miniature. An imaginative work, an artifice, an invention, stirs up forces that blend with disturbances in the outside world until no mind can tell the difference.

The "Mad Trist" serves as a magnet for critical attention. Colin Martindale holds that "both narrator and 'The Mad Trist' are not only integral parts of the tale but that their interpretation in terms of myth and depth psychology is essential to a full understanding."[30] Although Martindale's reading expands our awareness of an alt-narrative embedded within this story, it overlooks the tale before the narrator's reading of "Mad Trist." That story also contains the drama of confusion escalating into lost reason. Poe places these inner narratives one inside the other, like the *matryoshka*, Russian nesting dolls. The effect is a swirling story, an ongoing challenge to gain a rational perspective.

Like Usher, the narrator sits contained in his room, fighting terror, struggling for sanity. He is like the hermit who has abandoned the hut in the woods, leaving a dragon in charge. Usher comes "gently" into his room, a contrast with Ethelred's crash through the door, yet the effect of bursting into a contained self is the same. Usher tempts the narrator into confronting the ghastly miasma outside, a kind of stupefying dragon's breath. "I" tries to stand fast in his rationality, but the forces of disorientation are too overwhelming.

The narrator, like Ethelred, does claim a treasure. He escapes with a sliver of sanity. To close the overall narrative frame that began at the "short causeway" entrance, the narrator escapes from the collapsing Usher mansion over that same causeway, but just barely. He cannot figure out what just happened. As he had said when he first saw the decaying mansion, "analysis of this power lies beyond our depth."[31] The surreal experience lives in his memory as a nightmare, defying rational explanation.

Claudius and Hamlet fight over the rights to narrate the "true" story of transition to power. Similarly, the shocking demise of Roderick Usher within view of the narrating storyteller, who also nearly loses his sanity, finds strong parallels in our current national dilemma.

Poe's story captures the fall of the House of Trump. Like Usher, Trump is a once-privileged scion showing progressive cognitive decline. A vaporous evil cloud too powerful for onlookers to comprehend, the Russia probe, surrounds Trump Tower. The embedded story of the "Mad Trist," which is designed to distract from the clouds, replicates the false narrative about Trump's ascent to heroism. The shallow tale of the drunken knight, Ethelred the Unready, is a slapstick narrative about meaningless heroism. The tarnished knight slays a somewhat lazy dragon to claim gold. The shield, an official emblem of his heraldry and pedigree similar to the presidential seal, perhaps, clangs to the floor. This tale of heroism plays out as a distraction from the swirling disorienting cloud surrounding the house of Usher. For a modern interpretation, the cloud approximates not only the Russia probe, but Twitter and other social media as a source of vertigo-inducing experiences for national news media and alert public. The storyteller's ability to convey the tale and the listener's power to make sense of it remain in question.

Madeline Usher's appearance in Poe's tale likewise plays a part in the Trump saga. Madeline, a once-beautiful, feminine spirit, had been the only one capable of taking Usher out of himself. She was once, we assume, tall, willowy, dressed in white, as statuesque as a model, perhaps like First Lady

Melania Trump. The image of Madeline/Melania had been Roderick's, as well as Trump's, sole bid for an empathic self. Now she has aged. When Madeline claws her way out of the burial vault, she is the spirit of vengeance, images of FLOTUS, Trump's ex-wives, and former mistresses. Nondisclosure agreements cannot hold the padlock on the vault. In a broader interpretation, Madeline's blood-stained white robe suggests a tattered Lady Liberty. The figure is wounded, but not yet dead. Although exiled for a time, the figure comes back to gather up the weakened figure drawn to faux narratives and carry him from the scene.

The current occupant of the White House has cast vaporous clouds over major policies. The most serious allegation by far against Trump involves conspiracy with Russia to manipulate the US 2016 election. Therefore, the legitimacy of the Trump presidency has been called into question. As with Claudius sitting on the throne of Denmark, the official story of an ascent to power is tainted by poison, the most lethal of these being Russian interference.[32]

> Fact: Russia interfered in the US 2016 election.
>
> Challenge to the Fact: Tweet: "The illegal Mueller Witch Hunt continues in search of a crime. There was never Collusion with Russia, except by the Clinton campaign, so the 17 Angry Democrats are looking at anything they can find. Very unfair and BAD for the country. ALSO, not allowed under the LAW!" 9/16/18 10:20 AM Donald J. Trump@real Donald Trump[33]
>
> Resolution to the Fact: Unknown.

The ship of state now sails on uncharted waters. The special counsel's investigation into Trump-Russian ties faces an uncertain future. A Presidential pardon could effectively prevent former Trump campaign manager Paul Manafort from narrating his version of events to the special counsel. Another scenario is that the president could fire Attorney General Jeff Sessions or Deputy Attorney General Rod Rosenstein. The result of these dismissals could limit or end the Russia investigation. Political journalist Bob Woodward, author of *Fear: Trump in the White House*, is confident that "the truth will emerge."[34] However, the truth may never be known. As of this writing in late in September 2018, the investigation proceeds.

We expect our leaders to uphold democratic values. Yet this president's actions fly in the face of past political normalcy nearly on a daily basis. Since the start of 2017, the Trump administration has devised policies sowing seeds of chaos. Statements regarding immigration have stirred a festering political divisiveness. Claims that journalists are "disgusting" stir up cheers at rallies from Trump followers. Threats to pull out of global agreements have disrupted long-standing alliances. Policies on taxes and tariffs have sent shock waves through established economic structures. Indecisiveness over military initiatives has led to confusion among our allies. Threats to declassify sensitive intelligence documents have made our agents abroad vulnerable and exposed top-secret methods of spy craft. To be sure, these are actions from a politician promising change, but by most measures, the changes are not improvements. Those inclined to believe that Trump is beholden to Russia can do so with good reason. The behaviors of the current president have had the result of assisting Russia in breaking down our democracy from the inside.

A story woven with many story threads presents a rich view of human experience. An unreliable, deceptive narrator may demonstrate a shifting subjectivity to confuse the reader or explore depths of psychological perception. Likewise, in film and television, readers accept story shifts, reversals, and shuffled narratives because they are framed in a clearly labeled fictional context. Our tolerance for false narratives in the world of *realpolitik* is more limited.

This strategy of using fabrications in the 2016 Trump campaign and over the first year of this presidency has tarnished the usually valuable currency of presidential pronouncement. Alternative narratives in fiction have the power to question, obscure, and validate truth. When transferred into policy with real-world implications, false reports have an alienating effect. "Breaking News" comes across split images on television screens several times daily. A chyron running across the bottom of the screen carries a connotation at least, of a fractured dissonance, and at its worse, unstoppable dystopian destruction.

Our perceptions of history in this era of the Internet are changing fast. In the Twitterverse, all posts, unless deleted, exist for all time in a kind of suspended present or an absolutism of time. Reactions and objections are carved out in 140 characters and now 280, but these are mere pieces of information, hardly enough to contain depth or nuance. The structure of Twitter is both linear and circular. Threads and branches suggest a cause-and-effect line to thoughts, but comments repeated or retweeted from news accounts come across as information clouds. Twitter is a vast whirlwind. It seems akin to the vaporous glow of all living things that surrounds the Usher mansion. We may well echo the narrator's alarmed exclamation: "You shall not behold this!"

Trump began his public career as a reality show television star. His nearly constant presence on Twitter joins the vertiginous whirlwind of today's social media, amplifying the dangers of television's false narratives exponentially. Literally millions of clashing comments vie for a spot at jet speeds to claim a stake in what is "true." The compression of the tweet and its influence in the context of the Twitterverse carries an avalanche of ramifications. A presidential tweet appears. Then, just as readers, followers, tweeters, and retweeters begin to perceive the outlines of a position, another presidential tweet states a "walk back," and another avalanche of reactions clutters the social-media bandwidth.

We may find a path through the obscuring narratives of the Web with startling ideas from French media philosopher Jean Beaudrillard. His work on *Simulations and Simulacra* raises unsettling possibilities about this back and forth of discussion over facts and truth. Simulated images obscure the absence of reality or have no connection to reality at all.[35] The conclusion may be that there is no actual truth. As Poe's narrator points out in "The Fall of the House of Usher," the truth is beyond our understanding to grasp. It remains a "mystery insoluble."

In 2015, Professor Allan Lichtman, professor of history at American University in Washington, DC, accurately predicted Trump's election. Dr. Lichtman has also predicted Trump's impeachment. In addition to the stunningly serious allegation of conspiracy with Russia to undermine the 2016 election, Lichtman had foreseen and published articles last year on a long list of impeachable offenses stemming from Trump's presidency. These predictions are now coming to light.[36] A corrective such as impeachment cannot begin without courage and political will. In this case, that means the 2018 midterms must establish that Democrats take control of Congress. More challenging truths must come to the stage for our government to undergo a reset.

Voices of reason continue to affirm with certainty that repetitions of falsehoods are not facts. Rex W. Tillerson, former Secretary of State under the Trump administration, delivered a commencement address at Virginia Military Institute, Lexington, Virginia, in May 2018. "When we as people, a free people, go wobbly on the truth, we go wobbly on America."[37] In *The Soul of America: The Battle for Our Better Angels*, historian Jon Meacham asserts that we have indeed come through these times before. Our country improves its national interests when the president and forces of dissent work together, "to lift us to higher ground. In darker times, if a particular president fails to advance the national story—or, worse, moves us backward—then those who witness, protest, and resist must stand fast, in hope, working toward a better day."[38]

The river of history flows onward, but whorls, snags, and eddies churn the water. Suspense over the possibility that we are losing sight of the US narrative remains troubling. Challenges to established norms threaten to undermine the rule of law, access to voting, freedom of the press, and individuals' rights to free speech. What happens now along the banks of US history could significantly alter democratic institutions downstream. Whether the river diverges into new channels, floods its banks, or dries completely leaving a cracked riverbed depends on this pivotal moment in history.

NOTES

1. "Kellyanne Conway: Press Secretary Sean Spicer Gave 'Alternative Facts,'" *Meet the Press*. NBC News, January 22, 2017. YouTube. accessed https://www.youtube.com/watch?v=VSrEEDQgFc8 on September 5, 2018.

2. Rudy Giuliani: "Truth Isn't Truth," *Meet the Press*. NBC News, August 19, 2018. YouTube. Accessed https://www.youtube.com/watch?v=CljsZ7lgbtw on September 5, 2018.

3. "What you're seeing and what you're reading is not really happening," *BBC News*. July 25, 2018. Accessed https://www.bbc.com/news/av/world-us-canada-44959340/donald-trump-what-you-re-seeing-and-what-you-re-reading-is-not-what-s-happening on August 22, 2018.

4. "There isn't any obvious precedent for a former CIA head to publicly call a sitting U.S. president 'treasonous.'" This response refers to John Brennan's July 16, 2018 tweet about Donald Trump's comments at the Helsinki Summit with Russian Vladimir Putin. Shortly thereafter, Trump countered this charge with another unprecedented action, by revoking Brennan's top-security clearance, Katie Bo Williams, "Unprecedented Retaliation Draws Unprecedented Rebukes," *Defense One*. Accessed https://www.defenseone.com/politics/2018/08/trumps-unprecedented-retaliation-draws-unprecedented-rebukes/150652/.

5. Michiko Kakutani, "Why *1984* is a 2017 Must Read." *New York Times*, January 26, 2017. Accessed https://www.nytimes.com/2017/01/26/books/why-1984-is-a-2017-must-read.html on September 8, 2018.

6. Gerard Genette, *Narrative Discourse: An Essay in Meth*od, trans. Jane E. Lewin (Ithaca, NY: Cornell University Press, 1980). Accessed https://warwick.ac.uk/fac/arts/english/currentstudents/undergraduate/modules/fulllist/special/english19thcentnovel/genette_for_en245_pge.pdf on August 23, 2018.

7. Lucie Guillemete and Cynthia Lévesque, "Narratology," *Signo-Applied Semiotics Theories*, in *Signo* online, Louis Herbert (dir), Rimouski, Quebec, 2016. Accessed http://www.signosemio.com/genette/narratology.asp on August 22, 2018.

8. William Shakespeare, "*The Tragedy of Hamlet: Prince of Denmark*," ed. George Pierce Baker, William Allan Neilson text, 1906 (New York: The Macmillan Company, 1913).

9. Geoffrey Bullough, "The Murder of Gonzago: A Probable Source for 'Hamlet,'" *The Modern Language Review* 30, no. 4 (Oct 1935): 433–444. Accessed https://www-jstor-org.ezproxylocal.library.nova.edu/stable/pdf/3716252.pdf on September 3, 2018.

10. Bullough, "The Murder of Gonzago," 443.

11. Bullough, "The Murder of Gonzago," 440.

12. Garrett M. Graff, "The Untold Story of Robert Mueller's Time in Combat," *Wired* (May 15, 2018), a rchived from the original on May 16, 2018. Accessed August 15, 2018.

13. Brennan Weiss, Ellen Cranley, and Bryan Logan, "Here's everyone who has been charged and convicted in Mueller's Russia probe so far," *Business Insider* in late September 2018. Accessed https://www.businessinsider.com/who-has-been-charged-in-russia-investigation-mueller-trump-2017-12?IR=T#paul-manafort-former-trump-campaign-chairman-1 on September 10, 2018.

14. Edgar Allan Poe, "The Fall of the House of Usher" in *Great Tales and Poems of Edgar Allan Poe*, series ed. Cynthia Brantley Johnson (New York: Simon and Schuster, 2007), 64–89.

15. Poe, "The Fall of the House of Usher," 66.

16. Poe, "The Fall of the House of Usher," 65.

17. Poe, "The Fall of the House of Usher," 68.

18. D. H. Lawrence, *Studies in Classic American Literature*, "Edgar Allan Poe," Chapter 6. Accessed http://xroads.virginia.edu/~hyper/LAWRENCE/lawrence.html on September 3, 2018.

19. Poe, "The Fall of the House of Usher," 73.

20. Poe, "The Fall of the House of Usher," 77.

21. Poe, "The Fall of the House of Usher," 75.

22. Thomas Ollive Mabbott, "The Books in the House of Usher," *Books at Iowa* 19 (November 1973), 3–7, 17. Accessed http://digital.lib.uiowa.edu/bai/mabbottusher.htm

23. Poe, "The Fall of the House of Usher," 79.

24. Poe, "The Fall of the House of Usher," 83–84.

25. Poe, "The Fall of the House of Usher," 84.

26. *Encyclopaedia Britannica* online, "Ethelred the Unready." Accessed https://www.britannica.com/biography/Ethelred-the-Unready on September 18, 2018. Ethelred was a tenth-century ruler, who ascended to the throne by corrupt means. He was a weak, ineffectual leader.

27. Poe, "The Fall of the House of Usher," 85.

28. Poe, "The Fall of the House of Usher," 85.

29. Poe, "The Fall of the House of Usher," 88.

30. Colin Martindale, "Archetype and Reality in 'The Fall of the House of Usher,'" *Poe Studies* 5, no. 1 (June 1972): 9–11. https://doi.org/10.17077/0006-7474.1059

31. Poe, "The Fall of the House of Usher," 69.

32. Scott Shane and Mark Mazzetti, "The Plot to Subvert an Election: Unraveling the Russia Story So Far," *New York Times*, September 20, 2018. Accessed https://www.nytimes.com/interactive/2018/09/20/us/politics/russia-interference-election-trump-clinton.html on September 20, 2018.

33. Tweet: Donald J. Trump@realdonaldtrump, 9/16/18 10:20 AM. Twitter, accessed September 17, 2018.

34. Bob Woodward, *Fear: Trump in the White House* (New York: Simon & Schuster, 2018).

35. Jean Beaudrillard, *Selected Writings*, ed. Mark Poster (Stanford, CA: Stanford University Press, 1988), 166–184. https://epk.home.xs4all.nl/theory/Simulation/Baudrillard_Simulacra%20and%20Simulations.pdf.

36. James Varney, "Anatomy of the Impeachment Industry: Trump election predictor sees grounds but no politics," *Washington Times*, February 11, 2018. Accessed https://www.washingtontimes.com/news/2018/feb/11/allan-lichtman-sees-no-politics-donald-trump-impea/ on August 29, 2018.

37. Gardiner Harris, "In rebuke of Trump, Tillerson Says Lies Are a Threat to Democracy," *New York Times*, May 16, 2018. Accessed https://www.nytimes.com/2018/05/16/us/politics/tillerson-truth-lies-american-democracy-trump.html on September 4, 2018.

38. Jon Meacham, *The Soul of America: The Battle for our Better Angels* (New York: Random House, 2018).

Chapter Three

The Search for Sustainability Transitions in Science Fiction Futures

Jeffrey Barber

Science fiction (sf) is widely recognized for its role in imagining the future. Aside from its entertainment value, the genre offers a critical lens to reflect on and interrogate humanity's problematic condition and possibilities, having "most persistently and most daringly engaged environmental questions and their challenge to our vision of the future."[1] "Science fiction can," as Peter Paik explains, "serve as a vital instrument for the investigation of the contingencies governing political life, the forces that structure and dissolve collective existence, by providing the reader with visions in which familiar realities are destabilized and transformed."[2]

From the early musings on the consequences of biotechnology in Mary Shelly's *Frankenstein* (1818) and British colonialism in H. G. Wells's *War of the Worlds* (1897) to the dizzying rise of the Internet, nanotechnology, and complexity theory in post-cyberpunk and New Space Opera, sf continues to reflect the battles of competing perspectives and ideologies as well as the wonder, hopes, and fears of emerging technologies and changing political regimes.

Over the past two centuries, sf has accumulated a wide variety of approaches toward formulating the future, influenced by, as well as, influencing the time periods they inhabited. In particular, there is the task of building the *storyworld*—the context and environment within which the characters of a narrative operate. Whereas the traditional focus of the story is on a small set of primary characters and their process of moving through various obstacles and conflicts toward the anticipated climax and resolution, it is in the storyworld that the story of sustainability transition is expressed.

Placing their characters in a future setting, the writer is pressured to not only create a world new and different, whether constructing high-tech wonders or a postapocalyptic hell but to imagine the process that led to that future landscape and to ensure plausibility as well as sensibility. Darko Suvin referred to the *novum*, a scientifically plausible innovation and key element of *cognitive estrangement*, which "compels readers toward critical reflection on seemingly invisible everyday attitudes and habits."[3]

The challenge for the writer is building a future storyworld beyond a simplistic "Jetsons" approach of familiar present-day story arcs spiced with flying cars and robot nannies and to imagine one of many possible evolutions (or devolutions) of technology, politics, culture, consciousness, and ecosystems. In the early sf film *Forbidden Planet*, Earth's twenty-third-century technology is far surpassed by the remains of an advanced alien civilization in which thoughts are transmuted into material realities—an idea later appearing in *Star Trek* as the iconic replicator. Although the technology of rearranging subatomic particles into cups of Earl Gray tea has yet to be demonstrated, the evolving popular familiarity with nanotechnology and three-dimensional (3D) printing now evokes an increasing sense of possibility.

In contrast to the high-tech city of flying cars in *Blade Runner* and *Total Recall*, the film *Soylent Green* follows detective Frank Thorn walking around an overcrowded, polluted, class-divided New York in 2022, where the common-place amenities of fresh produce, meat, strawberry jam, and running water are extreme luxuries, available only to the wealthy elite and criminals. This film makes a point of portraying a future of increased scarcity, ecological collapse, and desperation raised as consequences in *Limits to Growth.*

The public sense of possibility with scenarios of modern civilization's collapse appears to be more widely accepted given the huge popularity of dystopian narratives in film, video, novels, and games. The question stands as to the possibility of transition to a postscarcity, sustainable, and egalitarian future.

STUDYING SUSTAINABILITY TRANSITIONS

Sf does not have a monopoly on imagining the future, a practice going back to the beginnings of human history, personified by shamans and prophets, military strategists, and caravan leaders. Currently, the theory and practice of "sustainability transitions" provides a resource for policy makers, advocates, educators, urban planners—as well as sf writers and movie producers—considering the forces shaping sustainable futures.[4]

According to the Sustainability Transitions Research Network, "a central aim of transitions research is to conceptualize and explain how radical changes come about in the way societal functions are fulfilled."[5] These highlight dynamics within and among three basic levels: niche (micro-level, e.g., changing individual choices, attitudes, and motivations), regime (meso-level) and landscape (macro-level, e.g., changing the nature of capitalism or nature-society interactions). Falcone's survey of sustainability transition approaches noted the importance of better understanding the role of power and politics as well as the long-term effects of specific policies.[6]

Whereas knowledge of narratives has increasingly been applied to studying transitions,[7] the study of transitions tends to be an underdeveloped resource for sf writers and producers. Yet the construction of possible future storyworlds could benefit from a better understanding and portrayal of the stories dealing with the politics and power struggles of actors actively engaged in these transition processes. One of the obstacles to sustainable cities is predominance of the automobile, locked in place not only by habit and convenience but by industry lobbyists, advertisers, and real-estate developers. Does futurist storytelling really need more variations of (flying) car chases and (laser) gun battles to successfully engage an audience's sense of wonder and possibility?

IMAGINING SUSTAINABILITY TRANSITIONS

In the early 1900s, Olaf Stapledon pointed out that humanity's overconsumption of natural resources would lead to its inevitable demise. That insight and warning has been raised repeatedly over the past century. Nevertheless, the practice, promotion, and ideology of limitless consumption and production, the disregard and abuse of the environment and natural resources upon which those practices depend, and the economic inequality and poverty rationalized as "human nature," remain primary obstacles and challenges.

The image of the wall is a useful metaphor of those obstacles. The Berlin Wall (1961–1989) has long been a symbol of the Cold War, the geopolitical separation between east and west and between socialism or communism and capitalism. The wall is also a symbol of those differences continuing to keep humanity divided within itself and its potential to become something more.

In Ursula LeGuin's 1974 novel, *The Dispossessed: An Ambiguous Utopia*, the wall on the planet Annares also represents major ideological differences, in this case between capitalism and anarchism. Physically, the wall on Annares circumscribes a sixty-acre landing field for ships loading and off-loading freight in exchange with the affluent capitalist planet Urras. One side announces Annaresti freedom from the rest of the universe's demands and constraints; the other side, a prison. The wall on Annares not simply separates two worlds and ideologies, wealthy and poor, but also the cultural barrier to understanding each other.

The capitalist system of Urras provides for the needs of its wealthy, ruling class but at the expense of its unhappy working, lower class, who hold a mass-protest demonstration but are violently suppressed. If there is concern about future generations, it is reserved for the children of the elite. It is not only the economic inequality that causes the main character Shevek to describe Urras as "Hell" but also the lack of freedom and human dignity:

> There is nothing here but States and their weapons, the rich and their lies, and the poor and their misery. There is no way to act rightly, with a clear heart, on Urras. There is nothing you can do that profit does not enter into, and fear of loss, and the wish for power. [8]

On the other hand, the anarchist world of Annares is no paradise. In fact, it is a harsh and desolate place, where the people often endure hunger and sacrifice; however, it also provides the freedom, dignity, and "splendor" that Urras lacks. As Shevek explains,

> You are rich, you own. We are poor, we lack. You have, we do not have. Everything is beautiful here. Only not the faces. On Anarres nothing is beautiful, nothing but the faces. The other faces, the men and women. We have nothing but that, nothing but each other. Here you see the jewels, there you see the eyes. And in the eyes you see the splendor, the Splendor of the human spirit. Because our men and women are free—possessing nothing, they are free. You the possessors are possessed. You are all in jail. Each alone, solitary, with a heap of what he owns. You live in prison, die in prison. It is all I can see in your eyes—the wall, the wall! [9]

The 1970s saw the publication of several future narratives about sustainability transitions. In the 1975 novel *Ecotopia: The Notebooks and Reports of William Weston* by Ernest Callenbach, a wall separates the states of Oregon, Washington, and Northern California from the rest of the United States from which it seceded:

> The actual frontier is marked by a picturesquely weathered wooden fence, with a large gate, obviously little used. When my taxi pulled up, there was nobody around. The driver had to get out, go over to a small stone guard-house, and get the Ecotopian military to interrupt their card game. . . . they checked my papers with an air of informed authority, and they passed the taxi through the gate—though only after making a point of the fact that it had required a special dispensation to allow an internal combustion engine to pass their sacred portals. [10]

Although similar to Annares in their rebellion against a hierarchical, capitalist system, Ecotopia takes shape on planet Earth. Formally seceding from the United States and establishing itself as a politically independent region in the year 1980, Ecotopia declares itself a "stable state" economy based not on fossil fuels but solar energy. They enjoy the fruits of resource sufficiency as opposed to the harsh scarcity endured by the Anarresti. Yet, like the Anarresti, they have eschewed the "profiteering," private-property ethos of US capitalism to embrace a more communitarian culture and way of life. "Naturally, the transition period that ensued," wrote Callenbach, "was hectic—though many people also remember it as exciting." As to the system they left behind:

> The burden of military outlays to support an enormous arms establishment caused economic disruption even after the citizenry lost the power to control them. The persistent inflation and recession of the seventies had caused widespread misery and undermined Americans' confidence in economic progress. . . . After the abortive antipollution efforts of the early seventies, the toll of death and destruction had resumed its climb. Energy crises had bred economic disruption and price gouging. And chronic Washington scandals had greatly reduced faith in central government.[11]

Two other feminist utopian narratives coincided around that time: Marge Piercy's *Woman at the Edge of Time* (1975) and *The Female Man* (1976) by Joanna Russ. Piercy's alternative society also takes place on Earth but in the distant future. Here the boundary is not a physical wall but time. For the main character, Connie, the world of Mattapoisett is just one future next to less desirable possibilities. This is not a glittery, loud urban future with super skyscrapers and flying taxis zipping past giant holographic advertisements. It is instead arcadian, peaceful, with goats and vegetable gardens, appearing to Connie more like the poor farmyard her family migrated from in Mexico. Otto describes how

> the ecotopian future town of Mattapoisett exhibits some estranging characteristics, if viewed from the perspective of mainstream modern society: cooperative technological planning, organic public gardens, compostable diapers for infants. Every one of these estrangements in the author's imaginary ecotopian community provokes cognitive reflection on the viability of what they are replacing, because contemplating them requires us to recall our own society's models.[12]

She wanted her novel "to show an ecologically sound society," Piercy later explains. "The lives and institutions and rituals of Mattapoisett all stress being a part of nature and responsible for the natural world."[13] It takes some time for her main character Connie to realize this is a future without the poverty, crime, inequality, and oppression so familiar to her "normal" world. In this future, there are no hungry poor or condescending rich. Work in this world also means something different from what she has known. Time traveling to and from the future community of Mattapoisett, Connie is encouraged to do what she can to ensure this particular future will take place. She is pointedly told (also a message to the reader):

> "You of your time. You individually may fail to understand us or to struggle in your own life and time. You of your time may fail to struggle together." His voice was warm, almost teasing, yet his eyes told her he was speaking seriously. "We must fight to come to exist, to remain in existence, to be the future that happens. That's why we reached you."[14]

In addition to sustainability norms, these three utopian visions emphasize an evolved and inclusive experience of freedom, highlighting behavior and structures celebrating gender and racial equality through a wide diversity of relationship types, social roles, and personal expression. These feminist ecotopian novels of the 1970s provide a window on the social-movement priorities of the time as well as normative elements vying for inclusion in the evolving definitions and agenda of "sustainability."

UTOPIAN MUTATIONS

Emerging in the middle of a decade of environmental activism, these three novels present alternative visions of future societies based on democratic localized participation, decentralized government, ecological principles, cooperation over competition, gender, racial,and sexual equality, and a demonetized economy putting human well-being above individual profit.

Although deemed "utopian," the meaning and context of this term has significantly mutated over the decades from its original classic ironic meaning of "no place." The contemporary popular meaning of "utopia" is saturated with suspicion. The Enlightenment promises of technological progress are more often associated with the disenchantments of nuclear war, authoritarianism, pollution, and fossil-fuel addiction. However, the need for hope persists, whether in "moving forward" or "making great again."

Although declaring "modern sf thus had no utopias to offer," James claims it is those "tantalizing fragments in the utopian tradition" that are "moving that genre in very new directions."[15] Baccolini and Moylan further note how, from this pessimism and the oppositional political culture of the late 1960s and 1970s, there emerged a "revival of distinctly eutopian writing, the first major revival since the end of the nineteenth century" which they labeled *critical utopia.*[16] This is a form of writing incorporating "an Enlightenment sense of critique, a postmodern attitude of self-reflexivity" with which authors "reclaimed the emancipatory utopian imagination while they simultaneously challenged the political and formal limits of the traditional utopia."

These critical utopian scenarios were in contrast yet resonant with their dystopian counterparts, such as Brunner's novel *The Sheep Look Up* and the film *Soylent Green*. These more pessimistic offerings visualized threats identified in the *Limits to Growth* report, which acquired more serious attention and legitimacy with the arrival of the 1973 energy crisis and global food crisis of 1972–1975.

Deepening public awareness and concern about the environment was apparent with the launch of the first Earth Day in 1970, taking formal shape in Richard Nixon's signing of the clean air, water, and other environmental acts and establishing the Environmental Protection Agency (EPA) and National Oceanic and Atmospheric Administration (NOAA). Internationally, the 1972 United Nations (UN) Conference on the Human Environment took place in Stockholm, launching the UN Environment Program and formalizing a global policy platform to advance sustainable development.

NEOLIBERAL BACKLASH

As the Berlin Wall stood its ground, a new wall obstructing sustainability transitions was being erected, taking shape in the anti-environmental backlash of the 1980s. This reversal embodied the economic-political paradigm of neoliberalism, which rose to dominate both US and UK governmental agendas for decades after. With the 1980s, the critical utopian tendency in fiction "came to an abrupt end."[17]

In 1981, newly elected Ronald Reagan appointed staunch anti-environmental and pro–fossil-fuel candidates to head top federal offices, notably James Watt as Secretary of the Interior and Anne Gorsuch as Administrator of the EPA, signaling an attack on the regulatory achievements of the previous decade and laying the foundations of the neoliberal agenda for future decades. "The events that led to Donald Trump's election," claims George Monbiot, "started in England in 1975" when Margaret Thatcher presented Frederick Hayek's *The Constitution of Liberty* as "what we believe."[18]

Hayek was one of the architects of neoliberal theory calling for reduction of government and regulations on corporations, opposition to trade unions, and tax cuts for the wealthy. His associate, Milton Friedman, became Ronald Reagan's economic advisor. Supporting this union was a network of conservative think tanks and wealthy funders dedicated to spreading the new political gospel, which helped boost the Republican party to power.

Reagan began his first year in office taking down the solar panels President Jimmy Carter had previously installed on the White House, followed by rolling back energy-efficiency standards and eliminating price controls and regulations on oil and natural gas. In the movie theaters, the film *Road Warrior* portrayed the apocalyptic collapse of civilization, marked by violent competition for the last remaining stores of oil.

As Reagan's "morning in America" unfolded, popular culture steadily moved away from utopian narratives, delivering instead a rich buffet of dystopian films such as *Escape from New York*, *Blade Runner*, *The Termina-*

tor, *Handmaid's Tale*, and the dystopian classic *Nineteen Eighty-Four* (*1984*). Futurist novels included *The Wild Shore*, *Ender's Game*, and William Gibson's cyberpunk classic, *Neuromancer*, described as "a novel that updated Orwell for the computer age."[19]

The 1980s was a time of transition for the sf genre. Between 1980 and 2000, the audience for sf "broadened and diffused," noted John Clute.[20] After 1980, there was some sense that sf was running on inertia and that too many of its creative thinkers had decamped. By around 1990, however, when the Internet began radically to shape our sense of the nature of the real world, sf as a set of arguments and conventions was in some disarray. It had been blindsided by the future. The only form of sf to grapple imaginatively with at least some aspects of the dizzying new order was cyberpunk.

Published in 1984, Gibson's *Neuromancer* inspired a new, cynical but energetic school of imaginative writers and filmmakers fusing new wave "inner-space" and film-noir styles with the latest socio-technical developments, exploring implications of the Internet, artificial intelligence (AI), neuro-pharmaceuticals, bioengineering, and transnational capitalism.

In 1984, Margaret Atwood traveled a somewhat different dystopian track from the cyberpunks. Composing on a manual typewriter in West Berlin, still encircled by the Berlin Wall, Atwood imagined a theocratic retro-future harkening back to the Puritan origins of US society. "The book mirrored the United States' embrace of conservatism," Jennifer Keishin Armstrong explains, "as evidenced by the election of Ronald Reagan as president, as well as the increasing power of the Christian right and its powerful lobbying organisations the Moral Majority, Focus on the Family and the Christian Coalition—not to mention the rise of televangelism."[21]

After the Reagan presidency, the fall of the Berlin Wall signaled the end of the Soviet Communist era. With the demise of the "evil empire," the campaign for the Strategic Defense Initiative (SDI)—also known as "Star Wars," lost its main target and rationale. However, this was quickly replaced by a new target—global-warming "alarmists." In pursuit of this new target, the Global Climate Coalition was launched, composed of Exxon, Mobil, Shell, and other members of the fossil-fuel and auto industries.

"CRY OF THE EARTH"

In 1990, environmentalists hoping to strengthen public attention to their agenda, looked to the twentieth anniversary of Earth Day, celebrated in 3,600 US cities. "Welcome to the first day of the green future," exclaimed an inspired Denis Hayes. "We hear the cry of the Earth, and we have come to heal her." Kim Stanley Robinson published *Pacific Edge*, a vision of small-town, postrevolution ecotopian life and politics in southern California in

2065. Iain M. Banks published *Use of Weapons*, his third novel in The Culture series, featuring a far-future, interstellar, postscarcity, egalitarian utopia. Hope for change was in the air.

Mood building around the Earth Day anniversary turned to disappointment because the media and public became absorbed instead with the Persian Gulf War. The neoliberal campaign to cut taxes and reduce government and regulations on corporations continued to build as greenhouse gas emissions and global temperatures increased, economic inequality deepened, and audience demand for dystopian stories grew to record highs.[22]

In 1992 governments and citizens, as well as corporate lobbyists, attended the UN Conference on Environment and Development in Rio de Janeiro. The "Earth Summit" attracted the biggest global civil society gathering in history up to that time; it also launched the UN Framework Convention on Climate Change, the UN Convention on Biological Diversity, the UN Commission on Sustainable Development, and the so-called blueprint for the future, *Agenda 21*.

While delegates in Rio discussed the plight of the Earth, Robinson published his extraterrestrial utopian novel, *Red Mars*, the first of a trilogy exploring different political philosophies and approaches to the goal of creating a sustainable society in an arid, cold, and airless environment. In this trilogy, Robinson took up the challenge posed by LeGuin in *The Dispossessed*—to imagine the complex political and emotional struggles of people attempting to forge a sustainable society.

PCSD YEARS

Bill Clinton began his two terms (1993–2001) establishing the White House Council on Environmental Policy and creating the President's Council on Sustainable Development (PCSD). The aim of the latter initiative was to develop "bold, new approaches to achieve our economic, environmental, and equity goals."[23] One of the PCSD task forces addressed the challenge of building sustainable communities, paralleling the post-Rio discussions around the world on developing "local Agenda 21s."

Unfortunately, the "Republican Revolution" of 1994, taking control of the US Congress, strengthened opposition to Clinton's sustainability efforts. Amplifying the conservatives' communication capacity, Rupert Murdoch launched Fox News, appointing Reagan's media consultant Roger Ailes as CEO.

Violent dystopias continued to pervade popular movie fare through this period, such as *Demolition Man*, *Fortress*, *The Stand*, *12 Monkeys*, *Ghost in the Shell*, *Johnny Mnemonic*, *Judge Dredd*, *Strange Days*, and *Escape from L.A.* Attention to climate change appeared in the films *The Fire Next Time* and *Waterworld* and the novels *Heavy Weather* and *Mother of Storms*, as well as in the background of the next two volumes of Robinson' s ecotopian saga. *Green Mars* and *Blue Mars* detailed different social and political experiments as Earth's cities flooded.

George Lucas reset the clock on his *Star Wars* franchise, beginning with the prequel *Phantom Menace*. This second trilogy (1999–2005) has been described as an allegory about the rise of the Bush–Cheney administration. Occurring simultaneously to the War on Terror, the prequels portray "a non-conflict blown up into something that represents absolute patriotism, and the gradual decline into the creation of the Galactic Empire."[24]

"FLIPPING THE BIRD"

The presidency returned to the Republicans in 2001 as world population reached six billion mark and greenhouse gases continued to grow. George H. W. Bush not only backed out on his campaign promise to cap emissions but formally renounced the Kyoto agreement in a letter hand-delivered by Vice President Dick Cheney to Congress. According to EPA Administrator Christine Todd Whitman, "[t]he way they did it was just flipping the bird to the rest of the world."[25] It soon became clear that the oil industry now called the shots. Although public criticism of oil-industry machinations mounted, they were soon overshadowed by the twin tower attacks on September 11.

In South Africa, nations gathered for the 2002 World Summit on Sustainable Development. The global campaign for sustainability faced industry lobbyists, a political "implementation gap," and a newly anxious and distracted public concerned with the new War on Terror.

Between the military invasion of Iraq and nature's invasion of the US Gulf Coast by hurricanes Katrina, Rita, and Wilma, the Hollywood blockbuster *Day After Tomorrow* appeared on movie screens around the country, providing dramatic if time-compressed imagery of the impacts of climate change, with tornadoes and tidal waves, and the iconic sight of a half-submerged statue of liberty, last seen in *Planet of the Apes*. In bookstores, Kim Stanley Robinson's *Forty Signs of Rain* initiated his climate trilogy (later combined as *Green Earth*) targeting Washington climate politics, providing readers with an optimistic scenario of US voters electing a climate-activist president.

As if timed for rebuttal, Michael Crichton's *State of Fear* showed ecoterrorists plotting mass murder to advance their climate alarmist agenda. The novel garnered high praise from conservative media, despite climate scientists' criticism of the book for its factual errors and distortions.[26] It was made required reading for members of the Republican-dominated Senate Committee on Environment and Public Works.

While hurricanes spread catastrophic damage to the Louisiana coast, killing more than 1,200 people, the Kyoto Protocol entered into force–minus the United States. As countries outside the United States discussed plans for national mitigation and adaptation strategies and initiatives, political debate in the United States grew more intense. Al Gore's *An Inconvenient Truth* received widespread attention and praise, refocusing attention on the challenge and need to take action.

"HOPE IS NOT BLIND OPTIMISM"

As the first African American president, Barack Obama was a symbol of hope and, as his campaign slogan promised, "change you can believe in." Yet when he entered the White House in 2009, he faced a Republican-controlled Congress and a financial crisis threatening to drag down the entire US economy. Confronting the sustainability crisis, if not as aggressively as many desired, he nevertheless raised fuel-efficiency standards, launched the Clean Power Plan, invested in green jobs, and signed the 2015 Paris Agreement on Climate Change.

In 2009, books on climate and sustainability were filling the shelves, notably Hansen's *Storms of My Grandchildren*, Jackson's *Prosperity Without Growth*, Giddens's *The Politics of Climate Change*; in fiction, Bacigalupi's *The Windup Girl*, Collins's *The Hunger Games*, and Atwood's *The Year of the Flood*. In the movie theaters *Avatar* raised emotions and debate: "global warming propaganda, hypocrisy or warning?"[27] *The Age of Stupid* painted a future retrospective of missed chances, asking why humanity failed to address climate change. To avoid that failure, scholars assembled in Amsterdam, launching the Sustainable Transitions Research Network.

Literature aiming to better understand the phenomena of climate skepticism increasingly appeared, such as Kingsolver's *Flight Behavior*, describing a poor Appalachian girl's self-education about climate change through her experience with the disturbed migration of Monarch butterflies while exploring some of the cultural and interpersonal dimensions of climate skepticism. Corporate disinformation campaigns on climate were examined in *Merchants of Doubt* next to a review of climate-denial mechanisms involved in *Don't Even Think About It: Why Our Brains are Wired to Ignore Climate Change*. A cluster of "cli-fi" novels and story anthologies also appeared.

UP AGAINST THE WALL

Trump's election victory came as a surprise to many. For sustainability advocates, it has been a growing nightmare. His first year in the White House recalled the Reagan years, attacking environmental gains, women's rights, labor unions and civil rights, and healthcare, and appointing candidates known for their antagonism and commitment to dismantling, not managing, regulatory and policy responsibilities. In addition to failing to honor the Paris Climate Agreement, Trump issued an executive order to dismantle Obama-era work on climate change, had "climate change" expelled from the Federal Emergency Management Administration's (FEMA's) strategic plan and the list of national security threats, cut the budget to eliminate climate and clean-energy programs, slashed Department of Education (DOE) funding for renewable energy and energy efficiency, ended National Aeronautics and Space Administration's (NASA's) Climate Monitoring System, placed a steep tariffs on imported solar panels, rolled back EPA's car emissions standards, and scrapped Obama's Clean Power Plan while praising "beautiful clean coal."

As Trump engaged in his exorcism of US commitments, Gore's *An Inconvenient Sequel: Truth to Power* hit US screens, reviewing the status of climate efforts and resistance. "How do you move forward on it?" a reporter from the *Miami Herald* asked. "In order to address the environmental crisis," Gore responded, "we're going to have to spend some time fixing the democracy crisis, because Big Money has so much influence now, it's been hacked." A recent study of industry lobbying on climate showed fossil-fuel interests outspending environmental advocates ten to one, more than $2 billion in the fight against US climate legislation.[28]

STILL ON THE EDGE OF TIME

At the moment of this writing, grand drama is taking place a few miles down the road where the congressional hearings on Trump's Supreme Court nominee are taking place. More than two hundred protestors have been arrested; some dressed as characters from *The Handmaid's Tale*, concerned that Bret Kavanaugh will provide the expected vote to overturn *Roe v. Wade*.

In her Introduction to the 2016 edition of *Woman on the Edge of Time*, Piercy writes "the early 1970s was a time of great political ferment and optimism among those of us who longed for change, for a more just and egalitarian society with more opportunities for all the people, not just some of them. Since then inequality has greatly increased."

As I write this, more people are poor, more people are working two or three jobs just to get by, and more people find that their savings and their future have been wiped out by bad health or losing their jobs. The homeless are everywhere, not just the single man or woman down on their luck or the shuffling bag lady but whole families with their children. There is less opportunity for the children of ordinary people to afford college; if they can go, they will be dragging huge debt through much of their adult lives.

Piercy adds that when she wrote the novel, women were gaining greater control of their bodies and their lives. Now however, in this Age of Trump, "not only has that momentum been lost, but many of the rights we worked so hard to secure are being taken from us by Congress and state legislatures every year." "In the wake of the recent American election, fears and anxieties proliferate," Atwood observed, reflecting on the changes since the publication of her book.[29]

Basic civil liberties are seen as endangered, along with many of the rights for women won over the past decades and, indeed, the past centuries. In this divisive climate, in which hate for many groups seems on the rise and scorn for democratic institutions is being expressed by extremists of all stripes, it is a certainty that someone, somewhere—many, I would guess—are writing down what is happening as they themselves are experiencing it. Or they will remember, and record later, if they can . Will their messages be suppressed and hidden? Will they be found, centuries later, in an old house, behind a wall?

THE NEW NEWSPEAK

Sales of *Nineteen Eighty-Four* skyrocketed after the Trump inauguration, especially after Kellyanne Conway introduced the concept of "alternative facts." Conway's dismissal of evidence contrary to Trump's claim his inaugural was the "biggest ever" elicited an immediate association with the "Newspeak" in Orwell's classic novel of authoritarianism.[30] As explained in the novel to central character Winston:

> Don't you see that the whole aim of Newspeak is to narrow the range of thought? In the end we shall make thought-crime literally impossible because there will be no words in which to express it. Every concept that can ever be needed will be expressed by exactly one word, with its meaning rigidly defined and all its subsidiary meanings rubbed out and forgotten.[31]

Trump's facility with the phrase "fake news," accusing the mainstream news media as "enemy of the people," caused some, like Sullivan, to declare "we've gone full Orwell." Unlike Big Brother's use of political language, which was pragmatic, intentional, and systematic, Trump's rhetoric tends to be more erratic, inconsistent, and improvisational. He speaks not to the broader public, but to his adoring base supporters.[32]

Some observers view the Age of Trump as living in a Philip K. Dick future, where "spurious realities are manufactured by the media, by governments, by big corporations, by religious groups, political groups—and the electronic hardware exists by which to deliver these pseudo-worlds right into heads of the reader."[33] This is a time when postmodernism has gone mainstream, where "truth is not truth" and the scales of justice are clearly tipping to the right, and "a golden age for dystopian fiction."[34]

Trump's presidency inspired references to Dick's novel, *The Man in the High Tower*, adapted by Netflix, featuring a fantasy of the United States ruled by a fascist government. The show's second season in 2016 "arrived amid a resurgence of real-life white nationalism, a post-election spike in hate crimes, and the bizarre spectacle of G.O.P. policymakers citing Second World War-era internment camps as legal precedent for a Muslim registry."[35] The novel and show disturbingly imagines Americans smoothly adapting to fascism.

Trump may be suffering from and exporting a "malignant normality" because of dangerous psychological issues.[36] However, the problem goes deeper than Trump, within the age and people which lifted him to power. "The assault on truth and reason that reached fever pitch in America during the first year of the Trump presidency had been incubating for years on the fringe right," says Kakutan.[37] It is also likely to go on after Trump, as well the impacts of climate change and deepening inequality, assuming other scenarios are not imagined and explored.

BEYOND THE WALL

As to why we are not seeing more critical utopian narratives, Piercy explained:

> Feminist utopias were created out of hunger for what we didn't have at a time when change felt not only possible but probable. Utopias came from the desire to imagine a better society when we dared to do so. When our political energy goes into defending rights, and projects we won and created now under attack, there is far less energy for imagining fully drawn future societies we might wish to live in.[38]

John Scalzi also complained about the difficulties of writing about the future during the Age of Trump, "when the world feels like it's on fire and everyone you know is trying to decide between hiding in a hole or taking up recreational alcoholism to get by." Noting that although sf stories are set in the future, the people writing and reading it are living in the present, that the stories and how they are understood "reflect the hopes and fears of whatever age the story is written in." Scalzi laments that "the challenge of making science fiction *not* seem like a bald ripoff of current headlines is much more of a task than it's been in a while."[39]

Asked how he felt promoting his book *New York 2140* during the new "Dark Age of Trump," Kim Stanley Robinson, described Trump as a blip and an aberration in a process of coming to grips with climate change that has been gathering momentum for about 20 years now. We've designed cleaner technologies for energy and transport and although installing them worldwide is a massive task, it can be done and it will be. It will be the work of human civilization in the 21st century. . . . It's true that Trump and his team are stupidly destructive of much that is good. They are tearing the social fabric, and enjoying that in the usual way of thugs and vandals. There's a sickness there that is disturbing to see. But we'll knit the fabric back together and carry on.[40]

Although we cannot predict the future, we have hindsight and the study of history to help us make sense of the present and project different possible scenarios of the future. We can imagine, as Robinson stresses, the kind of futures that might be possible, that we hope for our children. It is the business of sf to imagine life beyond the present, including beyond the Age of Trump.

LeGuin, in her acceptance of the Medal for Distinguished Contribution to American Letters at the National Book Awards in 2014,

I think hard times are coming when we will be wanting the voices of writers who can see alternatives to how we live now, and see through our fear-stricken society and its obsessive technologies to other ways of being, and even imagine some real grounds for hope. We will need writers who can remember freedom, poets, visionaries—the realists of a larger reality. Right now I think we need writers who understand the difference between the production of a market commodity and the practice of art.[41]

"Utopia is born of the hunger for something better," Piercy explained, "but it relies on hope as the engine for imagining such a future."[42]

NOTES

1. Ursula K. Heise, quoted in Eric C. Otto, *Green Speculations: Science Fiction and Transformative Environmentalism,* (Columbus: Ohio State University Press, 2012), 2.
2. Peter Y. Paik, *From Utopia to Apocalypse: Science Fiction and the Politics of Catastrophe,* (Minneapolis: University of Minnesota Press, 2010), 1–2.
3. Otto, *Green Speculations*, 7.
4. European Environment Agency, *Sustainability Transitions: Now for the Long Term* (Luxembourg: Publications Office of the European Union, 2016).
5. Sustainability Transitions Research Network, "A research agenda for the Sustainability Transitions Research Network," Amsterdam, December, 2017, 5. Accessedhttps://transitionsnetwork.org/wp-content/uploads/2018/01/STRN_Research_Agenda_2017.pdf on September 1, 2018.
6. Pasquale Marcello Falcone, "Sustainability transitions: A survey of an emerging field of research," *Environmental Management and Sustainable Development* 3, no. 2 (2014): 62–83.
7. Lukas Hermwille, "The role of narratives in socio-technical transitions: Fukushima and the energy regimes of Japan, Germany, and the United Kingdom," *Energy Research and Social Science* 11 (2016): 237–46.
8. Ursula Le Guin, *The Dispossessed: An Ambiguous Utopia* (New York: Harper and Row, 1974), 345–46.
9. Le Guin, *The Dispossessed*, 228–29.

10. Ernst Callenbach, *Ecotopia: The Notebooks and Reports of William Weston* (New York: Bantam Books, 1975), 7.

11. Callenbach, *Ecotopia*, 58–59.

12. Otto, *Green Speculations*, 9.

13. Marge Piercy, "Introduction to the 2016 Edition" in *Woman at the Edge of Time* (New York: Ballantine Books, 1976), location 66 in e-book.

14. Percy, "Introduction," 213.

15. Edward James, "Utopias and anti-utopias," *in The Cambridge Companion to Science Fiction*, eds. Edward James and Farah Mendlesohn (Cambridge: Cambridge University Press, 2003), 219.

16. Raffaella Baccolini and Tom Moylan, *Dark Horizons: Science Fiction and the Dystopian Imagination* (New York, Routledge, 2003), 2.

17. Baccolini and Moylan, *Dark Horizons*, 2.

18. George Monbiot, "Neoliberalism: the deep story that lies beneath Donald Trump's triumph," *The Guardian*, November 14, 2016. Accessedhttps://www.theguardian.com/commentisfree/2016/nov/14/neoliberalsim-donald-trump-george-monbiot on September 25, 2018.

19. Nathaniel Rich, "American dreams: Did William Gibson's 'Neuromancer' blueprint our reality?" *Daily Beast*, October 5, 2014. Accessedhttps://www.thedailybeast.com/american-dreams-did-william-gibsons-neuromancer-blueprint-our-reality on September 25, 2018.

20. John Clute, "Science fiction from 1980 to the present," in *The Cambridge Companion to Science Fiction*, 64.

21. Jennifer Keishin Armstrong, "Why the *Handmaid's Tale* is so relevant today," *BBC Culture*, April 25, 2018. Accessedhttp://www.bbc.com/culture/story/20180425-why-the-handmaids-tale-is-so-relevant-today on September 25, 2018.

22. Jill Lepore, "A golden age for dystopian fiction," *The New Yorker*, June 5, 2017. Accessedhttps://www.newyorker.com/magazine/2017/06/05/a-golden-age-for-dystopian-fiction on September 25, 2018.

23. President's Council on Sustainable Development, archived website, covering the period from June1993 and June 1999. Accessedhttps://clintonwhitehouse2.archives.gov/PCSD/ on September 25, 2018.

24. Lonnie Nadler, "Star Wars is more political than you think," *Huffington Post*, May 4. 2017. Accessedhttps://www.huffingtonpost.com/entry/star-wars-is-more-political-than-you-think_us_590b663de4b056aa2363d298 on September 25, 2018.

25. Peter Baker, "16 years later, Bush's climate pact exit holds lessons for Trump," *New York Times*, June 4, 2017. Accessedhttps://www.nytimes.com/2017/06/04/us/politics/trump-paris-accord-bush-kyoto.html on September 25, 2018.

26. Gavin Schmidt, "A review of the distorted science in Michael Crichton's State of Fear," *Grist*, February 2, 2005. Accessedhttps://grist.org/article/schmidt-fear/ on September 25, 2018.

27. Roberta Cruger, "Avatar: global warming propaganda, hypocrisy or warning?" *Treehugger*, December 18, 2009.

28. Robert J. Brulle. "The climate lobby: a sectoral analysis of lobbying spending on climate change in the USA, 2000 to 2016," *Climatic Change* 149, nos. 3–4 (2018).

29. Margaret Atwood, "What 'The Handmaid's Tale' Means in the Age of Trump," *New York Times*, March 10, 2017. Accessedhttps://www.nytimes.com/2017/03/10/books/review/margaret-atwood-handmaids-tale-age-of-trump.html on September 25, 2018.

30. Kimiko de Freytas-Tamura, "George Orwell's '1984' is suddenly a best-seller," *New York Times*, January 25, 2017. Accessedhttps://www.nytimes.com/2017/01/25/books/1984-george-orwell-donald-trump.html on September 25, 2018.

31. George Orwell, *Nineteen Eight Four* (New York: New American Library, 1949), 46.

32. Margaret Sullivan, "The traditional way of reporting on a president is dead. And Trump's press secretary killed it," *Washington Post*, January 22, 2017. Accessedhttps://www.washingtonpost.com/lifestyle/style/the-traditional-way-of-reporting-on-a-president-is-dead-and-trumps-press-secretary-killed-it/2017/01/22/75403a00-e0bf-11e6-a453-19ec4b3d09ba_story.html?utm_term=.fb660692a5c6 on September 25, 2018.

33. Henry Farrell, "Philip K. Dick and the fake humans," *Boston Review*, January 16, 2018. Accessedhttp://bostonreview.net/literature-culture/henry-farrell-philip-k-dick-and-fake-humans on September 25, 2018.

34. Lepore, "A golden age."

35. Aaron Bady, "Philip K. Dick's vision for resisting fascism in America," *The New Yorker*, January 17, 2017. Accessedhttps://www.newyorker.com/culture/cultural-comment/philip-k-dicks-intellectual-vision-for-living-in-a-fascist-america on September 25, 2018.

36. Bandy Lee, ed., *The Dangerous Case of Donald Trump: 27 Psychiatrists and Mental Health Experts Assess a President* (New York: Saint Martin's Press, 2017), location 58 in e-book.

37. Michiko Kakutani, *The Death of Truth: Notes on Falsehood in the Age of Trump* (New York: Tim Duggan Books, 2018), 26.

38. Piercy, location 92 in e-book.

39. John Scalzi, "During Trump's present, it's hard to write the future, says science fiction writer John Scalzi," *Los Angeles Times*, August 16, 2017. Accessedhttp://www.latimes.com/books/jacketcopy/la-ca-jc-scalzi-future-is-now-20170816-story.html on September 25, 2018.

40. Emily Temple, "The weirdness of promoting a book in the first year of Trump," *Literary Hub*, November 6, 2017. Accessedhttps://lithub.com/the-weirdness-of-promoting-a-book-in-the-first-year-of-trump/ on September 25, 2018.

41. Ursula Le Guin, "Books aren't just commodities," Speech at National Book Awards, *The Guardian*, November 20, 2014. Accessedhttps://www.theguardian.com/books/2014/nov/20/ursula-k-le-guin-national-book-awards-speech on September 25, 2018.

42. Piercy, location 132 in e-book.

Chapter Four

Resurrecting and Adapting *A Wrinkle in Time* in the Age of Trump

Emily A. O'Dell

In January 2017, Donald Trump was inaugurated as the forty-fifth president of the United States, and since then, his presidency has been surrounded by critical, satirical, and subversive commentary. These expressions of the First Amendment have manifested in a variety of forms from posts on social media to performance art, but one of the most interesting trends has been the "rediscovery" of twentieth-century works of literature that are subsequently adapted to reflect modern sentiments. For example, many Americans have chosen to express their perception of Trump's presidency in a negative, almost apocalyptic tone, which has resulted in filmmakers and writers adapting many dystopian works of literature to the big and small screens (e.g., Margaret Atwood's 1985 novel *The Handmaid's Tale* that was turned into a series on the streaming platform Hulu, a 2018 adaptation of Ray Bradbury's 1953 novel *Fahrenheit 451* into an HBO movie directed by Ramin Bahrani, and many others). However, a more optimistic example of this process of resurrection and adaptation can be found in Madeline L'Engle's Newbery Award winning young adult novel *A Wrinkle in Time* (1962), which became the basis for the 2018 Disney film of the same name. In this chapter, I will address how this particular twentieth-century novel, which is popularly marketed to young readers as a fantasy or science fiction novel, was strategically transformed into a film that reflects and responds to the modern social anxieties surrounding the Trump administration and the current political climate. To support this claim, I will compare and contrast the novel with the film, particularly regarding the strategic casting, narrative, and aesthetic choices that were made to modernize the story for a US audience in the twenty-first century. I will then demonstrate how these alterations contributed to the film's ability to symbolically reflect the need to resist conformity, hatred, and evil, while simultaneously encouraging the audience to practice racial and cultural inclusivity and embrace ideals that extend beyond the boundaries of traditional normative US society.

A Wrinkle in Time is the story of three children, Meg and Charles Wallace and Calvin, who embark on a quest across the universe to rescue Meg and Charles Wallace's father, Dr. Murry, from an evil presence. With the help of three supernatural beings, Mrs. Who, Mrs. Which, and Mrs. Whatsit, the children are able to "tesser" by "wrinkling" time or, in other words, manipulate time and travel into alternate dimensions to defeat "the darkness," which threatens to take over every planet, and return Dr. Murry to his home and family on Earth. Although the novel was previously made into a film in 2003, the 2018 Disney cinematic feature is unique in that it strategically alters or suppresses elements from the novel to more clearly reflect the current anxieties of US society in a way that the previous adaptation did not.

The majority of US adults are familiar with *A Wrinkle in Time* because it has been popular among adolescents ever since its publication. However, the book has the potential for greater cultural import than the average work of young adult fiction because, as the author herself has noted, it is much more than a book for children.

> I've never written a book for children in my life, nor would I ever insult a child by doing so. The world is even more confused now than it was when I first discovered story as a medium for meaning, and story is still, for me, the best way to make sense out of what is happening, to see 'cosmos in chaos' (as Leonard Bernstein said).[1]

L'Engle evidently considers works of children's literature to be influential for herself and for her readers as a means of clarifying the world; however, her readers are not restricted to any age group. Or, as the children's literature theorist Emer O'Sullivan explains,

> More than one implied reader can be discerned in certain children's books which address both child and adult readers. . . . Although it is unavoidable to speak of "adults" and "children" as readers, it should be made clear that these two groups of readers are nothing more than constructs.[2]

Therefore, *A Wrinkle in Time* is more-or-less universal in its ability to reach a large number of Americans of all ages, which is why it is intriguing that Disney chose to adapt this story at such a tumultuous moment in US history under the direction of an African American woman and encouraged strategic casting, narrative, and aesthetic choices to represent the classic story of good versus evil in such a way that it mirrors social and political circumstances.

The reason that the casting of the film version of *A Wrinkle in Time* is so pertinent is because the filmmakers purposefully assembled an ethnically and racially diverse cast to represent the characters, despite the fact that they are all described as Anglo Americans in the novel. This fits into the discussion of modern political anxieties because, since the beginning of President Trump's term, there has been undeniable tension surrounding the subjects of race, immigration, and ethnic discrimination. Because of numerous official and unofficial discriminatory comments and the approval of policies that have impacted and diminished the social freedoms of racial minorities and immigrants, the discussion of race, immigration, or diversity in connection to President Trump's administration frequently provoke responses of uncertainty, fear, and at times, hostility. For instance, President Trump's travel ban has been popularly interpreted as discriminatory toward people from predominately Muslim countries, and he famously referred to majority black nations as "shithole countries,"[3] both of which inspired racial, religious, or ethnic minorities in the United States to feel as though their identities were not valued and their interests were not represented by the US president. Trump has also openly endorsed the construction of a wall that will separate the United States and Mexico to limit immigration from South and Central America, he has defended legislation that separated immigrant children from their parents at the US–Mexico border, and he famously chose the campaign slogan "Make America Great Again," which has been popularly interpreted as "Make America White Again"[4] because it implies an effort to revert to a prior historical period during which the United States was considered to be a more powerful global power, but minorities had extremely limited rights and faced discrimination. Other tactics used by the current president include emphasizing crimes committed by African Americans and immigrants, threatening to roll back Obama-era affirmative-action guidelines for colleges and universities, and making disparaging comments about the former president, Barack Obama, including questioning whether or not Obama was born in the United States.

> I have people that have been studying [Obama's birth certificate] and they cannot believe what they're finding. . . . I would like to have him show his birth certificate, and can I be honest with you, I hope he can. Because if he can't, if he can't, if he wasn't born in this country, which is a real possibility . . . then he has pulled one of the great cons in the history of politics.[5]

As a result of these statements and many others, in response to a poll querying whether the US public believes that President Trump is racist, CNN reported that "among all women respondents, 56% reported that yes, they think Trump is a racist, while 39% reported that no, they do not; Millennials (18 to 34 years old) said yes: 56%, no: 40%; blacks 79% to 19%, Hispanics

58% to 40%."[6] Although much of President Trump's racist ideology is implied, it has nevertheless resulted in a gradual normalization of racism in US society that the president is indirectly promoting.

Therefore, in light of what is perceived as President Trump's disregard for anyone who is not a Caucasian male, it becomes clear that the multicultural cast that was chosen for the 2018 adaptation of *A Wrinkle in Time* is a deliberate attempt by the filmmakers, particularly the African American director Ava DuVernay, to infuse the story with diversity to assert the integral role of minorities in a country where non-white individuals are persecuted or generally undervalued by society.

> Despite observed declines in crime and much talk of criminal justice reform, the United States continues to incarcerate a large segment of the population. . . . In the United States, incarceration is disproportionately concentrated among African-American and Latino men. . . . The concentration of incarceration in racial and ethnic minority groups is due to shifts in policing, prosecution, and sentencing that disproportionately affect historically disadvantaged groups.[7]

In response to the racial and ethnic discrimination against people of color in the United States, the cast members of the Disney film were chosen to place minorities in a positive light. According to Sean Bailey, who oversees Disney's live-action features, "[i]nclusivity is not only a priority but an imperative for us, and it's top of mind on every single project."[8] As a result, the character of Meg, who is described in the novel as "baring a mouthful of teeth covered with braces," wearing glasses, and having "mouse-brown hair,"[9] is portrayed in the film by the African American actress Storm Reid, who, with the exception of wearing glasses, is the physical opposite of the character in the novel. Charles Wallace's character, who is described in the book as bearing a striking resemblance to his father, who is Caucasian, is played by the Filipino American actor Deric McCabe in the film, which required that the character become an adopted member of the Murry family. Meg and Charles Wallace's mother, Mrs. Murry, who is described as having "flaming red hair, creamy skin, and violet eyes with long dark lashes"[10] in the novel is played by Gugu Mbatha-Raw, a British citizen of black South African descent, in the film. Similarly, other characters including Mrs. Which (played by Oprah Winfrey), Mrs. Who (played by Mindy Kaling), and a few minor characters in the film including Principal Jenkins (played by André Holland) likewise do not reflect their physical descriptions in the novel. Although some have critiqued this attempt at inclusivity because it is not a faithful adaptation of the novel to the screen, it serves the purpose of bringing minority groups and immigrants to the forefront of Hollywood cinema and asserting their agency within the artistic spheres of the industry:

> DuVernay, the first woman of color to direct a live-action film with a production budget over $100 million, intentionally cast non-white actors in lead roles (Storm Reid will play Meg, and Deric McCabe will play her younger brother Charles). In 1962, it was radical to see a young girl in charge. Now a new generation of black girls (and boys) can see themselves on screen and dream of saving the world.[11]

Like the cast of actors chosen for the film, the soundtrack of the film similarly reflects the influence of minority groups on the US entertainment industry. It features the Mexican American singer Demi Lovato, the Palestinian American DJ Khaled, the Nigerian Sade Adu, the African American Kehlani, the multiracial US hip-hop group Freestyle Fellowship, the African American Chloe x Halle, and the Iranian German composer Ramin Djawadi. According to Jon Burlingame, "[Djawadi] pulled out all the stops, assembling a 71-piece orchestra, a 40-voice choir and a 24-voice children's choir, then adding synthesizers and solo instruments from around the world—the sonic equivalent of DuVernay's multicultural, multiethnic cast."[12] As a result of including racially and ethnically diverse US and international artists on the soundtrack, it contributes to the recognition and valorization of minorities and immigrants in the creation of US popular culture.

Another reflection of the cultural import of ethnically and racially diverse people in the United States is evident in the deliberate selection of quotations used by Mrs. Who, Mindy Kaling's character, in the film. In both the film and the novel, it is explained that Mrs. Who "finds it so difficult to verbalize. . . . It helps her if she can quote instead of working out words of her own."[13] As a result, in the novel, she quotes Euripides, Cervantes, Delille, the words of Jesus Christ from the King James' Bible, Dante, Shakespeare, and many other classical figures of Western philosophical and literary ideology: "*Come t'è picciol fallo amaro morso*! Dante. *What grievous pain a little fault doth give thee!*"[14] However, in the film, although Mrs. Who continues to use quotations to express herself, she almost exclusively employs the words of modern or non-European individuals such as Gibran (Lebanese), Rumi (Persian), Buddha (Nepali), OutKast (a US hip-hop duo), Tucker (an African American actor/comedian), and Miranda (a Puerto Rican American composer and performer) to convey her meaning to the human children.

> In the novel the enigmatic Mrs. Who speaks to Charles, Meg, and Calvin through a series of French, German, and Latin quotes all rooted firmly in classical Western philosophy. Through actress Mindy Kaling, DuVernay once again tessers our expectations: Kaling's Mrs. Who draws wisdom from influential people of color, including Rumi, Lin-Manuel Miranda, and OutKast. New wisdom is unveiled, new universes unfolded.[15]

Although it would have been entirely possible and expected to use the majority of the sayings that were originally quoted in the novel, it is significant that the filmmakers elected to include the contributions of non-European artists and thinkers to reinforce the importance of nontraditional ideals to emphasize diversity as a defining feature of US culture.

> We now are creating a country, the first country in world history which literally has to represent all of the world, which is to say it is not just Protestant, Catholic and Jewish; it is now Hindu, Buddhist and Muslim, along with Catholic, Protestant and Jewish. It is not just four or five languages, it is 150 languages. We have the challenge and the opportunity to create the first country in world history which literally is a reflection of the entire world.[16]

In addition to celebrating the contributions of US and international artists of color, Disney's *A Wrinkle in Time* also symbolically represents the evil that has caused what Prewitt calls the "unpleasant and nasty" state of the nation through the description of the "IT." In both the book and the film, the IT is an unfeeling entity represented as a giant brain capable of mind control that borders on possession. The IT rules the dystopian planet of Camazotz under the philosophy that conformity is the key to happiness, "Why do you think we have wars at home? Why do you think people get confused and unhappy? Because they all live their own, separate, individual lives. . . . Camazotz is ONE mind. It's IT. And that's why everybody's so happy and efficient."[17] The ultimate goal of the IT is to spread the darkness, which is visually manifested as a black cloud that represents jealousy and hatred, across the universe until everything and everyone is under IT's control.

Many of the details from the novel pertaining to the IT and the darkness are preserved in the film, with the exception of one small temporal change. More specifically, in the novel Dr. Murry has been living away from home for many years while working on various projects for the government, but he has only been living as a prisoner on Camazotz for one year. However, in the film adaptation Dr. Murry has been missing and living under the control of the IT/the Darkness for four years. This seems too conspicuous not to be a deliberate choice on the part of the filmmakers to equate Dr. Murry's absence with the exact length of time as an US presidential term. As a result of this minor change in the narrative timeline, it is possible to interpret the IT's attempts to control Dr. Murry's intelligence and independent thinking as symbolic of the president's attempts to control or destroy everything that Dr. Murry represents (e.g., light, intelligence, independent thought, etc.) in US culture.

Similarly, the darkness, which is the power used by the IT to take over the universe, is, according to Mrs. Who, Mrs. Which, and Mrs. Whatsit, capable of causing "fear which turns to rage which turns to violence."[18] Its power becomes particularly apparent when the IT possesses Charles Wallace and compels him to convince Meg that their father abandoned them by choice. The IT uses Charles Wallace as a mouthpiece to make Meg doubt what is true and convince her to succumb to IT's power. These plot elements contribute to the potential to read the IT as President Trump because they both use darkness (i.e., fear, hatred, uncertainty) to manipulate minds and suppress independent thoughts and actions. In Trump's case, this is accomplished by way of inspiring Americans to doubt what is true or to believe false and potentially destructive information, including the discrediting of information delivered by major news networks by labeling it "fake news" or liberal propaganda whenever they report something with which the president disagrees. Through these manifestations of darkness, President Trump, like the IT, gains control of people's minds and inspires them to conform to his beliefs and expectations for a successful society.

This idea of conformity, which the IT considers the key to happiness, is demonstrated in both the novel and the film version of *A Wrinkle in Time*, although to different ends. In both representations, Meg persists throughout the story in seeing herself as abnormal because of her appearance and her mental aptitude, which her teachers misinterpret as laziness because she is single-minded in her understanding of math and science, yet seemingly incapable of grasping information in her Language Arts and Social Studies classes. The film version of Meg's character, like in the novel, wears glasses and her teachers misunderstand her intellectual aptitude, which causes them to resent her because she does not apply herself and physically confronts other students to defend the honor of her family. However, unlike in the novel, Meg's insecurities about her appearance in the film are primarily because she has the naturally curly hair of an African American and, as DuVernay explains, "[h]air is a big deal for black women. . . . There's the European standard of beauty that we're all exposed to and bombarded with that says, '*My hair needs to look like a Caucasian woman's hair: straight.*'"[19] In both representations Meg is incapable of finding an emotional/mental balance or "happy medium" that will help her conform to gendered societal expectations for a well-behaved girl, but the traits that she perceives as her "faults" are what make her unique and partially contribute to the possibility for her to participate in the quest to find her father and defeat the IT.

Like Meg, Charles Wallace's character in both the film and the novel is also unable to conform to societal expectations, but unlike Meg he does not struggle with emotions, so the source of his difference is his supernaturally extreme intellect and ability to understand the inexplicable. In the novel, he is described as being so quiet that people believe he lacks the ability to speak: "I think it will be better if people go on thinking I'm not very bright. They won't hate me quite so much."[20] However, he also has the ability to understand "the wind talking with the trees"[21] and consistently tries to understand the feelings of Meg and their mother. In the film, Charles Wallace demonstrates his unique personality by talking to everyone he meets and by unapologetically understanding things about the universe that he cannot fully communicate to anyone except Mrs. Whatsit. However, whereas Meg's inability to conform to gendered expectations make it possible for her to defeat the IT, Charles Wallace's exceptional qualities make him a target for the IT because the ruler of Camazotz is a purely cerebral entity that is interested in taking over Charles Wallace's exceptional mind and can only be defeated by positive emotion (e.g., love), which Charles Wallace is unable to demonstrate in a conventional manner.

The question of conformity becomes particularly apparent in both the novel and the film when, during their quest, the children encounter a neighborhood on Camazotz where all of the children are dressed similarly and play in rhythmic synchronicity until their eerily similar mothers beckon them to come inside. However, the novel and the film depict two different results to this alternative reality where people look and behave uniformly. For instance, in the novel, Meg, Charles Wallace, and Calvin witness one young boy who bounces his ball, drops it, and is immediately ushered into the house by his mother. When the children ring the doorbell to return the boy's ball, the woman rejects the object and tells them "the children in our section *never* drop balls! They're all perfectly trained. We haven't had an Aberration for three years."[22] This response indicates that abnormality is something to be feared because it will result in punishment at the hands of the all-powerful IT.

In contrast to the novel, the film does not depict aberrant behavior, instead the equivalent scene concludes when one of the mothers asks Meg, Charles Wallace, and Calvin if they would like to come and eat dinner at her house. Although the male characters want to accept the invitation, Meg is suspicious of the kindness of others and rejects the offer, which inspires the entire neighborhood to collapse, revealing that it was a virtual reality that never actually existed. This is an interesting contrast to the original scene from the book because, unlike the fear of punishment for transgressing the expectations of the IT through independent action or thought represented in the novel, the film demonstrates that the sheer concept of conformity is an illusion and is therefore entirely unattainable by any means. Therefore, by extension, the darkness that represents the influence of the IT is also an illusion that is capable of being disassembled if approached strategically.

One element that is emphasized in the film but is entirely absent in the book is the idea of "enfolding," which has significance when interpreting the film as a reflection of the sentiments of the modern US public. At the beginning of the film, when Meg's parents are preparing to pick up their newly adopted son, Charles Wallace, they gift Meg with a paper origami fortune teller that has a heart drawn on one of its many sides, which is meant to symbolize their love for her. Meg then manipulates the paper contraption, which causes the heart to disappear and reveal a new drawing meant to represent the vast universe. Her parents explain that even when she doesn't see their love, it is still there; it has just been enfolded or hidden from sight. Much later in the movie, this concept reappears when Mrs. Who gifts Meg with glasses that have the ability to reveal what has been enfolded. These glasses make it possible for Meg to recognize elements that allow her to access the hidden chamber where the IT has imprisoned (or enfolded) her father.

The concept of enfolding is an interesting one because it is unique to the film, and it implies that something can exist even when it is not apparent. Because the ability to see that which is enfolded makes it possible for Meg to find her father, it is possible to extrapolate that Dr. Murry represents that which is presently missing from US society, but it is merely enfolded within the darkness of the present government. However, like Meg's parents' love for her, the good qualities that Dr. Murry represents (i.e., intelligence, independent thought, love, and light) are not gone; therefore, it is possible to recover them once the IT (i.e., Trump) has been defeated by someone courageous enough to challenge him.

The courage to defeat the IT in the film is derived from feminine strength, which is another theme that is emphasized more within the film than the novel. For example, in the novel the three children and Dr. Murry cause the ultimate downfall of the IT. However, in the film it is just Meg who is forced to confront the IT and save Charles Wallace. This alteration can be interpreted as an exaggeration of the feminist undertones in the novel or an indication of the significant role that young African Americans will play in defeating the evils of the world. Although the film features other strong female characters (i.e., Mrs. Who, Mrs. Which, and Mrs. Whatsit), they only provide Meg with the instructions and physical tools to defeat the IT. Ultimately, it is she alone who can save others with the power of her love. This is particularly significant when interpreting the IT as President Trump who has earned a reputation for being a misogynist as a result of famously belittling Hilary Clinton during his presidential campaign, using derogatory language when discussing women in interviews, and for generally underestimating women and being negative, hateful, and hostile toward them. Therefore, it is Meg's feminine power that allows her to feel, which protects her from the IT's mind control and makes it possible for her to save her younger brother.

In addition to feminine power, Meg is also empowered by her position as an African American. As previously discussed, under the Trump administration African Americans have suffered significantly, and many of them feel increasingly unsafe because of an increase in police brutality and a lack of judicial and social support. However, the fact that the only African American human involved in the quest to Camazotz is the person charged with saving Charles Wallace indicates that Meg has an ability that neither her Caucasian companions, Calvin or her father, or her Asian brother, Charles Wallace, possesses. Therefore, the message of the film could also be interpreted as a motivational message for younger generations of African Americans. Meg's ability to defeat the IT and keep the Earth from being entirely engulfed in darkness can be interpreted as an indication that young African Americans will be able to defeat the current climate of fear and hatred (i.e., the darkness), release the love and light that still exists but has been enfolded, and restore hope for the future by understanding that they deserve to give and receive love.

Through the process of resurrection and adaptation, the story of Meg, Charles Wallace, and Calvin's journey to rescue Dr. Murry in *A Wrinkle in Time* has become a vehicle for representing the anxieties and concerns surrounding President Trump's administration. The 1962 young adult novel represents a dystopian reality that results from conforming to the expectations of a powerful entity that wishes to control the goodness and intelligence in the world. The 2018 Disney film adapts the original story to valorize the ideas and people that have been most affected by the current political climate. Through the deliberate valorization of minorities and immigrants, the addition of new concepts, and the adaptation of existing details within the story achieved through strategic casting, narrative, and aesthetic choices, *A Wrinkle in Time* becomes both a warning and a source of hope for the US public. It warns of the dystopian future that will result from conformity, while proposing the potential for underrepresented groups to halt the spreading of hatred, fear, and violence that has resulted from President Trump's power and restore the light and love that have been enfolded within his presidency.

NOTES

1. Quoted in D. Norton, S. Norton, and A. McClure, eds., *Through the Eyes of a Child: An Introduction to Children's Literature*, 6th ed. (Columbus, OH: Merrill Prentice Hall, 2003), 298.

2. Emer O'Sullivan, *Comparative Children's Literature*, trans. Anthea Bell (London: Routledge, 2005), 16, 18.

3. Josh Dawsey, "Trump Derides Protections for Immigrants From 'Shithole' Countries." *Washington Post*, January 2, 2018. Accessed https://www.washingtonpost.com/politics/trump-attacks-protections-for-immigrants-from-shithole-countries-in-oval-office-meeting/2018/01/11/bfc0725c-f711-11e7-91af-31ac729add94_story.html?noredirect=on&utm_term=.88a83564eeed on June 4, 2018.

4. Eugene Robinson, "Trump Can't Make America White Again," *Washington Post*, July 5, 2018. Accessed https://www.washingtonpost.com/opinions/try-as-he-might-trump-cant-make-america-white-again/2018/07/05/0634e02e-8088-11e8-b0ef-fffcabeff946_story.html?utm_term=.10a4bb376d83 on August 12, 2018.

5. Quoted in Gregory Krieg, "14 Of Trump's Most Outrageous 'Birther' Claims—Half From After 2011," *CNN*, September 16, 2016. Accessed https://www.cnn.com/2016/09/09/politics/donald-trump-birther/index.html on July 22, 2018.

6. Roxanne Jones, "That Poll Is Not Just About Whether Or Not Trump Is Racist," *CNN*, July 6, 2018. Accessed https://www.cnn.com/2018/07/06/opinions/trump-racism-poll-opinion-jones/index.html on August 12, 2018.

7. Beck Pettit and Bryan Sykes, "Incarceration," *State of the Union 2017*, The Stanford Center on Poverty and Inequality. Accessible at https://inequality.stanford.edu/sites/default/files/Pathways_SOTU_2017_incarceration.pdf

8. Quoted in Rebecca Ford, "Black Santa and Hip-Hop 'Oliver Twist': Disney's Diversity Push," *The Hollywood Reporter*, November 2, 2016. Accessed https://www.hollywoodreporter.com/news/black-santa-hip-hop-oliver-twist-disneys-diversity-push-942983 on August 1, 2018.

9. Madeleine L'Engle, *A Wrinkle in Time* (New York: Square Fish, 2007), 10.

10. L'Engle, *A Wrinkle in Time*, 16–17.

11. Natalie Escobar, "Girl Power: How *A Wrinkle in Time* Liberated Young Adult Liter Lature," *Smithsonian* 48, no. 9 (January 2018), 9, *MasterFILE Complete*, EBSCO*host*, 12.

12. Jon Burlingame, "How Ava DuVernay Collaborated With Ramin Djawadi On 'A Wrinkle In Time' Score," *Variety*, March 7, 2018. Accessed https://variety.com/2018/artisans/production/wrinkle-in-time-music-1202720210/ on June 16, 2018.

13. L'Engle, *A Wrinkle in Time*, 69.

14. L'Engle, *A Wrinkle in Time*, 62.

15. Brian Bantum and Wendi Dunlap, "Wrinkling a sacred text: What makes *A Wrinkle in Time Christian*?" *The Christian Century* 135, no. 10 (May 9, 2018), 12–13, *ATLA Religion Database*, EBSCO*host*.

16. "First Measured Century: Interview: Ken Prewitt," *PBS*. Accessible at http://www.pbs.org/fmc/interviews/prewitt.htm

17. L'Engle, *A Wrinkle in Time*, 157.

18. *A Wrinkle in Time*, directed by Ava DuVernay (USA: Disney, 2018), DVD.

19. Kyle Buchanan, "Ava DuVernay on Meg Murry's Hair Journey in *A Wrinkle in Time*," *Vulture*, March 12, 2018. Accessed http://www.vulture.com/2018/03/ava-duvernay-on-megs-natural-hair-in-a-wrinkle-in-time.html on June 15, 2018.

20. L'Engle, *A Wrinkle in Time*, 36.

21. L'Engle, *A Wrinkle in Time*, 36.

22. L'Engle, *A Wrinkle in Time*, 118.

Chapter Five

The Medium Is the Massacre

Deceit, Desire, and Patrick Bateman's Trumpian Dystopia

Daniel Adleman

In an essay about the intimate connection between utopias and dystopias, science fiction writer Ursula Le Guin writes that "[e]very utopia since [Thomas More's] *Utopia* has also been, clearly or obscurely, actually or possibly, in the author's or in the readers' judgment, both a good place and a bad one. Every utopia contains a dystopia, every dystopia contains a utopia."[1] Since Thomas More wrote his ground-breaking fictional account of the imaginary "well ordered" island *polis* of Utopia, the term has undergone significant semantic drift away from signifying "no place" (*u-topos*). In recent history, it has often come to represent "[a]n imagined place or state of things in which everything is perfect."[2] But Le Guin's point is that each utopian vision (from More's to Mao's) is necessarily partial, and by extension, so, too, is the experience of its habitat as smooth functioning and pleasurable. One group's "perfect place" at one moment may be, or ultimately become, another's prison. Nowhere is this Moebius-strip-like relationship between well-ordered utopian enclosures and dystopias more pronounced than in Bret Easton Ellis's *American Psycho*.

A great deal has been said about the violence of the novel. Patrick Bateman, the notorious *dystagonist* of Easton Ellis's *American Psycho*, is an obtrusively sexist, racist, classist serial killer, and ostentatious consumer. Perceiving most of those around him as excremental "dirt," he sets out on a mission to violently expel the human "trash" from his personal urban utopia, a sterile, hypermediatized bubble of chauvinistic privilege organized around the fetishization of expensive trinkets and trendy restaurants. Because of the story's apparent glorification of baroque acts of violence, critics occupying the right and left side of the conventional political spectrum have united in panning it. As Donna Lee Brien and Julian Murphet observe, many early critics of Easton Ellis's novel (and Mary Harron's brilliant film adaptation) hastily overlooked the profound allegorical quality of *American Psycho*. The ostentatious violence that permeates the narrative should be understood in the spirit of critique, rather than pornographic celebration, of the callous cultural logic that underpins the utopian ideology of the US neoliberal project.

In one graphic example, Bateman attacks a homeless black man, admonishing him to pluck himself up by the bootstraps and "get a job."[3] As Bateman puts it, the destitute man's unforgivable offence is not having "anything in common"[4] with him. As Thomas Heise frames the matter, *American Psycho* is fundamentally a "late-1980's portrait of class hatred and power."[5] For Heise, the novel lays bare "the violence that underwrites the utopian fantasy of neoliberal free market economics in which impoverishment is rewritten as a personal choice and a sign of personal failure and crimes against others (the poor, gays and lesbians, sex workers) are rewritten as punishment for the crime of being Other."[6] In other words, Bateman's actions represent the "invisible" systemic violence (at least to its perpetrators and beneficiaries) that subtends the supposedly smooth-functioning, well-regulated gentrification of urban utopian enclaves. Far from depicting events transpiring "no place," the novel narrows its gaze on the odious violence bound up with the rapid gentrification of urban spaces such as Manhattan and, more broadly, the corporate homogenization of turn-of-the-millennium United States.

This being the case, it should come as no surprise that Bateman's mimetic mentor, his aspirational role model, is 1980s' New York real-estate developer and celebrity author, Donald Trump, who is directly and indirectly referenced more than thirty times throughout the story. In fact, Bateman's wholesale *investment* in Trump leads Javier Martín Párraga to describe him as "a distorted, parodic, and highly exaggerated alter ego of Trump himself."[7] To articulate the dystopian Trumpian logic of *American Psycho*, it will be necessary to explore the uncoordinated nexus of mediation and mimicry that really calls the shots in *American Psycho*.

WHAT PIERCES THROUGH PATRICK BATEMAN?

Given his violent predilections, it should come as no surprise that Bateman works at a firm called "Pierce and Pierce." This is, not incidentally, also the name of putative "master of the universe" Sherman McCoy's Wall Street trading firm in Tom Wolfe's satirical 1987 novel, *The Bonfire of the Vanities*. Above and beyond the fact that Bateman is a serial killer, the novel's alignment of his occupation, as a Wall Street executive, with hyperbolic violence is a consistent motif throughout the narrative. For instance, at a trendy sushi restaurant, he tells a model that he works in the field of "murders and executions," rather than mergers and acquisitions. He also attends an office Halloween party in the "costume" of a mass murderer (i.e., himself, adorned with the blood of his most recent victim). And during an exchange of business cards, he is thrust into a cycle of depression and rage over the slightly superior aesthetic of his colleagues' nearly identical off-white business cards; Bateman's is a slightly different shade, "bone" white, connoting the eerie admixture of whiteness and death that saturates his murderous occupational-recreational domain (wherein he is constantly hacking, sawing, and grinding the bones of his victims); but it also exemplifies the impossibility of substantive distinction within a field completely overdetermined by the homogenizing tendencies of corporate capitalism.

One implication of this chain of hyperbolic figurations is that Easton Ellis's novel translates the systemic violence of Wall Street finance and the decadence it affords, into what Slavoj Žižek calls "subjective violence," violations that are readily perceptible to empirical experience as emerging from a particular locus or agent.[8] Bateman's pathologically narcissistic universe is one in which aesthetic and social slights are deemed potentially fatal, whereas *actual* violations of people, animals, and even entire neighborhoods are construed as inconsequential. In this regard, *American Psycho* must be understood as a potent critique of Reagan-era decadence, the advent of yuppie culture, and the utopian neoliberal valorization of "the free market" as the solution to the problems in the United States. It also, importantly, serves as a remarkably prescient narrative about Trump's uncanny role as an avatar for the US *Zeitgeist* in not just the 1980s but also the digital twenty-first century.

It is noteworthy that Bateman, the quintessential garish 1980s yuppie, almost never seems to work. His occupation as a Wall Street executive is little more than a sinecure. Instead of attending to the proper demands of his profession, he devotes most of his time and cognitive bandwidth to recreating, fantasizing about recreation, and planning to recreate. Inasmuch as he seems to operate under the duress of an impossible utopian injunction, it is a perverse variant of the Lacanian "injunction to enjoy."[9] We might even refer to it, emphasizing a different connotation of *jouissance*, as a mandate "to play." That is to say that Bateman is slavishly subordinate to the Culture Industry's impossible commands to optimize his jouissance under the conditions of media modernity. Part of what makes anything resembling fulfillment or gratification impracticable is that his hedonism does not operate under a unified categorical imperative. Instead, the terms of Bateman's enjoyment are dictated by a cacophonous spectral tribunal. This punitive superegoic media chorus demands increasingly exclusive and intense forms of consumer enjoyment from the simulacral spoils of 1980s' New York as he moves about in a continuous network of limousines, office spaces, opulent apartments, clubs, and trendy dining establishments within his bubble of privilege. This bubbleworld is what media philosopher Peter Sloterdijk refers to as "the World Interior of Capital," a densely mediated, securitized capitalist ecosystem that systematically cleaves the have-nots from the lifeworlds of the rich and famous.

SMASH CUTS AND STEREO TYPES

It is easy enough to misrecognize Bateman as a smug "master of the universe." He is an ostentatiously wealthy chauvinist who violently commands his immediate environment's conformity with his pathological narcissistic desires. But a proper accounting of Bateman's agency necessitates an analysis of the extent to which these self-centred demands emanate, somewhat paradoxically, out of his utter subordination to an overriding mimetic gravity field. This perspectival illusion does not exculpate him (or anyone cut from his ornamental chauvinistic cloth) from the consequences of his behavior so much as articulate the contours of an ongoing historical moment when the Culture Industry has so much sway over human orientation that we are compelled to completely rethink notions like "the human," "the good life," "sovereignty," and "utopia."

The novel begins with Bateman and Price, one of Bateman's many rich white male colleague doppelgangers, traveling in a limousine across Manhattan. Price, who is engaged in the same Wall Street occupation as Bateman (and can be understood as one of Bateman's multiple alternate personalities), is complaining about how much he hates his job. Serving as an echo chamber of Bateman's concerns, he feels he is not sufficiently appreciated, which is to say, *compensated* (although, as this analysis will show, in the simulacrally gluttonous world of *American Psycho*, no amount of money, luxury, or prestige is ever enough): "I'm resourceful. . . . I'm creative. I'm young, unscrupulous, highly motivated, skilled. In essence what I'm saying is that society cannot *afford* to lose me. I'm an *asset*. . . . I mean am I alone in thinking we're not making enough money?"[10] The appropriately named *Price*, like everyone else in Bateman's microcosm, views his personal attributes and education only in terms of their exchange value. Cultural, symbolic, and social capital are merely instrumental to the accrual of and fungible with financial capital; *Price* is an *asset* that society supposedly can't *afford* to dispense with. He espouses a neoliberal appreciation of the economic realm as, in Foucauldian terms, the ultimate "site of veridiction" (that is to say, of verity—or truth value—and "proper" jurisdiction) of all cultural activity, as evinced in every line of the novel. Within the diegetic space of *American*

Psycho, a novel that hyperbolizes the era's paroxysms of ostentatious consumption and status fixation, there is no life outside of *the Market*.

The passage continues, "Like in a movie another bus appears, another poster for *Les Misérables*. . . . His voice stops, he takes in a breath and then quietly says, his eyes fixed on a beggar at the corner of Second and Fifth, 'That's the second one I've seen today. I've kept count.'"[11] This scene underscores the extent to which their experience of their utopian bubble-world, of which the limousine is an acute node, is that of haughty consumer spectators for whom everything and everyone is reduced to the status of commodities and consumable spectacles. Through this commodifying lens, the actual "beggars" on the street occupy the same reified position as the play posters for *Les Misérables* (which is, in turn, a musical remediation of Hugo's novel about the plight of the homeless rendered sonorous for the purpose of entertainment), as though the limousine window were itself a video screen and the "beggars" merely insentient cartoons or avatars mobilized by an entertainment algorithm.

The cocooned limousine thus takes on the trappings of what Sloterdijk characterizes as insulating "caravans,"[12] the kind of mobile immunitary media habitat that vehiculates all intercommunal conquests, from transnational colonialism to urban gentrification (both of which are of import to *American Psycho*). What Murphet refers to as Bateman's full-spectrum "gentrifying agenda"[13] operates through a mobile, securitized caravan network that protects the decadent rich from overproximity to everyone else in 1980s' Manhattan. As such, Bateman figures as an incarnation of the systemic Reagan-Trump-era forces that transformed Manhattan into the playground for the rich that it remains to this day. Above and beyond that, it eerily anticipates the present-day xenophobic project to build a prophylactic wall around Fortress America to keep the "beggars" out.

The limo scene is one of many explicit and implicit references to Bateman's pathological cinematic experience of his life. Throughout the novel, his narration is peppered with references to the fact that his experience of the world around him is "like a movie" and mediated through cinematic devices; for instance, on his way back from the video store (a central node of his media environment), he feels his pharmaceutical cocktail kick in and takes in his surroundings as different elements are brought in and out of relief: "the crying bum, . . . the honking taxis, the decent-looking babe in the Betsey Johnson dress, all of that *fades* and in what seems like *time-lapse photography* but in *slow motion, like a movie*—the sun goes down, . . . and all I can see is the red Lamborghini and all I can hear is my own even, steady panting."[14] Bateman's "time-lapse" experience of the scene sets up a callous chain of equivalences that reduces everything around him—the "bum," the play (which is, not incidentally, about the plight of the poor), the car, the "babe," and her dress—to hollowed-out commodity spectacles, all interchangeable cartoon characters in the service of his filmic experience of the world.

In addition to other explicit references to Bateman's experience being "like a movie,"[15] there are countless subtler articulations of his mediatic experience of the supposedly immediate: sometimes transitions from scene to scene are effected with cinematic devices like the "dissolve"[16] and "[s]mash cut"[17] ; when the consistent fabric of his immediate experience breaks down, he sometimes experiences the rupture in "slow motion"[18] ; and he even later describes an intense sexual experience as a "hardcore montage."[19] Commenting on this *a-priori* mediality of Bateman's innermost experience, Murphet points out that his perceptions and sensibility are ventriloquized by "the technology, economics and spectacularity of film and television. . . . [and] most of what he tells us is [likely] a vividly related version of a cinematic fantasy flickering through his own psyche."[20] What we might refer to as Bateman's "psyche" —including his capacity for attention, desire, cognition, memory, feeling, perception, and recognition—is so subordinate to the coordinates of his media environment that, at a relatively reflexive moment about the issue, he acknowledges that what plays on his television "is [his primary] reality. Everything outside of this is like some movie [he] once saw."[21]

NARCI-SCHISM: A TASTE FOR VIOLENCE

Whenever the group of Bateman doppelgangers deliberates about where to eat dinner, Bateman immediately consults his trusty pal "Mr. Zagat" to resolve the quandary. This rhetorical anthropomorphosis of media is a figuration that gets repeated throughout the novel (in which *Zagat*, to take one example, is mentioned thirteen times). In fact, Bateman's aesthetic judgements are so exaggeratedly overdetermined by the mandates of the mass media that he is depicted as lacking the ability to "immediately" like anything. For example, writes Mark Storey, in addition to his inability to decide which restaurant to visit without consulting the *Zagat* guide, "he cannot offer an opinion on something without first having read a review of it. The constant listing of brands, makes, and models is unmistakably evocative of catalogue-speak or a consumer guide."[22]

If "life for Bateman . . . is one long film,"[23] it is clearly one that remediates the stuff of trusted print media (*Zagat*, *GQ*, *New York Magazine*, *Gentlemen's Quarterly*, store catalogs, consumer guides, etc.), whose opinions, recommendations, and instructions he passively regurgitates (as well as the content and formal features of television shows, commercials, music videos, and cinema). In so doing, he not only anthropomorphizes his media (e.g., "Mr. Zagat") but also brand-objectifies himself through it: he *is* "*total GQ*."[24] On this point, Frances Ferguson highlights the fact that Bateman is so thoroughly constituted by the ether of media injunctions and brand-name commodities that "the constant search for excessive distinctiveness . . . issues in its opposite, the inability of any individual to perform an action that can be connected with his name by other people."[25]

This leads to another important point. Under the homogenizing mandates of the Culture Industry, everyone in the novel seems to be interchangeable with everyone else: Bateman confuses most every man in his circle with another and is, in turn, so confused by his peers; by the same token, the women are reduced to interchangeable "hardbodies" whom their boyfriends' indistinguishable friends take turn sleeping with behind the boyfriends' backs: Bateman is sleeping with Luis Carruthers's girlfriend, and Price is likely conducting an affair with Bateman's, and so on.

Storey points out that this economy of interchangeability loosely conforms to René Girard's concept of "mimetic rivalry," a dynamic that compellingly explains Bateman's murder of Owen, who, among all the doppelgangers, represents the most perfect manifestation of the Bateman personality complex. Owen has captured the prized Fisher account, has a better apartment than Bateman, and has no difficulty getting into Dorsia (the Holy Grail of elite restaurants in Bateman's universe). All this leads Murphet to conclude that "[Owen] is the sun around which Bateman and his interchangeable companions circle in emulation and envy."[26] Such a Girardian understanding provides a preliminary framework for understanding yet another layer of mediation in Bateman's life.

In *Deceit, Desire, and the Novel*, Girard hypothesizes two interoriented modalities of mimetic mediation. The first category is "internal mediation," which operates roughly at the level of the psychoanalytic "ideal ego." In the history of Western literature, internal mediation often plays out as a rivalry between relative mirror images, "mimetic rivals," over a shared object of desire. In *American Psycho*, this would describe Bateman's envy-bound relationship with relatively interchangeable doppelgangers like Van Patten, Carruthers, and especially, Owen.

The one proximal colleague toward whom Bateman experiences no envy is Tim Price, who hovers on the periphery of the internal mediation and, the text suggests, may even be a pure hallucination. Bateman has an intense mimetic attachment first to Price and then Owen as arbiters, or at least nodes, of taste and distinction, but he splits them into good and bad manifestations. Price is "the most interesting person [Bateman] know[s],"[27] and he even seems to be unfazed by the fact that Price may be conducting an affair with his girlfriend Evelyn; of course, according to the Girardian formulation of mimetic rivalry, such an affair should be anathema to Bateman and amplify his interest in Evelyn (which it does not). This may well be because Bateman's mirror images are simply that, alter egos that do not exist outside of his imagination. Or it may be that Girard's optics provide an imperfect heuristic for articulating the modality of mimesis at play here. Nonetheless, Bateman's ultimate mimetic rival, in strictly Girardian terms, is undeniably Paul Owen, the most perfect immediate manifestation of Bateman's neoliberal ideal, and Bateman murders him "on this account."

TRUMPING SELF-MASTERY

Girardian "external mediation" operates at something like the level of the psychoanalytic "ego ideal." According to Girard's formula, the subject does not experience mimetic rivalry toward their distal external mediator: "The hero of external mediation proclaims aloud the true nature of his desire. He worships his model openly and declares the true nature of his desire."[28] Such external mediators as often serve as respected, benevolent figures constituting the high-water mark of taste and distinction. As such, "[n]o rivalry with the mediator is possible."[29] In Bateman's case, this is the upper pantheon occupied by celebrity investor Donald Trump, whose iconic book, *The Art of the Deal*, he keeps on his desk and recommends to Detective Kimball as he investigates the murder of Owen.

In *Fire and Fury* author Michael Wolff's words, "[in the 1980s and 1990s] Trump was both symbol of and punch line for this new era of excess and celebrity and the media's celebration of those things. . . . The story of Trump was the story of how he tried to make himself a story."[30] Apropos of Trump's own recursive obsession with his image, Bateman's preoccupation with the Trump brand is bound up with his own misguided aspiration for distinction and manifests itself as a constant alertness for any sign of Donald, Ivana, or even their car. Trump is always on the tip of Bateman's tongue: he tries and fails to get himself invited to the Trump Christmas party; at one point he speculates that women would be more attracted to him if he claimed to be Trump's "close personal friend"; and he even introduces himself to a limousine driver, however sarcastically, as none other than Donald Trump.

This mimetic fixation on Trump explains Bateman's momentary confusion when he is told that the pizza he has just fastidiously disapproved of is actually Trump's favourite. After being presented a Xerox copy of an article (tellingly, referred to merely by the corporation's name—"a Xerox") in which Trump himself praises the pizza in question, he reverses his assessment and praises it in lock-step with his external mimetic medium. Trump, then, figures as the ultimate external medium and arbiter of *taste* (conducted through the simulacral medium of a photocopy of a newspaper or magazine article) that, like *Zagat*, "trumps" Bateman's own "immediate" sense perception: "Well . . . I think I have to *re*taste the pizza," Bateman concedes, "if the pizza is okay with Donny. . . . it's okay with me."[31]

Rajeev Balasubramanyam claims that Trump's role as Bateman's prevailing aesthetic and ethical authority functions to both quash any compunctions he might have about his violent behavior and, at least temporarily, keep total psychotic breakdown at bay. Whenever Bateman is called to account for his actions, asserts Balasubramanyam, "he tries to resolve the crisis by invoking Trump's name or form as one might a god's."[32] The Trump brand functions, for Bateman, like a sacred talisman that wards away what he construes as evil. After perpetrating countless violent crimes, he wanders among the "filth" of Manhattan like a newfangled Travis Bickle (the dystagonist of Martin Scorsese's *Taxi Driver*), observing that "everyone on the street looks sad, the air is full of decay, bodies lie on the cold pavement, miles of it, some are moving, most are not. History is sinking and only a very few seem dimly aware that things are getting bad."[33] But he is suddenly heartened, Balasubramanyam observes, by an abrupt encounter with his moral compass and beacon of hope: "I notice the skyline has changed only recently. I look up, admiringly, at Trump Tower, tall, proudly gleaming in the late afternoon sunlight."[34]

GRABBING HARDBODIES IN STORMY WATERS

Yet another infernal fold of mediation resides in Bateman's remarkably Trumpian interactions with women. His interaction with those in his circle bespeaks a lifeless world in which, as Murphet articulates the scene, "[m]en and women do not so much talk to each other . . . as pile up meaningless, irreconcilable lists on dishes garnished with indifference."[35] Ultimately, this is because Bateman views the women around him as mere commodity instruments, the acquisition of which garners him little more than the fleeting gratification of conquest and orgasm.

His subordination of women is at its most acute in his trysts with prostitutes and "hardbodies" that he meets at nightclubs. But, even here, Bateman is far from master of his own house. It is scenes such as these that have caused some critics to speculate that the gratuitous sex and violence that so define the narrative are little more than feckless Bateman's fantasies of omnipotence. Storey observes that, in Bateman's impudent litanies of sexual conquest, his "real-life sexual acts become intertwined with the pornography he freely admits to watching, to the extent that in his own narrative the line between the two is obliterated."[36] For example, when Bateman describes a scene from a favorite pornographic film, *Inside Lydia's Ass*, he refers to it "in exactly the same uninflected, cool prose in which he later describes the 'real' sex. As a result, the sex, like the violence, becomes less realistic; for the most part, it reads like a certain type of male fantasy. . . . Bateman even describes a threesome as a 'hard-core montage.'"[37]

It is important to dwell on the fact that Bateman's own experiential "film" is peopled in no small part by sex trade workers who are reduced to the status of mere performers in his fantasy. This fantasy is so overdetermined by commodification and, as Murphet points out, the "heavily stereotyped language of mass-marketed porn"[38] that, whether these carefully choreographed vignettes "actually" transpire at all (within the diegetic space of this fictional novel), there is rarely much pleasure to be had for anyone involved. Murphet, invoking Fredric Jameson, characterizes this state as "the waning of sexual feeling under the regime of commodities in which he functions."[39] In keeping with this Lacanian-Jamesonian reading, it should come as no surprise that fragments of mass-media scripts constitute the fantasies that frame the scene. These are the basic coordinates of all human desire in the electronic (and digital) media sphere. But Bateman has such privileged access to the "objects" of his desire that the minimal distance which usually feeds and sustains desire is obliterated, and he is subjected to a libidinal economy of diminishing returns within his homogenizing media cocoon. No "hardbody" conquest, no rarefied dish, no cinematic mise-en-scène is adequate to the task of feeding his impetuous demands for (and addiction to) the enjoyment of prestige.

Bateman's neoliberal utopia would seem to be defined by its paradoxically simultaneous licentiousness and sterility. Writing on this conjuncture and the vicissitudes of utopian worlds, Terry Eagleton asserts that there are two basic forms of utopia.

> There are carnivalesque societies in which, instead of working, everyone will drink, feast and copulate from dawn to dusk. In one such 18th-century fantasy, men and women bereft of all body hair leap naked into fountains, while the progressively minded narrator watches on. . . . There are also more austere utopias, in which everything is odourless and antiseptic. . . . In these meticulously planned countries of the mind, the natives tend to jaw on for hours about the efficiency of their sanitary arrangements or the ingenuity of their electoral system.[40]

In resonance with Eagleton's account and Le Guin's observations about the intimate relationship between utopia and dystopia, the dystopian world of *American Psycho* seems to congeal both fantasies of perfection that Eagleton articulates—the libidinal and the biopolitical—into a single nightmarish vision. Even though there are almost no limits to Bateman's licentious pursuits within the confines of his automated media environment, the experience afforded is so "antiseptic" that even he does not stand to benefit in a meaningful way. The perverse logic of his superficial desires dictates that the plenum he pursues become more and more elusive and illusory and the more aggressively he pursues it. Even the would-be "master of the universe" is a peculiar variety of slave to the infernal cultural logic of media modernity. Abandon faith all ye who enter the fancy restaurant at "the end of history."

TRUMP'S GREATEST APPRENTICE: MAKING AMERICA HATE AGAIN

At the beginning of the novel, Bateman announces his avowed political beliefs to his cadre. His hypocritical sound bites are not a far cry from the kind of cynical doublespeak one would expect to hear from Trump at various stages of his career.

> We have to end apartheid for one. And slow down the nuclear arms race, stop terrorism and world hunger. Ensure a strong national defense, prevent the spread of communism in Central America, work for a Middle East peace settlement, prevent U.S. military involvement overseas. We have to ensure that America is a respected world power . . . [and] strengthen laws to crack down on crime and illegal drugs. . . . But economically we're still a mess. We have to find a way to hold down the inflation rate and reduce the deficit. We also need to provide training and jobs for the unemployed as well as protect existing American jobs from unfair foreign imports. We have to make America the leader in new technology. At the same time we need to promote economic growth and business expansion and hold the line against federal income taxes and hold down interest rates while promoting opportunities for small businesses and controlling mergers and big corporate takeovers. . . . We have to stop people from abusing the welfare system. We have to provide food and shelter for the homeless and oppose racial discrimination and promote civil rights while also promoting equal rights for women but change the abortion laws to protect the right to life yet still somehow maintain women's freedom of choice. We also have to control the influx of illegal immigrants. We have to encourage a return to traditional moral values and curb graphic sex and violence on TV, in movies, in popular music, everywhere.[41]

His speech is little more than a regurgitated cache of hollow, often mutually contradictory, campaign talking points of the sort that circulate widely during the US election cycle. Of course, Bateman's sounding board, Price, who knows him better than any of the other *doppel*s, is incredulous because these claims are so hypocritical, so disingenuous, there is no way that, *deep down*, he could earnestly stand behind them.

But Bateman anticipates the twenty-first-century politician Trump in that he seems to appreciate that there need not be any substance underlying these empty promises. As he acknowledges, in one of the novel's rare apostrophic moments, there is no "deep down" interiority or reality to Bateman. There is merely, he avers, "an idea of a Patrick Bateman, some kind of abstraction, but there is no me, only an entity, something illusory, and though I can hide my cold gaze and you can shake my hand and feel flesh gripping yours and maybe you can even sense our lifestyles are probably comparable: I simply am not there."[42]

As for Trump, if *The Art of the Deal* is to be taken at face value (despite that it was actually written by ghostwriter Tony Schwartz), we have good reason to be as incredulous as Price.

> The final key to the way I promote is bravado. I play to people's fantasies. People may not always think big themselves, but they can still get very excited by those who do. That's why a little hyperbole never hurts. People want to believe that something is the biggest and the greatest and the most spectacular. I call it truthful hyperbole. It's an innocent form of exaggeration, and a very effective form of promotion.[43]

Appealing to people's utopian fantasies has proven to be a startlingly effective form of self-promotion on the campaign trail. Le Guin would undoubtedly have a great deal to say about their dystopian undergirdings. After all, Trump's most effective "hyperbole" is subtended by the racist, classist, and sexist fantasies of both magically repelling putatively toxic visitors at the country's borders and going back in time to an imaginary Edenic moment to "make America great again." A psychoanalyst might refer to such misguided fancies as a particularly schizoid modality of magical thinking, especially when Americans start to hallucinate that this immunizing purge has somehow accomplished its constitutively impossible mission.

ONTOGENY RECAPITULATES REAGANOMY (RATHER THAN NIXONOMY)

At the end of *American Psycho*, Bateman and Price are watching the inauguration of George H. W. Bush on television. In the wake of the Iran-Contra hearings, Ronald Reagan, President of the United States for most of the 1980s, has been betrayed as corrupt, wildly hypocritical, or senile: "[L]ike Bateman himself, Reagan is the 'psycho' of the novel's title, selling arms to Iran to back genocide in Nicaragua."[44] As the paternal signifier who guaranteed the integrity of an entire decadent yuppie form of life and its utopian theology of the Invisible Hand of the Market, Reagan's unhinging is replete with significance. Though Bateman seems unfazed, Price, his proximal arbiter of value and values, is a mess: "How can [Reagan] lie like that? How can he pull that shit?"[45] Given his mimetic proximity to Bateman, Price's outrage betokens a potential irreparable schism in the American psycho's soul. The scandalous unhinging of the president, the figure whose rhetorical *ethos* was supposed to stand as the fiat currency of a new US century, would seem to presage a radically new understanding of the United States and its relationship to the world. Like Bateman, many in the western world may still be immune to the more penetrating implications of this rupture. But such obliviousness is not likely sustainable.

THE GREAT UNHINGING: CAESAR OR CAESURA

Rhetorician Lynette Hunter points out that the term "allegory" is "derived from *allos* and *agoreuein*, signifying 'other speaking', other than what is said, or, what is not said."[46] Hunter goes on to suggest that, among the rhetorical tropes, allegory might harbor a unique relationship with otherness and alienation. If *American Psycho* is what Hunter would call an allegorical "event" about the trajectory of the United States at the turn of the millennium, it is one that figures as both a warning of and uncanny augury about the World Interior of Capital's hardening optics on "otherness." The novel can be understood as a sustained critique of an increasingly dystopian neoliberal media environment that (far from uniting humanity in a harmonious Global Village) precipitates violent, acrimonious class, race, and gender relations while representing this state as the fault of those that have been placed squarely in its scapegoating crosshairs.

Commenting on the bizarre torsion at play in the nucleus of the utopian US project, Sloterdijk observes that the Western Imaginary seems to be invested in a special relationship between the figure of the sovereign lawmaking individual and the trajectory of the body politic as a whole.

> You see this in American Westerns, where the good sheriff has to imagine the not-yet-existent state in his own private morality. But Trump is a degenerate sheriff. He acts as if he doesn't care if the state comes into being or not and mocks the upright townsfolk. What makes Trump dangerous is that he exposes parts of liberal democracies that were only shadowily visible up until now. In democracies, there is always an oligarchic element, but Trump makes it extremely, comically visible.[47]

If any popular Fukuyamist delusion about vibrant democracies' inherent compatibility with unfettered neoliberalism survived the Bush and Obama presidencies, Trump would seem to represent the utter extirpation of such a parochial utopian fantasy. At a time when conventional wisdom dictated that the "upright" heir to the two-party consensus would swoop in and maintain the polite fantasmatic semblance, an obscene sheriff showed up, seemingly from out of the digital media ether, to snuff it out once and for all.

It is hard to believe that any crystal ball could have anticipated that the caricaturish Trump brand would not only survive Reagan's great unhinging but also gather enough steam to run roughshod over the entire political and media establishment to assume a simulacral version of Reagan's place. *American Psycho* enjoins us to ask what precisely it is about Trump that makes him such a numinous techno-epistemic figure for this historical moment. As a celebrity businessman and author who became a popular game show host and WWE professional wrestler before rerouting the presidential election cycle through his *Twitter* feed, he seems to function as a charismatic avatar for, and indivisible remainder of, three successive media regimes: print culture, television, and the Internet. Trump is not just an obscene sheriff; he also plays one on TV and every other existing media channel.

Future historians may well look back on the short period spanning neoliberalism's gestation as a utopian idea to its manifestation and dystopian digital actualization as "the Reagan Era." Just as, according to Hegel, Julius Caesar finally became enshrined in the order of things as caesarism after his assassination, perhaps Trump's repetition of Reagan—a media celebrity and charismatic public manipulator who became president before publicly descending into scandal and dementia—constitutes the perfection of the contingent model under more conducive political-mediatic circumstances. It is also conceivable that the name *Trump* marks an absolute caesura. If so, perhaps "the Trump Era" will be defined by its perverse escape velocity from the turn-of-the-century techno-epistemic horizon (including neoliberal Reaganism) toward a new, still-coalescing state of political-mediatic affairs.

However the silicon dust settles, *American Psycho* is an uncannily prescient allegory about the Trumpian Spirit of the Age. As such, it also harbors what we might call modest *thanatopian* potentials about our present circumstances. That is to say that the novel serves as the locus of a peculiar narrative event, a thanatotic break in the discourse network that potentially jolts the reader out of their complacency and complicity with the efficiencies and pleasures of neoliberalism's psychotic, rudderless model of "the good life." But rather than offering utopian panaceas embedded in the theology of invisible hands and universal wills, *American Psycho* importunes Americans to rethink the vortex of values, orientations, goods, mentors, kin, rivals, and violence that constitutes both their own proximal media ecosystems and that of the lumbering, confused US body politic at the turn of the millennium. In the meantime, as the obscene "oligarchic element" envelops the space once reserved for the *demos*, Sloterdjik warns, "[t]he playground for madness is vast."[48]

NOTES

1. Ursula Le Guin, *No Time to Spare: Thinking About What Matters* (New York: Houghton, Mifflin, Harcourt, 2017), 85.
2. *Oxford Dictionaries*, s.v. "utopia." Accessed https://en.oxforddictionaries.com/definition/utopia on July 20, 2018.
3. Bret Easton Ellis, *American Psycho* (New York, Picador, 1991), 130.
4. Easton Ellis, *American Psycho*, 130.
5. Thomas Heise, "*American Psycho*: Neoliberal Fantasies and the Death of Downtown," *Arizona Quarterly: A Journal of American Literature, Culture, and Theory* 67, no. 1 (2011): 136.
6. Heise, "Neoliberal Fantasies," 138.
7. Javier Martín Párraga, *Fear, Trauma and Paranoia in Bret Easton Ellis' Oeuvre* (Newcastle: Cambridge Scholars, 2017), 48.
8. Slavoj Žižek, *Violence: Six Sideways Reflections* (New York: Picador, 2008), 2.
9. Georgina Colby, *Bret Easton Ellis: Underwriting the Contemporary* (New York: Palgrave Macmillan, 2011), 88.

10. Easton Ellis, *American Psycho*, 3 (my italics).
11. Easton Ellis, *American Psycho*, 3–4.
12. Peter Sloterdijk, *The World Interior of Capital*, trans. Wieland Hoban (Cambridge: Polity, 2013), 120.
13. Julian Murphet, *Bret Easton Ellis' American Psycho: A Reader's Guide* (New York: Continuum, 2002), 59,
14. Easton Ellis, *American Psycho*, 114 (my italics).
15. Easton Ellis, *American Psycho*, 61, 114, 245, 343.
16. Easton Ellis, *American Psycho*, 8, 24.
17. Easton Ellis, *American Psycho*, 11.
18. Easton Ellis, *American Psycho*, 62, 86
19. Easton Ellis, *American Psycho*, 303.
20. Murphet, *Reader's Guide*, 85-6.
21. Easton Ellis, *American Psycho*, 345.
22. Mark Storey, "'And as Things Fell Apart': The Crisis of Postmodern Masculinity in Bret Easton Ellis's *American Psycho* and Dennis Cooper's *Frisk*," *Critique: Studies in Contemporary Fiction* 27, no. 1 (2005): 61.
23. Storey, "And as Things," 61.
24. Easton Ellis, *American Psycho*, 90.
25. Frances Ferguson, *Pornography, the Theory: What Utilitarianism Did to Action* (Chicago: University of Chicago Press, 2004): 33.
26. Murphet, *Reader's Guide*, 44.
27. Easton Ellis, *American Psycho*, 21.
28. Rene Girard, *Deceit, Desire, and the Novel: Self and Other in Literary Structure* (Baltimore: Johns Hopkins University Press, 1976), 10.
29. Girard, *Deceit*, 9.
30. Michael Wolff, *Fire and Fury* (New York: Henry Holt, 2018), 74.
31. Easton Ellis, *American Psycho*, 110.
32. Rajeev Balusubramanyam, "Donald Trump, *American Psycho* Muse: How the *Art of the Deal* Elitist Became a Poor Man's Patrick Bateman—and Now He's a Real Threat," *Salon*, May 14, 2016. Accessed http://www.salon.com/2016/05/14/donald_trump_american_psycho_muse_how_the_art_of_the_deal_elitist_became_a_poor_mans_patrick_bateman_and_now_hes_a_real_threat/ on May 9, 2018.
33. Easton Ellis, *American Psycho*, 385.
34. Balusubramanyam, "Donald Trump."
35. Murphet, *Reader's Guide*, 30.
36. Storey, "And as Things Fell Apart," 61.
37. Storey, "And as Things Fell Apart," 61.
38. Murphet, *Reader's Guide*, 38.
39. Murphet, *Reader's Guide*, 38.
40. Terry Eagleton, "Utopias, Past and Present: Why Thomas More Remains Astonishingly Radical," *The Guardian*, Oct 16, 2015. Accessed https://www.theguardian.com/books/2015/oct/16/utopias-past-present-thomas-more-terry-eagleton on May 7, 2018.
41. Easton Ellis, *American Psycho*, 15.
42. Easton Ellis, *American Psycho*, 377.
43. Donald Trump, *The Art of the Deal* (New York: Ballantine, 1987), 58.
44. Murphet, *Reader's Guide*, 54.
45. Easton Ellis, *American Psycho*, 397.
46. Lynette Hunter, "Allegory Happens: Allegory in the Arts post-1960," in *The Cambridge Companion to Allegory*, eds. R. Copeland and P. T. Struck (Cambridge University Press, 2010), 266.
47. Peter Sloterdijk, "A Celebrity Philosopher Explains the Populist Insurgency," interview by Thomas Meaney, *New Yorker*, Life and Letters, February 26, 2018.
48. Sloterdijk, "A Celebrity Philosopher."

Chapter Six

"Horror Movies Are Already Telling the Story" . . . of Trump's America

Todd K. Platts and Kibiriti Majuto

One month before Donald Trump won the presidency, media critic Matthew Monagle noted, "if there's any upside to this presidential election, it's the next wave of horror movies dealing with all these issues we've raised."[1] Monagle was not alone in seeing the potential cathartic function of horror in response to one of the most polarizing elections in recent memory. Indeed, in the wake of the election, other critics echoed Monagle's proclamation: "What America Needs Now Is Horror Movies,"[2] "Why Horror Movies Will be the Most Exciting Art Form of the Donald Trump Era,"[3] and "Has Horror become the Movie Genre of the Trump Era?"[4] Likewise, even the reviews of individual horror films mentioned Trump in their titles, "*Get Out* Proves the Vitality of Horror in the Trump Era"[5] and "*Green Room* Is a Horror Movie for Trump's America."[6] This is not to mention the hoopla over Trump's 2020 campaign slogan, "Keep America Great," being used to promote 2016's *The Purge: Election Year*. In short, critics saw the specter of Trump haunting the narratives of innumerable horror films in the years 2016 and 2017. In the words of Matt Kim, "Horror Movies Are Already Telling the Story" . . .[7] of Trump's America.

To make sense of the torrent of commentary linking Trump to horror cinema, this chapter follows recent scholarship that examines the work performed by film critics and observers. Where prior literature has discussed how critics decipher and relay the racial content of films to audiences, this chapter explores how critics implicitly and explicitly inform their audiences of current political events.[8] Specifically, it will examine how various critics reckoned with candidate, then President, Trump through reference to horror cinema in general and specific horror films in the years 2016 and 2017.

Although scholars debate the meaning of films in academic literature, often for years after their release, it is significant to understand how film texts are grappled with in a broader context. The fact that professional critics evaluate films for a living gives their words significant weight and, arguably, turns them into barometers of how movies are understood contemporaneously.[9] As Thomas Schatz points out, critics and industry observers "set the terms of critical discussion on American film, and their writing is especially useful when dealing with recent (and still current) films" because they "provide the first phase of evaluation, theoretical formulation, and canon formation."[10] That is, the cultural job of critics and observers is to translate complex texts in ways that make sense to lay audiences. To give further credence to their work, the late film critic Roger Ebert was named "the most powerful pundit in America" in 2007 by *Forbes* magazine, in part, because his reviews were seen as intelligent and perceptive.[11] The continued relevance of critics is demonstrated by a recent Nielsen report that found, "eight out of 10 moviegoers still refer to movie reviews at least some of the time when they're considering what films to see."[12] Accordingly, the manner in which critics inform their readers becomes a vital site of inquiry. Before investigating how Trump appeared in reviews of horror films, however, it is important to pause and consider both the general functions of horror and its recent history. This will allow us to gain perspective on how so many critics turned to the genre as Trump rose to power.

HORROR AND SOCIETY

One of the best ways to gain insight into how a society grapples with large-scale social change is through reference to horror cinema—the very genre designed to scare, unsettle, and otherwise disturb its audience.[13] Horror cinema ebbs and flows in accordance with diffusely felt trauma, whereby it functions as a conduit for negative sentiment.[14] The genre gives voice and form to a society's "shared fears"[15] and "collective nightmares,"[16] in the process providing a "versatile barometer for gauging a society's most basic truths."[17] Horror films often accomplish their task by drawing on "social upheaval, anxieties about natural and manmade disasters, conflicts and wars, [and] crime and violence"[18] to animate their narratives.

Since the 1960s, horror cinema has frequently commented upon contemporary US life and institutions and has done so by locating monstrous threats within rather than away from us.[19] In short succession, horror films from the 1960s and 1970s dramatized the horrors of the Vietnam War and the growing nihilism of the countercultural left.[20] During the 1980s, slasher films like *Halloween* (1978) and *Friday the 13th* (1980) came to prominence. With their plots organized around the gory deaths of hedonistic teenagers, slashers have been seen as a reactionary riposte to liberalized sexual attitudes of the 1960s and 1970s as well as endorsement of conservative values.[21] In the 1990s, horror films akin to the *Scream* series (1996–2011) responded to the growing media savvy of younger audiences by sporting storylines with characters aware of the fact they were in a horror film.[22] The terrorist attacks of September 11, 2001 and the ensuing War on Terror are seen as catalyzing torture porn films like the *Saw* franchise (2004–2017) and *Hostel* (2005) as well the resurgence of zombie cinema. Where torture porn films wrestled with ambivalence over the Bush administration's use of enhanced interrogation techniques, the imagery of zombie films strongly paralleled with the aftermath of a terrorist attack.[23] The hope and optimism many on the left placed in President Barack Obama was not echoed in horror cinema.[24] Instead, the financial anxieties associated with the 2007–2008 recession became the driving force of the genre. Films like the *Paranormal Activity* franchise (2007–2017) and the *Insidious* (2010–2018) and *The Conjuring* series (2013–2016) "implicitly and explicitly reference the financial crisis [that] has adversely affected the lives of millions of ordinary American families."[25]

For many, the 2016 presidential election was a horror film incarnate with "a lot of people [finding themselves] genuinely afraid of losing their livelihoods, their liberties, and the lovely graces of their planet."[26] During the campaign, candidate Trump nakedly trafficked in horror(ific) tropes. Across his speeches and rallies, he painted images of horror through claims that democrats had left (white) Americans destitute and alienated from politics; he evoked images of horror by likening Washington, DC, to a swamp in need of draining, with its worst embodiment, Hillary Clinton, in need of going to jail; and he stoked up real horror with racial animus, a flagrant disregard for environmental science, and a seeming hell-bent desire to dismantle public education and reputable news coverage.[27] What is more, Trump ran a campaign of "prideful ignorance and alarmist bravado" with "no rational ideas about how to govern the United States."[28] Concurrent, and perhaps inspired by Trump's campaign sloganeering, 2016 saw a rise in hate crimes, xenophobia, bullying, and white nationalism.[29]

The parallels to the 2016 presidential campaign and horror noted in the opening paragraph did not take long. As Monagle noted, horror films perform their cultural work best with low budgets and high concepts,[30] making the genre ideally suited to comment upon what cultural critic Douglas Kellner dubbed the "*American Horror Show*."[31] Thus, starting in 2016, many commentators began to view President Trump as the primary animating force behind the genre; a view shared by famed horror producer Jason Blum, "the current administration's been terrific for the scary-movie business." Blum even credited Trump with the commercial success of *Get Out*, "I think *Get Out* did four times the business it would have done if Hillary had been president."[32]

While it is tempting to view the horror films of 2016 and 2017 as a direct response to the horrors of Trump's ascendency, these films had been in development for years. It is, thus, more appropriate to suggest the films discussed demonstrated an anticipatory function by providing "artistic visions of the world that might transcend the social context of the moment and articulate future possibilities."[33] Though this chapter only covers the films released during the campaign and immediately after the election, it is arguable that 2018 marks the year when horror films began to explicitly respond to Trump's America. For instance, *Winchester* (2018) represents an attempt to grapple with issues of gun violence, *Unsane* (2018) responds to issues over sexual harassment and assault raised by the Me Too Movement, *A Quiet Place* (2018) dramatizes the risk of living in a society where one's speech can put them at risk of losing their life, and *The First Purge* (2018) depicts a political future wherein the federal government has declared a de facto war against the poor. Given the volume of commentary on the association between Trump and horror cinema, the ensuing discussion favors breadth over depth. As well, discussions of each film are meant to be illustrative, not exhaustive.

HORROR FILMS DURING THE CAMPAIGN, OR HORROR AND THE POTENTIAL HORRORS OF TRUMP

During the campaign, several films were seen as offering an uncanny resemblance to the underbelly of Trump's rise to power. Reviewers saw Trump supporters as being represented in *Green Room* (2016), the potential future United States under President Trump was given haunting voice in *The Purge: Election Year*, and *31* (2016) was seen as satirizing how the frailties of racism are used to maintain a gilded class system.

Green Room tells the story of a struggling punk band who take a last second gig at a white nationalist bar in backwoods Oregon. After witnessing a murder, the band is held hostage in the bar's green room. A strong subtext of the film is the idea that the white nationalists, under the leadership of Darcy Banker (Patrick Stewart), are planning a large-scale social movement. This facet of the film gave it a strong resonance to many critics. According to Jason Bailey of *Flavorwire*, with its "vile white supremacist and his lockstep followers, [*Green Room*] is a horror that seems, in this election season, uncomfortably close to reality."[34] *GQ*'s Scott Meslow took the observation further, stating *Green Room* "is the only movie I've seen this year that actually centers on characters who would almost certainly be Trump supporters . . . confident that his coronation would usher in a new age of American culture in which white supremacy would be widely accepted."[35] For his part, director Jeremy Saulnier seemed penitent regarding the resonance of the film, "it's now more relevant than it should be. That wasn't my attention. I'm sad that it is so relevant."[36]

The Purge series (2013–) depicts a dystopian future where once a year nearly any crime, including murder, is legal for twelve hours. *The Purge: Election Year*, the third film in the series, centers around an upcoming presidential election that pits the New Founding Fathers of America's (the fictional political party behind the purge) Edwidge Owens (Kyle Secor) against the anti-purge candidate Charlie Roan (Elizabeth Mitchell), who witnessed her entire family slaughtered eighteen years before the film's start. Jia Tolentino's *New Yorker* review of *The Purge: Election Year* described the first two films in the series as cartoonish embellishments of US politics, something that could only happen in the movies. For her, the third movie, unfortunately, hit too close to home in that it "arrives at a time when nightmare politics have already bent real life."[37] This was a sentiment shared by B. Alan Orange of *Movieweb*, "the real-life presidential campaign looks like something out of a movie, so should it come as any surprise that it has inspired one?"[38] and *Forbes*'s Scott Mendelson who called it "sadly topical."[39] For some, the film spoke to the worrying aspects of Trump's supporters, "the film echoes some of the violence that has been a recurring concern for Donald Trump's campaign."[40] In fact, this facet of the film became part of its advertising, "the marketing has been deviously brilliant, with frighteningly authentic campaign videos running during the GOP debates."[41] In a retrospective piece on *The Purge* series, Scott Mendelson noted that Trump, "played to the very worst instincts of people who otherwise might consider themselves good and decent," and this allowed *The Purge: Election Year* to serve as "a de facto warning call."[42] With Trump adopting "Keep America Great" as his 2020 campaign slogan, a phrase used to promote *The Purge: Election Year*, *Vulture*'s Jordan Crucchiola opined that the fourth installment is "practically writing itself."[43] Indeed, *The First Purge* was released July 1, 2018, and is rife with potshots at Donald Trump.[44]

Though set in 1976, the plot of *31* reverberates with the spirit of 2016. In the film, which was given a limited theatrical run, five traveling carnival workers are kidnapped and forced to play a survival game called 31. The game is run by wealthy aristocrats who hire hitmen dressed as clowns to kill the game's participants. Luke Thompson's *Forbes* review drew parallels between the film and the tactics of Trump, "the free-loving carnies and the carnage-loving clowns all arguably ought to be on the same side, as they're at the same level of income"; however, they are not because, "some on the clown side are racist, sadistic, abusive, horrible people" who are "being played by rich jerks for some minor amusement."[45]

Trump's presidential victory surprised nearly everyone. Films like *Green Room*, *The Purge: Election Year*, and *31* were supposed to be warnings; after all, the white nationalists are killed in *Green Room* and an anti-purge candidate wins in *The Purge: Election Year*. Instead of warning us of Trump, they predicted his rise. After the election, newly released horror films began being interpreted in light of Trump's presidency or its potential destructiveness.

FILMS AFTER THE CAMPAIGN, OR HORROR AND THE HORRORS OF TRUMP

After Trump's victory, perhaps in an attempt to come to grips with what just happened, commentators began witnessing Trumpian allusions in a variety of horror films. Some commentators, however, did not join this trend. Kenneth Turan of the *Los Angeles Times*, for instance, went so far as to blame Hollywood for President Trump.[46] He was joined by *Forbes*'s Rob Cain who wrote, "Hollywood has been foreshadowing the possibility of a moment like this for decades, both in horror movies and dystopian fiction"[47] and *Huffington Post*'s Brian Ross suggested our focus on reel horrors distracted us from real horrors.[48] These critics, though, were outflanked by those critics who opted to look to new horror films to make sense of the election. *The Awl*'s Seyward Darby was perhaps the most forthright, suggesting that the US populace needed horror cinema for its ability to grapple "with our base fears and instincts."[49] Writing for *W Magazine*, Max Lakin summed the prevailing view of critics thusly, "the horror genre is responding to [Trump] faster and more successfully than most other art forms today."[50] Such statements allowed critics to see Trump "appearing" in horror films as varied as *A Cure for Wellness* (2017), *XX* (2017), *Get Out*, *Life* (2017), *The Belko Experiment* (2017), *It Comes at Night* (2017), *It* (2017), and *Mother!* (2017).

Though a box-office bomb and garnering more attention for its use of fake news sites for promotion,[51] *A Cure for Wellness*'s story of a vampiric operator of a wellness clinic who slowly leaches the life away from his clients was seen by *Huffington Post*'s Matthew Jacobs as containing "Trumpian parallels." with the film's lead antagonist Dr. Heinreich Volmer, a "deceptive despot," as providing a stand-in for Trump.[52]

The Trumpian parallels in the anthology *XX* come not from a critic, but from one of the film's directors, Karyn Kusama. Kusama's segment of *XX*, "Her Only Living Son," involves a single mother and the coming eighteenth birthday of her rebellious son, who is a spawn of Satan. Kusama saw the boy as resembling the character of Trump, "I was writing about the devil's presence at the end of that film as this petty, easily insulted childish force that just sort of needed a spanking, needed to just be resisted and screamed back at and told, 'no, get out of my life'" before adding that the current political environment was a "sadly way too literal manifestation of what I just described."[53]

Get Out, a film about a seemingly liberal white family who kidnaps blacks to transplant their life essence into whites, was heralded by *New York*

Times's Frank Bruni as "the movie for the age of Trump."[54] The film was understood as offering a biting commentary on the rise of Trump, "In an era of Donald Trump and Black Lives Matter, it taps into America's racial tensions in the most unsettling and yet compelling fashion."[55] John DeFore's *Hollywood Reporter* review seconded this idea, "[the film] exploits racial fears that have become substantially more potent (not to mention more comprehensible for many white Americans) since the events of Nov. 8 [the day of the 2016 Presidential election]."[56] The Associated Press's Jake Coyle piggybacked on the praising of *Get Out*, noting that few films approached "its firm grip of the [racial] zeitgeist."[57]

On the surface, the plot of *Life*, which sees a blobby alien life form affectionately named Calvin devour the crew of a space shuttle, seems to offer no commentary on Trump. However, *Los Angeles Times* critic Justin Chang likened the film's monster to Trump's campaign itself. At first, the campaign, like Calvin, started out small, innocent, and seemingly harmless . . . maybe even funny. Before long, and to everyone's surprise, both transformed into uncontrollable monsters.[58]

In *The Belko Experiment*, eighty American white-collar workers stationed in an office building in Bogotá, Colombia, are tasked with killing each other in a morbid game of survival. One of the film's stars, Tony Goldwyn, compared the plight of *The Belko Experiment*'s protagonists fight for survival to the current political climate.

> [W]e find ourselves in a political environment where there's this divide where there are people who want to solve our impractical problems with blunt force. The appeal of Trump in America is: 'These problems, were [*sic*] gonna fix 'em. Some people are gonna get hurt but we're tired of being politically correct and empathetic to everyone—we're going to fix this and get this done.' There are people on the other side saying, 'Wait a minute, what about the people who are going to suffer?' We're in this dialectic in the Western World between these extreme approaches to problem-solving.[59]

Nylon's Hayden Manners suggested the film demonstrated how humans will stoop to their lowest levels when the basest fears are stoked, something Trump fanned in his campaign.[60]

It Comes at Night focuses on the tribulations of close-knit family living in the aftermath of an unidentified apocalypse. The family's encounter with another living person gives rise to extreme tension, which Angie Han of *Mashable* claimed, "it only takes a short leap to see the uncomfortable parallels between our world and theirs" where "a thick air of paranoia poisons even the most innocuous-seeming interactions."[61] Justin Chang further quipped how the film's postapocalyptic backdrop gave it a stronger resonance because we live "at a moment when environmental decay and nuclear/chemical warfare are no longer the distant prospects they once were."[62] The film offers an unflinching portrait of despair that "goes straight for the jugular of contemporary American politics and slices clean through."[63] Such subtexts made the film "seem super-relevant in the age of Donald Trump."[64]

It was the most financially successful horror film of 2017, and one of the most successful horror films of all time.[65] Adapted from a Stephen King novel of the same name, *It* takes place in the fictional town of Derry, Maine, in 1988 where Pennywise, a soul-devouring clown, awakens from his twenty-seven-year slumber to prey on the town's children. Trump's sociopathic nature was seen as being reflected in Pennywise, something noted by King at a women's march in Sarasota, Florida "we just elected Pennywise President."[66] According to director Andy Muschietti, "[f]ear is used as a tool these days to divide and control and conquer. And hate is a tool. And that's something Pennywise does, so that's something resonating in our society right now."[67] Samantha Becker wrote a lengthy guest column for *Entertainment Weekly* where she compared the seven members of the Loser's Club (the film's main protagonists) to groups President Trump has castigated.[68] The singling out of each Loser's Club member's weakness led Justin Chang to claim that the film represented a "thinly veiled parable of life in Donald Trump's America."[69]

Darren Aronofsky's *Mother!* is a transparent retelling of creation (and destruction), and arguably, a parody of Christian fundamentalism. The film's God character, Him (Javier Bardem) is a vainglorious narcissist who cares not for the well-being of his creation, but only cares for their love of him. Chauncey DeVega's *Salon*'s mostly negative review of *Mother!* connected the dots between the devotees of Him and Trump: "scenes of chaos, destruction and slavish devotion to 'Him' in *Mother!* inescapably evoke the way Trump serves as a savior or godhead for his 'deplorables.'"[70] DeVega (2017) then pinpointed Trump as an example of the film's allegory, likening the president to "a man with fascist tendencies and overtly racist views, who as a matter of routine violates almost every idealized norm of 'Christian' behavior, [and] was swept into the White House with the overwhelming support of white Christian evangelicals."[71]

To be sure, more horror movies were released in the two years covered in this chapter. However, not all of them were seen as reacting to the forces that helped elect President Trump. For instance, *IndieWire*'s Eric Kohn singled out *Rings* (2017) as socially irrelevant, despite the film offering a potentially relevant computer hacking subplot. Kohn cautioned against reading the film as "a potential metaphor for the real-world hacking scandals plaguing modern times" before stating "simply acknowledging contemporary circumstances isn't the same thing as doing something innovative with them."[72] Similarly, *Geostorm* (2017) was seen as failing to offer the commentary it desperately wanted to. Tasha Robinson's review for *The Verge* noted how the film's message seemed forced with parts of it "feel[ing] like . . . self-conscious reference[s] to Trump's 'make America great again' speeches" that fail "to examine the impact of these kinds of politics."[73]

CONCLUSION

In his recent overview of the horror genre, scholar Murray Leeder wrote, with some hesitancy, "only time will tell if the Trump era proves the fertile ground for horror filmmakers as other conservative periods."[74] The commentary from the film critics summarized in this chapter would suggest a resounding yes. Beyond that, critics have high hopes for the genre's future. Much of this hope stems from the notion that horror films respond to civil unrest and social upheaval. Jordan Crucchiola predicts "horror will be our most powerful form of on screen activism in this period of raw and rampant social unrest."[75] Justin Chang adds that the genre draws on the social divisions that President Trump exploited.[76] Thus, Matt Kim's observation from 2017 that "horror movies are already telling the story . . . "[77] of Trump's America can be extended to "horror films are continuing to tell the story of Trump's America."

NOTES

1. Matthew Monagle, "The Post-Donald Trump Horror Films Are Going to Be Epic," *Film School Rejects*, October 7, 2016. Accessed https://filmschoolrejects.com/the-post-donald-trump-horror-films-are-going-to-be-epic-6266f1287330/ on August 12, 2018.

2. Seyward Darby, "What America Needs Now Is Horror Movies," *The Awl*, February 16, 2017. Accessed https://www.theawl.com/2017/02/what-america-needs-now-is-horror-movies/ on August 12, 2018.

3. Max Lakin, "Why Horror Movies Will Be the Most Exciting Art Form of the Donald Trump Era," *W Magazine*, March 17, 2017. Accessed https://www.wmagazine.com/story/horror-movies-social-thrillers-get-out-the-purge/ on August 12, 2018.

4. Justin Chang, "Has Horror Become the Movie Genre of the Trump Era?" *Los Angeles Times*, October 15, 2017, E6.

5. Jordan Crucchiola, "*Get Out* Proves the Vitality of Horror in the Trump Era," *Vulture*, February 24, 2017. Accessed http://www.vulture.com/2017/02/get-out-proves-horror-will-be-vital-in-the-donald-trump-era.html/ on August 12, 2018.

6. Jason Bailey, "*Green Room* Is a Horror Movie for Trump's America," *FlavorWire*, April 13, 2016. Accessed http://flavorwire.com/571081/green-room-is-a-horror-movie-for-trumps-america/ on August 12, 2018.

7. Matt Kim, "6 New Cinematic Monsters that Will Emerge in 2017: Horror Movies Are Already Telling the Story of 2017," *Inverse*, December 30, 2016. Accessed https://www.inverse.com/article/25769-cinematic-monsters-in-2017/ on August 12, 2018.

8. See, for example, Matthew W. Hughey, "The White Savior Film and Reviewers' Reception," *Symbolic Interaction* 33 (2010): 475–96; Alicia Anderson and Scott Grether, "Reviewing the Reviews: Discussions of Race by Film Reviewers," *Sociological Spectrum* 37 (2017): 188–204; Todd K. Platts and David Brunsma, "Reviewing *Get Out*'s Reviews: What Critics Discussed and How Their Race Mattered," in *Approaches to Jordan Peele's* Get Out, ed. Dawn Keetley (Columbus, OH: Ohio State University Press, in press).

9. Barrie Gunter, *Predicting Movie Success at the Box Office* (New York: Palgrave MacMillan, 2018), 209, 222.

10. Thomas Schatz, "2008: Movies and a Hollywood too Big to Fail," in *American Cinema of the 2000s: Themes and Variations*, edited by Timothy Corrigan (New Brunswick: Rutgers University Press, 2012), 195.

11. Tom Van Riper, "The Top Pundits in America," *Forbes*, September 24, 2007. Accessed https://www.forbes.com/2007/09/21/pundit-americas-top-oped-cx_tvr_0924pundits.html#7d79a0bb54c4/ on August 12, 2018.

12. *Nielsen*, "#twothumbsup: Moviegoing at a Theater Near You," March 24, 2014. Accessed http://www.nielsen.com/us/en/insights/news/2014/twothumbsup-moviegoing-at-a-theater-near-you.html/ on August 12, 2018.

13. Mathias Clasen, *Why Horror Seduces* (New York: Oxford University Press, 2017), 3.

14. Victoria McCollum, "Rednecks, Racism, and Religion: King and Darabont's Precarious Prophecy of Obama's Coming," in *Movies in the Age of Obama: The Era of Post Racial and Neo-Racist Cinema*, ed. David Garrett Izzo (Lanham, MD: Rowman and Littlefield, 2015), 85.

15. Charles Derry, *Dark Dreams 2.0: A Psychological History of the Modern Horror Film from the 1950s to the 21st Century* (Jefferson, NC: McFarland, 2009), 22.

16. Robin Wood, "An Introduction to the American Horror Film," in *Planks of Reason: Essays on the Horror Film*, ed. Barry Keith Grant and Christopher Sharrett (Lanham, MD: Scarecrow Press, 2004), 117.

17. Jeremy Marshally, "What President Trump Could Mean for the Future of Horror," November 16, 2016. Accessed https://www.dreadcentral.com/news/200003/what-president-trump-could-mean-for-the-future-of-horror/ on August 12, 2018.

18. Brigid Cherry, *Horror* (New York: Routledge, 2009), 11.

19. Todd K. Platts, "The New Horror Movie," in *Baby Boomers and Popular Culture: An Inquiry into America's Most Powerful Generation*, ed. Brian Cogan and Thom Gencarelli (Denver, CO: Praeger, 2015), 148.

20. Platts, "The New," 152–54.

21. Vera Dika, *Games of Terror:* Halloween, Friday the 13th, *and the Films of the Stalker Cycle* (Madison, NJ: Fairleigh Dickinson University Press, 1990), 123–39.

22. Valerie Wee, "The *Scream* Trilogy, 'Hyperpostmodernism,' and the Late-Nineties Teen Slasher Film," *Journal of Film and Video* 57 (2005): 44–61.

23. Todd K. Platts and Mathias Clasen, "Scary Business: Horror at the North American Box Office, 2006–2016," *Frames Cinema Journal*, May 2017. Accessed http://framescinemajournal.com/article/scary-business-horror-at-the-north-american-box-office-2006-2016/ on August 12, 2018.

24. See, for example, Derry, *Dark Dreams 2.0*, 283; McCollum, "Rednecks, Racism, and Religion," 86.

25. Bernice Murphy, "'It's Not the House that's Haunted': Demons, Debt, and the Family in Peril Formula in Recent Horror Cinema," in *Cinematic Ghosts: Haunting and Spectrality from Silent Cinema to the Digital Era*, ed. Murray Leeder (New York: Bloomsbury, 2015), 243.

26. Josh Dickey, "Apocalyptic Movies are Peaking at the Worst Possible Time," *Mashable*, November 14, 2016. Accessed https://mashable.com/2016/11/14/apocalypse-movies-donald-trump-armageddon-end-of-the-world/#hoOHAFh_osqm/ on August 12, 2018.

27. Steven Bruhm, "Anchors Away! Horror in the Age of Pessimism," *Horror Studies* 8 (2017): 3.

28. Chuck Bowen, "Is It Time for a Horror Movie about the Evils of Donald Trump?" *The Guardian*, July 5, 2016. Accessed https://www.theguardian.com/film/2016/jul/05/donald-trump-horror-movie-they-live-john-carpenter/ on August 12, 2018.

29. Samantha Becker, "Stephen King's *It* is a Parable for Life Under Donald Trump," *Entertainment Weekly*, September 22, 2017. Accessed https://ew.com/movies/2017/09/22/stephen-kings-it-is-a-parable-for-life-under-donald-trump-guest-column/ on August 12, 2018.

30. Monagle, "The Post-Donald Trump Horror Films are Going to Be Epic," *Film School Rejects*.

31. Douglas Kellner, *American Horror Show: Election 2016 and the Ascent of Donald Trump* (Boston, MA: Sense Publishers, 2017), passim.

32. Maureen Dowd, "In the Time of Trump, a Horror-Movie Maker Rules Hollywood," *New York Times*, November 2, 2017, D8.

33. Douglas Kellner, *Cinema Wars: Hollywood Film and Politics in the Bush-Cheney Era* (Malden, MA: Wiley-Blackwell, 2010), 14.

34. Jason Bailey, "*Green Room* is a Horror Movie for Trump's America," *Flavorwire*, April 13, 2016. Accessed http://flavorwire.com/571081/green-room-is-a-horror-movie-for-trumps-america/ on August 12, 2018.

35. Scott Meslow, "*Green Room*: The Movie that Anticipated the Rise of Trump," *GQ*, November 15, 2016. Accessed https://www.gq.com/story/green-room-rise-of-trump/ on August 12, 2018.

36. Quoted in Rich Juzwiak, "'It's More Relevant Than It Should Be': *Green Room* Director Jeremy Sauliner on His Skinhead Horror Bloodbath in Backwater Oregon," *Gawker*, April 14, 2016. Accessed http://gawker.com/its-more-relevant-than-it-should-be-green-room-direc-1770995053/ on August 12, 2018.

37. Jia Tolentino, "Watch *The Purge* in Our Year of Nightmare Politics," *The New Yorker*, July 27, 2016. Accessed https://www.newyorker.com/culture/jia-tolentino/watching-the-purge-in-our-year-of-nightmare-politics/ on August 12, 2018.

38. B. Alan Orange, "*The Purge 3* was Inspired by Donald Trump and Hillary Clinton," *Movieweb*, April 2, 2016. Accessed https://movieweb.com/purge-3-election-year-inspiration-donald-trump-hillary-clinton/ on August 12, 2018.

39. Scott Mendelson, "Review: *The Purge: Election Year* Is (Sadly) Summer's Most Timely Sequel," *Forbes*, June 29, 2016. Accessed https://www.forbes.com/sites/scottmendelson/2016/06/29/review-the-purge-election-year-is-sadly-summers-most-timely-sequel/ on August 12, 2018.

40. Mia Galuppo and Meena Jang, "Rapid Round: *The Purge: Election Year* Directory on How the Violence at Donald Trump's Made Its Way Into His Movie," *Hollywood Reporter*, July 1, 2016. Accessed https://www.hollywoodreporter.com/news/rapid-round-purge-election-year-908136/ on August 12, 2018.

41. Mendelson, "Review."

42. Scott Mendelson, "*The Purge* Trilogy was the Political Satire of Our Time, For Our Time," *Forbes*, October 4, 2016. Accessed https://www.forbes.com/sites/scottmendelson/2016/10/04/the-purge-trilogy-was-the-political-satire-of-our-time-for-our-time/#160dc85059a9/ on August 12, 2018.

43. Crucchiola, "*Get Out* Proves the Vitality of Horror in the Trump Era."

44. Phil Hornshaw and Phil Owen, "All the Ways *The First Purge* Skewers American and Donald Trump," *The Wrap*, July 4, 2018. Accessed https://www.thewrap.com/ways-first-purge-skewers-america-donald-trump/ on August 12, 2018.

45. Luke Y. Thompson, "Review: Rob Zombie's *31* Is Bloody And (Perhaps Unintentionally) Relevant," *Forbes*, September 2, 2016. Accessed https://www.forbes.com/sites/lukethompson/2016/09/02/review-rob-zombies-31-is-bloody-andperhaps-unintentionally-relevant/#2b1335bc18b8/ on August 12, 2018.

46. Kenneth Turan, "How the Movies Gave Us Donald Trump," *Los Angeles Times*, January 8, 2017, E3.

47. Rob Cain, "American Horror Story: Three Movies That Presaged Trumpocalypse Now," *Forbes*, November 11, 2016. Accessed https://www.forbes.com/sites/robcain/2016/11/11/american-horror-story-three-movies-that-presaged-trumpocalypse-now/ on August 12, 2018.

48. Brian Ross, "The Real American Horror Story is Political. Call All Heroes," *Huffington Post*, June 27, 2017. Accessed https://www.huffingtonpost.com/entry/the-real-american-horror-story-is-political-calling_us_5951353be4b0326c0a8d0a2b/ on August 12, 2018.

49. Seyward Darby, "What America Needs Now Is Horror Movies," *The Awl*, February 16, 2018. Accessed https://www.theawl.com/2017/02/what-america-needs-now-is-horror-movies/ on August 12, 2018.

50. Max Lakin, "Why Horror Movies Will be the Most Exciting Art Form of the Donald Trump Era," *W Magazine*, March 17, 2017. Accessed, https://www.wmagazine.com/story/horror-movies-social-thrillers-get-out-the-purge/ on August 12, 2018.

51. Liam Stack, "To Lure Moviegoers, 20th Century Fox Dangles Fake News," *New York Times*, February 16, 2017, B1, B4.

52. Matthew Jacobs, "What Donald Trump and Dick Cheney Have in Common with *A Cure for Wellness*," *Huffington Post*, February 17, 2017. Accessed https://www.huffingtonpost.com/entry/a-cure-for-wellness-donald-trump_us_58a6f932e4b045cd34c0b4d7/ on August 12, 2018.

53. Kate Erbland, "Karyn Kusama on Making Horror Films and Fighting Evil in the Age of Trump," *IndieWire*, February 15, 2017. Accessed https://www.indiewire.com/2017/02/karyn-kusama-horror-films-donald-trump-xx-1201783181/ on August 12, 2018.

54. Frank Bruni, "The Horror of Smug Liberals," *New York Times*, March 19, 2017, SR3.

55. Andrew Anthony, "Jordan Peele on Making a Hit Comedy-Horror Movie out of America's Racial Tensions," *The Guardian*, March 4, 2017. Accessed https://www.theguardian.com/film/2017/mar/04/jordan-peele-interview-get-out-its-about-purging-our-fears-horror-film-daniel-kaluuya/ on August 12, 2018.

56. John DeFore, "*Get Out*: Film Review," *Hollywood Reporter*, January 24, 2017. Accessed http://www.hollywoodreporter.com/review/get-review-967922/ on August 12, 2018.

57. Jake Coyle, "In Sensation of *Get Out*, Hints of a Trump-Effect," *Associated Press*, March 13, 2017. Accessed https://www.apnews.com/18b36e0e9af042c99c 4f6d26ac297015/ on August 12, 2018.

58. Chang, "Has Horror become the Movie Genre of the Trump Era?" E6.

59. Quoted in Jackie Strauss, "Tony Goldwyn on How *The Belko Experiment* Speaks to Trump's America," *Hollywood Reporter*, March 17, 2017. Accessed http://www.hollywoodreporter.com/heat-vision/belko-experiment-star-tony-goldwyn-says-horror-movie-resonates-trumps-america-986828/ on August 12, 2018.

60. Hayden Manders, "What 'Raw' and 'The Belko Experiment' Say about the World Today," *Nylon*, March 16, 2017. Accessed https://nylon.com/articles/raw-belko-experiment-horror-2017/ on August 12, 2018.

61. Angie Han, "*It Comes at Night* Director on His Cautionary Tale for the Current Era," *Mashable*, June 18, 2017. Accessed http://mashable.com/2017/06/18/it-comes-at-night-socially-relevant-horror-trey-edward-shults/#n1VQ6QJXBkqS/ on August 12, 2018.

62. Justin Chang, "Has Horror become the Movie Genre of the Trump Era?" *Los Angeles Times*, October 13, 2017. Accessed http://www.latimes.com/entertainment/movies/la-ca-mn-horror-movies-trump-20171013-story.html/ on August 12, 2018.

63. Aja Romano, "*It Comes at Night* is a Terrifying, Uncomfortably Relevant Horror Masterpiece," *Vox*, June 8, 2017. Accessed https://www.vox.com/culture/2017/6/8/15739132/ it-comes-at-night-review-dystopia-politics/ on August 12, 2018.

64. Han, "*It Comes at Night* Director on His Cautionary Tale for the Current Era."

65. See, for example, Tom Brueggemann, "*It* is a Box Office Sensation—But 'It' Is Not the Record Breaker Everyone Thinks," *IndieWire*, September 26, 2017. Accessed http://www.indiewire.com/2017/09/it-top-horror-movies-stephen-king-box-office-1201879912/ on August 12, 2018.

66. Samantha Becker, "Stephen King's *It* Is a Parable for Life Under Donald Trump," *Entertainment Weekly*, September 22, 2017. Accessed http://ew.com/movies/2017/09/22/stephen-kings-it-is-a-parable-for-life-under-donald-trump-guest-column/ on August 12, 2018.

67. Becker, "Stephen King's *It*."

68. Becker, "Stephen King's *It*."

69. Chang, "Has Horror become the Movie Genre of the Trump Era," E6.

70. Chauncey DeVega, "Your God will not help you: Darren Aronofsky's *Mother!* in the Age of Trump," *Salon*, September 24, 2017. Accessed https://www.salon.com/2017/09/24/your-god-will-not-help-you-darren-aronofskys-mother-in-the-age-of-trump/ on August 12, 2018.

71. DeVega, "Your God."

72. Eric Kohn, "*Rings* Review: A Dull Sequel Nobody Needed, But There's a Lesson to Its Failure," *IndieWire*, February 3, 2017. Accessed https://www.indiewire.com /2017/02/rings-review-horror-1201777580/ on August 12, 2018.

73. Tasha Robinson, "For Those Who Want to Watch the World Burn, There's Geostorm," *The Verge*. October 20, 2017. Accessed https://www.theverge.com/2017/10/20/16512214/geostorm-movie-review-gerard-butler-jim-sturgess/ on August 12, 2018.

74. Murray Leeder, *Horror Film: A Critical Introduction* (New York: Bloomsbury, 2018), 88.
75. Crucchiola, "*Get Out* Proves the Vitality of Horror in the Trump Era."
76. Chang, "Has Horror become the Movie Genre of the Trump Era?" E6.
77. Kim, "6 New Cinematic Monsters that Will Emerge in 2017."

Chapter Seven

Beautiful and Damned

Tech Noir, *Neoplatonism, and Existential Crises in* Blade Runner 2049

Sue Matheson

As G. W. F. Hegel points out in his 1832 *Lectures on Aesthetics*, our sensory appreciation of art concentrates on its appearance or "form." Art, he says, communicates truth through idealized or Beautiful images of human beings.[1] Dystopic aesthetics, however, demand their viewer appreciate the Ugly. Designed to transmit social and political disharmony, they assign negative values, condemning the repression and violence found in dystopic visions that depict "a hell on earth, an absurd, death-bound social-political system where the elite deliberately conspires against its own people."[2] Throughout the twentieth century, urban dystopias on film have been filled with ugly images of degraded, dissociated, and chaotic cityscapes filled with disorder and, paradoxically, incorporations of diversity into dreary sameness. Among the alienated, dehumanized hordes that inhabited these cities, there has been at least one Beautiful individual determined to rise above social and political wreckage. Weimar cinema's representations of urban dystopias set the stage for these romantic ascents. Using German Expression's visual style to critique the degradation of urbanization,[3] Fritz Lang's highly influential *Metropolis* (1927), showcases the lovely Maria's (Brigitte Helm) efforts to ascend from an industrial hell buried beneath her employer's city to the streets above that resonate with German New Objectivity's approach to machines and industry and are filled with art deco buildings.[4] In the 1940s and 1950s, Hollywood film noir followed in Lang's footsteps—like the underground in *Metropolis*, its crime-ridden cities, lit in low-key, are crowded with grotesquely proportioned, decaying buildings. Thirty years later, Ridley Scott revitalized Lang's vision. Highly influential, *Blade Runner* (1982)[5] introduced audiences to a new hardboiled genre, *tech noir*,[6] a cynical and sophisticated hybrid of film noir and science fiction known for its stylish dystopias presented within the tonal frameworks of German Expressionism's shadowed lighting and unbalanced compositions. As Paul Meehan remarks in *Tech Noir: The Fusion of Science Fiction and Film Noir*, tech noir is now "an established, commercially viable form . . . explored by a number of talented directors including Steven Spielberg, David Cronenberg, Tim Burton, James Cameron, Ridley Scott, Terry Gilliam, and Alex Proyas."[7] Inspired by Ridley Scott's *Blade Runner*, James Cameron's *Terminator* (1984) and William Gibson's bleak, dystopian novel *Neuromancer* (1984), tech noir in the late 1980s and 1990s included box office successes like Cameron's *Terminator 2: Judgement Day*, Peter Verhoeven's *Robocop* (1987) and *Total Recall* (1990), Terry Gilliam's *12 Monkeys* (1995), and The Wachowski Brothers' *The Matrix* (1999).

Given the popularity of tech noir, it was surprising that following in *Blade Runner*'s footsteps, *Blade Runner 2049* grossed only $92,054,159 during its seventeen-week run in the United States. *Blade Runner 2049*'s failure to boot up at the box office has been attributed to the slow-moving tonal poem's length, the difficulty of its premise, and its marketing as an action.[8] Arguably, *Blade Runner 2049*'s box office failure, however, has been offset by its critical success. Reviewers agree that its ruined, dystopic world was stunningly represented. Christopher Orr of *The Atlantic* declares the film is "a splendor of the first order . . . breathtaking . . . a gorgeous ruin . . . [f]rom the grayed-out countrysides over which the sky has closed like a lid; to the drizzly neon decadence of Los Angeles; to a San Diego refashioned as a waste dump worthy of *WALL-E*; to the Ozymandian wreckage of Las Vegas."[9] Peter Bradshaw of *The Guardian* lauds *Blade Runner 2049*'s "mind-boggling, cortex-wobbling, craniofacial-splintering images," deeming the movie "a narcotic spectacle."[10] *Rolling Stone*'s Peter Travers judges it "an instant classic"—"a visual feast to gorge on."[11] Even A. O. Scott of *The New York Times* thinks *Blade Runner 2049*'s aesthetics are "sumptuous."[12]

Set in postapocalyptic Los Angeles, *Blade Runner 2049* is the story of a replicant, KD6–3.7 (Ryan Gosling), employed as a bladerunner who finds the bones of Rachel Rosen (Sean Young) thirty years after she and Rick Deckard (Harrison Ford) fled from San Francisco. Rachel's remains reveal that she died in childbirth. Assigned the job of erasing all the traces of Rachel's pregnancy, K finds himself competing with Niander Wallace and the Wallace Association as he hunts for Rachel's child. Wallace's replicant manufacturing company needs the "perfect specimen" that Rachel produced to create millions of androids for human beings to colonize the stars. Believing he himself may be that child, K locates Deckard before Wallace's operatives do. Later, he, learns that Rachel's child was a girl and takes Deckard to meet the daughter he has never seen. In the end, K is offered no hope of transcending his condition or escaping Los Angeles. He dies tragically—alone in the snow on the steps of the Stelline Laboratories.

Blade Runner 2049's aesthetics draw heavily on familiar dystopic tropes found in Ridley Scott's *Blade Runner* based on Philip K. Dick's dystopic masterpiece, *Do Androids Dream of Electric Sheep?* but present viewers with a radical departure from tech noir's hopelessness and stylish cynicism. Returning to Neoplatonic notions of Beauty and Ugliness, Villeneuve reintroduces classical questions of value and judgment into his consideration of dystopia and calls for a serious reexamination of human nature. Tracking the trajectory of aesthetics (and ethics) from *Do Androids Dream of Electric Sheep?* and *Blade Runner* to *Blade Runner 2049*, this chapter also considers Villeneuve's use of John Milton's *Paradise Lost* to empower his call for social change.

There is no Beauty to be found in *Do Androids Dream of Electric Sheep?* Consisting of decayed empty buildings filled with radioactive dust, "tattered gray wall-to-wall carpeting," "broken and semi-broken appliances, and "fly-specked" ceilings,[13] Dick's San Francisco is little more than a gigantic garbage dump. As Deckard leaves home to go to work, the very air belches around him "spilling over with radioactive motes, gray and sun-beclouding."[14] Organically disordered and psychically imbalanced, the city's inhabitants are equally unattractive. Living in radioactive pollution, one becomes a "chickenhead" like John Isidore,[15] a special who carries "distorted genes" and has "failed to pass the minimum mental faculties test."[16] Dick's narrator notes that there are many "chickenheads infinitely stupider than Isidore, who . . . hold no jobs at all" and remain "in custodial institutions quaintly call 'Institute of Special Trade Skills of America.'"[17]

As Plotinus points out in *The Enneads* 1.6, "beauty cannot arise from ugly things."[18] Dick's unattractive human beings behave unpleasantly. *Do Androids Dream of Electric Sheep?* begins with a domestic dispute that escalates from "irritability" to "outright hostility."[19] All of his relationships are toxic. His wife endures him, his neighbor patronizes him, and his boss bullies him. Throughout, his appearance is instructive—"not a demi-god in shape,"[20] he is a modern Everyman. "[A] medium man" with a "[r]ound face and hairless smooth features,"[21] he is not a heroic figure. He instead resembles the toad he discovers at the novel's end. Sadly, his attempt to bond with the animal fails—ironically, the amphibian he brings home turns out to be synthetic. In *Do Androids Dream of Electric Sheep?* replicants' physical appearances and behaviors also correspond with one another. Rachel, a Nexus-6 modeled on "the Celtic type of build, anachronistic and attractive," should be beautiful, but her proportions are "odd."[22] After her affair with Deckard, her actions are as questionable as her looks. She tosses his prized goat off the roof of his apartment building. Since Plotinus linked beauty with virtue,[23] Beauty has been equated with the idea of the Good and Ugliness with the idea of Evil.[24] Given the mediocrity of Deckard's unsightliness and Rachel's irregular features, it seems appropriate that the two undertake what must be considered only a tepid affair.

Blade Runner's well-worn cinematic tropes employ expressionist techniques pioneered by Fritz Lang in *Metropolis*. Expressing the toxicity of Los Angeles in 2019, Ridley Scott's *noir* palette of shadow and light renders the city a dripping darkness, filled with grey, slippery streets choked with crowds of nameless, anonymous people and slimy, steaming alleys patrolled by scavengers and vagrants. With the exception of Dr. Eldon Tyrell (Joe Turkel), a powerful replicant manufacturer, San Francisco's citizens live in garbage-filled streets and gothic structures like the romanesque Bradbury Building.[25] Situated above the city's squalor in a pseudo-Egyptian compound, Tyrell rules his corporation like an ancient pharaoh. The mammoth proportions of his inner sanctum not only replicate those of Frederson's in *Metropolis*, conveying the enormous corporate power he wields, they also remind the viewer of the occult and nightmarish nature of his work. Outside the Tyrell Corporation, light and darkness are awarded positive and negative values as twenty-foot futuristic billboards bursting with exotic color and Asian faces contrast sharply with Deckard, a larger-than-life American somberly dressed in clothes the colors of the streets. *Blade Runner*'s low-key contrasts, grotesquely canted buildings, and gigantic billboards point to the abnormal minds housed in this urban dystopia.

Unlike Dick's dystopic vision which is unremittingly repulsive, Scott's visualization of mankind's Ugly future is tempered by Beauty. Scott's principle characters in particular provide a sharp contrast with the unpleasantness that is Los Angeles. Played by an actor who has been voted thirteen times the sexiest man alive,[26] Scott's Deckard is a handsome, hardboiled, hard-drinking bachelor, the antithesis of Dick's hairless, hen-pecked bureaucrat. Concerned with the optics of the noir femme fatale, who is always mysterious, seductive, and irresistibly desirable, Scott cast Sean Young whom he saw as "a classic beauty in the mold of Vivien Leigh" as Rachel.[27] Scott's femme fatale is so physically perfect that Dick himself was captivated by Sean Young's looks and "asked Jeff Walker, one of the movie's publicists, if he could meet her, calling her the "super destructive cruel beautiful dark-haired woman that I eternally write about and now I've seen a photograph of her and I know that she exists and I will seek her out and presumably she will destroy me."[28] Upending Dick's expectations of the femme fatale, Rachel proves to be as good as she is Beautiful, maintaining the intrinsic value awarded her ideal proportions. Aptly, it is love for Rachel that enables Deckard to transcend his dystopic environment. As the film narrative ends happily, the lovers leave the Ugly environs of San Francisco and travel to a pristine portion of the Rockies.

Scott's decision to cast the handsome Dutch star, Rutger Hauer, as Roy Baty also complicates the film's aesthetic argument. Appreciating Scott's nod to the Nazi inspiration for *Do Androids Dream of Electric Sheep*"[29] Dick approved of Hauer's sculpted Nordic qualities, even though Baty in *Do Androids Dream of Electric Sheep?* is described as having "flat, Mongolian features which gave him a brutal look."[30] Hauer's blonde good looks reminded Dick of "the Nordic superman that Hitler said would come marching out of the laboratory"[31] Viewing Baty as a Nazi übermensch naturally leads audiences to award unpleasant motives to the character—when Baty and Leon (Brion James) interrogate Hannibal Chew (James Hong) at his eye lab, it can be assumed that Chew will be murdered after he talks. Baty's drama of ascent, however, overturns expectations like these at the film's end. After he proclaims himself Luciferian by misquoting lines from *William Blake's America: A Prophecy*, he inexplicably spares Deckard's life.[32] In the end, Baty, too, becomes one with the Good, proving to be as virtuous as he is handsome.

Promoting *Blade Runner 2049* before its theatrical release, Denis Villeneuve assured DeepMind CEO Demis Hassabis that some parts of the film would be "very close aesthetically" to *Blade Runner*.[33] "[I]t's still a detective *film noir*," he said, "You have to be in that kind of aesthetic zone."[34] Like *Do Androids Dream of Electric Sheep?*'s and *Blade Runner*'s aesthetics, *Blade Runner 2049*'s contentions rest on the values assigned by an object's, event's, or state of affairs' capacity to elicit pleasure (hence Beauty's positive value) or displeasure (hence the Ugly's negative value). Its dystopic cityscapes are as degraded and chaotic as Dick's and Scott's—Los Angeles' rusty industrial structures, unpleasant landfills, and mountains of trash exude an ugly negativity; Las Vegas's gigantic ruins bathed in radioactive dust emit a palpable toxicity. Villeneuve's sophisticated treatment of Beauty in this dystopia, however, complicates the Ugliness that marks the film. At first, the women of *Blade Runner 2049* appear to be simple types—madonnas and whores, angels and devils—but, as the Beauty of their faces and bodies realigns the movie's moral compass, appreciating them becomes a frightening and infernal experience.

In *Blade Runner 2049*, Beauty is coupled with Pleasure, but neither principle is necessarily awarded intrinsic positive values. Every female replicant is stunningly Beautiful. The streets of Los Angeles, for example, are filled with twenty-foot tall holograms of the beautiful Joi companion, a perfectly proportioned hologram designed to please her partner in a world in which people are starved for human contact. One "tacky erotic version" of a giant ad reads: "Whatever you want. Joi."[35] Clothed or unclothed, Joi (Ana de Armas) is a popular product and significantly a companion that Deckard can afford. Intrinsically good, she satisfies the needs of her partner. Complicated by what appears to be her sense of autonomy, her relationship with K is harmonious. Never actualized, Joi remains an abstract concept caught in a simulated reality—loving and obedient. Her love for K, however, enables her to transcend her condition. Before her app is deleted, she sacrifices her life for K's well-being. As *Blade Runner 2049*'s writer Hampton Fancher remarks, Joi's love for K "becomes real as opposed to programmed."[36] Because of love, she "escapes her own limitations (the digital limitations), and becomes totally real for herself."[37] In short, she acquires a soul.

K's Joi is beautiful and Good, but other stunningly attractive female characters in *Blade Runner 2049* are not. As Mackenzie Davis points out, Villeneuve's perfectly proportioned Doxies are "built to be used as pleasure models,"[38] entry-level workers in BiBi's Bar, "an unabashed sex den," that services patrons who "enter to taste and experience with no more shame than they would the vending machines."[39] Designed to elicit physical pleasure, Davis's Punk Doxie Mariette is best avoided. A mole for the Wallace Association, she "discreetly tags an almost imperceptible device in one of K's jacket pockets."[40]

Niander Wallace's personal assistant, Luv (Sylvia Hoeks) is also good-looking and at first appears to embody positivity. Completely faithful to her blind Maker, the stunning brunette is a perfect office wife, Joi's corporate counterpart, meeting Wallace's clients with "her hands tucked. Suit sensible. Every aspect immaculate. The flawless representative."[41] A complex figure, Luv is beautiful *and* deadly, a femme fatale dressed unsuitably in white. In the archive banks of the Wallace Tower, she seems to be the model of propriety, telling K, "the ancient models give the entire endeavour a bad name." Ironically, she then attempts to seduce him after he has retrieved Rachel's data from the Wallace Association's Memory Vaults and later beats him to a pulp because he has been a "bad dog." She is said by Wallace (Jared Leto) to be an "angel," but *Blade Runner 2049*'s shooting script explicitly associates her with the demonic. Determined not to disappoint her Maker, Luv proves to be much worse than the ancient models. She is the most brutal and violent of the female replicants. Described as "a wild crazed thing sent from the pit,"[42] she is a sadist, deriving pleasure from the suffering of her victims, maiming single-mindedly and killing indiscriminately.

Plotinus points out in *The Enneads* 1.8 that extreme viciousness is evidence of the Essential Evil that leads one to Hades.[43] Given her behavior, it is entirely appropriate that Luv is a fallen angel, and her home, the Wallace Association, a corporate hell. Its foyer, "a wide open space of sandstone and lit by artificial sunbeams," designed to be an antechamber to the nether regions, looks not "like the lobby of a corporation but the interior of a Nabatean tomb." Ringing with Miltonic undertones, Wallace's ambitious plan to produce millions of replicants to help trillions of human beings, "meant to reach beyond the firmament," colonize and "own the stars" makes him more than a simple business man. Seated in what he calls "the kingdom of heaven," he tells Luv that she is "[t]he best angel of all" the "Angels" his company makes "[i]n service of Civilization." Explicitly Luciferian, Wallace misquotes Satan in John Milton's *Paradise Lost.* Unable to solve the puzzle of procreation that Tyrell left him "in adamantine chains and penal flames,"[44] he declares his latest replicant's abdomen "the seat that we must change for Heaven."[45] Needing to model his work on a "perfect specimen," Wallace instructs Luv to bring him Deckard's daughter, so he may "storm Eden and retake her."

Like Satan in *Paradise Lost*, Wallace is "armed in Adamant and Gold."[46] His darkened private office, made of golden sandstone, is filled with ripples of yellow light waves that are also found in other offices, storage spaces, and passageways in his Towers. Everything the billionaire creates seems to be golden. Even the new female replicant he examines is "[c]overed in a viscous liquid, like honey."[47] According to Villeneuve, the yellow associated with the Wallace Association "is linked with madness. It's a subconscious point of view, not something you are supposed to understand: it's something you receive and feel."[48] A monomaniac, Wallace is always associated with the color yellow. The golden light waves that are reflected and refracted on the polished walls of the corporate headquarters mirror "the sensation of light that moves in front of his eyes like a pattern." Manifested in the world, the burning pattern that plays inside Wallace's head as Luv walks down a corridor that leads her to him, she appears to be walking through fluid waves of yellow. The means by which Wallace makes his Miltonic "darkness visible,"[49] this golden light also illuminates Wallace's office.[50] Villeneuve's use of simulated brightness reveals not only the space and its furnishings but also the darkness within its inhabitant's psyche. Recreating the "fiery Gulf" in which Satan found himself at the beginning of *Paradise Lost*,[51] the waves of gold turn to yellow flames flickering on the office's walls and are reflected, burning in the water surrounding his workspace. Seated in what appears to be Milton's "heart of Hell to work in Fire,"[52] Wallace counsels Deckard not to be afraid and tempts the ex-bladerunner, offering him Rachel remade. Like a dark specter, the reconstructed replicant, dressed in an adamantine suit, emerges, rising out of the water mounting the staircase hidden beneath the waves. Haloed by a mandorla of dancing flames as she approaches Deckard on the floating platform, she appears to have risen from the pit itself, "an angel, made again."

Fallen or rebel angels are often attractive romantic figures whose struggles to transcend the human condition are admirable. Although their efforts are doomed to failure, the romantic individuals' desire to rise above their condition is a marker of their humanity. Luv, however, is not a romantic individual—she is eye-catching, but no "friend to man" explicating Beauty to be truth and "truth beauty."[53] Created by Man, not God, she is perverse in her impulses. A pathological liar and murderer, she acts in bad faith, resorting naturally to falsehood and violence as she works for Wallace. She informs Coco (David Dastmalchian) that she has the required paperwork and that proper channels have been followed as she steals Rachel's bones from the police morgue. She warns Lieutenant Joshi (Robin Wright) that although androids can never lie or disobey, she has every intention of doing so, saying to the policewoman she is "going to tell Mister Wallace you tried to shoot me first. That's why I had to kill you."

As Plotinus points out, Evil appears "necessarily bound around with bonds of Beauty like some captive bound in fetters of gold" so Man is "not destitute of Images of the Good and Beautiful for their Remembrance."[54] Thus, when viewers consider Luv, Villeneuve's aesthetics insist they distinguish between the types of Beauty that Plotinus outlines in *The Enneads* 1.6. In *Blade Runner 2049*, one type of Beauty belongs to external and sensible things and may therefore said to be embodied. The other is the Beauty that Plotinus says is bodiless, belonging to man by virtue of his possessing a soul, and which manifests itself in action, intellectual love, character and virtue. At variance with her vicious and unethical behavior, Luv's Beauty is merely embodied. Joi's Beauty, on the other hand, is embodied *and* bodiless. "Being like a real human because that's what [K] needs,"[55] she makes dinner for him every day, creating a harmonious and concordant life away from work.

Dick points out in "The Android and The Human," being human or "Good" is evident in "what you do with the bits and pieces of meaningless, puzzling, disappointing, even cruel and crushing fragments all around us that seem to be pieces left over, discarded, from another world entirely that did, maybe, make sense."[56] In ordering her home, Joi, an angel of the hearth, experiences the principle that marks humanity, evidences her soul, and makes the world around her beautiful. The Beauty she creates around her transmits the authenticity of her existence. Creating order in the world is also the province of the bladerunner. As Joshi remarks to K, the making of social order, in part, belongs to the police. "The world's built on a wall that separates kind," she says, "There's an order to things. That's what we do here, we keep order." Here, Villeneuve again complicates the nature of Beauty, for the Ugliness of San Francisco maintained by the police state calls Joshi's claims to order and virtue into question. K discovers the State's dystopic unlinking of Beauty and virtue as he himself reorders the world throughout the film narrative. Reconstructing the history of Deckard's lost child, he rejects Joshi's vision as unprincipled and recognizes the family unit, whose mediating principle is love as society's ordering norm. Reuniting Deckard with his daughter, his behavior proves itself, in the end, to be virtuous and ethical.

A romantic figure, K, like Joi, wishes to change his lonely, alienated existence and "dream a little." However, as he remarks, such dreams are not for him. He is not Rachel's child. K's attempt and inability to transcend his condition defines human agency, subjectivity, and the place of institutions in

Blade Runner 2049 because Villeneuve's are meant to be "a mirror of ourselves."[57] As Villeneuve remarks, "[t]hey represent our anger to our maker, our human condition."[58] With this in mind, the existential nature of the human condition that K and Joi wish to experience could not be more provocative. Wallace, holding Rachel's skull as a *memento mori*, offers Deckard the opportunity to return to a perfect past with Rachel, but Deckard, a loving father, values his child and prefers to remain human. He knows "what's real."

As Mircea Eliade points out in *Myths, Dreams and Mysteries: The Encounter Between Contemporary Faiths and Archaic Realities*, nostalgia for Paradise expresses the desire for the beatitude lost in Man's Fall into Time and History. A prevalent theme throughout *Do Androids Dream of Electric Sheep? Blade Runner*, and *Blade Runner 2049*, this nostalgia is most clearly expressed at the conclusion of *Blade Runner*. Deckard and Rachel's escape from Scott's urban dystopia takes them to their own country, a paradise on Earth, the pristine, natural garden of the US wilderness. In *Do Androids Dream of Electric Sheep?* the desire to return to Eden is expressed obliquely. As Eliade points out in *The Myth of the Eternal Return*, the renewal of friendship with and spontaneous mastery of animals signifies a recovery of the paradisiac condition.[59] In *Do Androids Dream of Electric Sheep?* Deckard is desperate to own an animal and experience its friendship. Unhappy owning a synthetic sheep, he goes deeply into debt to purchase a Nubian goat. After he loses the beautiful goat, he contents himself with the ugliest of creatures, a toad he found in the desert—ironically, this toad turns out to be a replicant, and Deckard is unable to experience *illud tempus*. In *Blade Runner 2049*, Deckard's nostalgia for the perfect past is evident in his acquiring a dog as a companion underground. Wallace too longs for beatitude. His desire to storm Eden also expresses fallen man's existential crisis in the twenty-first century.

At its base, Villeneuve's dystopic vision insists that every individual is, as Eliade would say, "a being destined to death, issuing from Nothingness and on his way to Nothingness."[60] Be they replicant or human, the Beautiful, "inescapably devoured by Time,"[61] are the damned. With this in mind, Hegel would doubtless agree that Beauty in *Blade Runner 2049* enables us to bring to mind the truth about ourselves, and so become aware of who we truly are. Beauty's inability to mediate between man and the Good in *Blade Runner 2049* also makes us aware that there are no simple, straightforward solutions to our social and political problems, even in the Age of Trump. In final analysis, Villeneuve's sophisticated aesthetic (and moral) argument marks a radical departure from tech noir's hopelessness and stylish cynicism. Introducing classical problems of value and judgment, *Blade Runner 2049* calls for a serious reexamination of human nature *and* social change. Villeneuve's treatment of Beauty reminds us that even in a dystopia, living authentically is possible. Like K and Joi, we need only order where we are to make a heaven out of hell. And if everyone lived lives ordered by acts of love, what a wonderful world that would be.

FILMOGRAPHY

12 Monkeys, directed by Terry Gilliam (1995; Hertfordshire, UK: Arrow Video, 2018), DVD.

Blade Runner, directed by Ridley Scott (1982; Burbank, California: Warner Bros, 2007), DVD. Theatrical Cut.

Blade Runner 2049, directed by Denis Villeneuve (2017; Burbank, California: Warner Brothers Home Entertainment, 2017), DVD.

China Girl, directed by Henry Hathaway (1942; Century City, California: Twentieth Century Fox Corporation, 2012), DVD.

D.O.A., directed by Rudolph Maté (1950; Montreal, Quebec: Image Entertainment, 2012), DVD.

Marlowe, directed by Paul Bogart (1969; Burbank, California: Warner Bros, 2011), DVD.

Metropolis, directed by Fritz Lang (1927; New York, New York: Kino International, 2010), DVD.

Robocop, directed by Peter Verhoeven (1987; Beverly Hills, California: MGM, 2003), DVD.

Terminator, directed by James Cameron (1984; Beverly Hills, California: MGM, 2010), DVD.

Terminator 2: Judgement Day, directed by James Cameron (1991; Santa Monica, California: Universal Music Group, 2000), DVD.

The Matrix, directed by The Wachowski Brothers (1999; Burbank, California: Warner Home Video, 2007), DVD.

Total Recall, directed by Peter Verhoeven (1990; Toronto, Ontario: Mongrel Media, 2014), DVD.

The White Cliffs of Dover, directed by Clarence Brown (1944; Beverly Hills, California: MGM, 2010), DVD.

NOTES

1. Hegel, "Hegel's Lectures on Aesthetics, Vol. 1. Part I, The Idea of Artistic Beauty or The Ideal," *marxists.org*. Accessed https://www.marxists.org/reference/archive/hegel/works/ae/part1.htm on September 2, 2018. Discussing aesthetics, Hegel posits that Beauty is "a specific way of expressing and representing the true."

2. Erika Gottlieb, *Dystopian Fiction East and West: Universe of Terror and Trial* (Montreal: McGill-Queen's Press, 2001), 18.

3. German Expressionist painters reject the naturalistic depiction of objective reality, and often portray distorted figures, buildings, and landscapes in a disorienting manner that disre-

gards the conventions of perspective and proportion. The jagged, stylized shapes and harsh, unnatural colors convey subjective emotions.

4. Sarah Leedom, *Metropolis—A Case Study.* Accessible at http://metropolis-vixfx.blogspot.com/2007/. Last modified October 5, 2007.

5. Throughout this chapter, I will be considering only the 1982 theatrical cut of Ridley Scott's *Blade Runner*.

6. In "The Battle for Blade Runner," Michael Schulman also points out that Blade Runner's visual legacy has extended beyond the tech noir genre. Elements of Scott's tech noir in Blade Runner are found in " the stylized cyberpunk chic of The Matrix, the nocturnal manga of Ghost in the Shell, and the apocalyptic noir of countless video games. Filmmakers from Guillermo del Toro to Christopher Nolan cite [*Blade Runner*] as an influence, and its aesthetic DNA has permeated everything from George Michael's 'Freeek!' video to Jean Paul Gaultier's 2009 fall couture show and Raf Simons's recent collection of futuristic rainwear" (see *Vanity Fair*. Accessed https://www.vanityfair.com/hollywood/2017/09/the-battle-for-blade-runner-harrison-ford-ridley-scott on September 14, 2017.)

7. Paul Meehan, *Tech Noir: The Fusion of Science Fiction and Film Noir* (Jefferson, NC: McFarland, 2008), 9.

8. See Nathan Osborne's "We can't blame audiences for BLADERUNNER 2049's failure." Accessed https://www.filminquiry.com/blame-blade-runner-2049-failure/ on November 20, 2017; Scott Mendelson's "What 'Failure of Blade Runner 2049' Says About U.S. Box Office." Accessed https://www.forbes.com/sites/scottmendelson/2017/10/26/what-blade-runner-2049s-failure-says-about-u-s-box-office/#1cd84e44169f on October 26, 2017; Scott Mendelson's "Box Office: Why 'Jumanji' Was A Hit but 'Blade Runner 2049' Was A Flop." Accessed https://www.forbes.com/sites/scottmendelson/2017/12/28/box-office-why-jumanji-is-a-hit-but-blade-runner-2049-was-a-flop/#2fdc1ce96a04 on December 28, 2017; Christian Gentolia's "Three Reasons why Blade Runner 2049 Failed in Theatres." Accessed https://popmediauf.wixsite.com/popmediatv/single-post/2017/11/20/Three-Reasons-Blade-Runner-2049-Failed-in-Theaters on November 20, 2017; Alice Vincent's "Blade Runner 2049 flopped at the box office—here are six reasons why." Accessed https://www.telegraph.co.uk/films/2017/10/09/blade-runner-2049-has-flopped-box-office-six-reasons/ on October 9, 2017; Zack Sharf's "Ridley Scott Knows Why 'Blade Runner 2049' Bombed At The Box Office: It's Slow. Long. Too Long." Accessed https://www.indiewire.com/2017/12/ridley-scott-blade-runner-2049-box-office-bomb-1201910964/ on December 26, 2017. For another perspective on *Blade Runner 2049*'s failure to draw audiences, see Hoai Tran-Bui's "Why 'Blade Runner 2049' Failed at the Box Office, According to Director Denis Villeneuve." Accessed https://www.slashfilm.com/blade-runner-2049-failed/ on November 23, 2017.

9. Christopher Orr, "*Blade Runner 2049* Is a Worthy Heir to a Classic," *The Atlantic*. Accessedhttps://www.theatlantic.com/entertainment/archive/2017/10/blade-runner-2049-is-a-worthy-heir-to-the-classic-original/542205/ on October 6, 2017.

10. Peter Bradshaw, "*Blade Runner 2049* review—a gigantic spectacle of hallucinatory craziness," *The Guardian*. Accessed https://www.theguardian.com/film/2017/sep/29/blade-runner-2049-review-ryan-gosling-harrison-ford-denis-villeneuve on September 29, 2017.

11. Peter Travers, "'Blade Runner 2049' Review: Sequel to Sci- Fi Landmark Is an Instant Classic," *Rolling Stone.* Accessed https://www.rollingstone.com/movies/movie-reviews/blade-runner-2049-review-sequel-to-sci-fi-landmark-is-an-instant-classic-253371/ on September 29, 2017.

12. A. O. Scott, "Review: In 'Blade Runner 2049,' Hunting Replicants Amid Strangeness," *The New Yorker.* Accessed. https://www.nytimes.com/2017/10/02/movies/blade-runner-2049-review-ryan-gosling-harrison-ford.html on October 2, 2017.

13. Philip K. Dick, *Do Androids Dream of Electric Sheep?* (New York: Del Rey, 2017), 19.

14. Dick, *Do Androids*, 8.

15. Dick, *Do Androids*, 18.

16. Dick, *Do Androids*, 19.

17. Dick, *Do Androids*, 19.

18. Plotinus, "Enneads 1.6." Accessed http://www.phx-ult-lodge.org/The_beautiful.htm on August 25, 2018.

19. Dick, *Do Androids*, 3.
20. Dick, *Do Androids*, 201.
21. Dick, *Do Androids*, 201.
22. Dick, *Do Androids*, 171.
23. In "On Beauty," Plotinus describes the pleasurable experience of viewing physical beauty as the first step of man's ascent to the Good. See *Plotinus on the Beautiful*. Accessed http://www.phx-ult-lodge.org/The_beautiful.htm on August 20, 2018.
24. According to Plotinus, the lowest type of beauty is physical beauty. Following Plato in *Symposium*, Plotinus traces a hierarchy of beautiful objects above the physical, culminating in the Forms themselves. Their source, the Good, is also the source of their beauty (I 6. 7).
25. No relation to the science fiction writer Ray Bradbury, *The Bradbury Building* was the brainchild of Lewis Bradbury, a mining and real-estate millionaire. An architectural movie star in Los Angeles, *The Bradbury* has served as an exotic setting, making its first on-screen appearance in 1942, in *China Girl* when it played a Burmese hotel. In 1944, it played a London military hospital in *White Cliffs of Dover*. It was the background in the *noir* thriller *DOA* (1950). And in the 1969 movie *Marlowe*, Bruce Lee steps into an office of the Bradbury and kicks all the furniture apart. For more information about The Bradbury, see "This Building is the Biggest Architectural Movie Star in Los Angeles." Accessed http://www.slate.com/blogs/the_eye/2015/07/15/the_bradbury_building_is_the_biggest_architectural_movie_star_in_los_angeles.html on July 15, 2015.
26. Ariana Quiñónez, "13 times Harrison Ford was the sexiest man alive," *Screener*. Accessed http://screenertv.com/movies/13-times-harrison-ford-was-the-sexiest-man-alive/ on November 21, 2015.
27. Schulman, "The Battle for Blade Runner."
28. Schulman, "The Battle for Blade Runner."
29. Schulman, "The Battle for Blade Runner."
30. Dick, *Do Androids*, 141.
31. Dick, *Do Androids*, 141.
32. Alexis Harley, "America, a Prophecy: When Blake meets Blade Runner," *Sydney Studies in English* 31 (2005): 63. In her excellent study, Harley points notes that Baty complicates his character in Blade Runner, saying: "Fiery the angels fell; deep thunder rolled around their shores; burning with the fires of Orc." Identifying with the angels who actually rose from the fires of Orc, Baty proclaims himself a fallen angel, embodying the spirit of rebellion. This misreading, she points out, also evokes John Milton's account of the angels' fall from heaven in *Paradise Lost*, further associating Baty with Lucifer and his rebel angels.
33. "Denis Villeneuve: 'Blade Runner 2049,'" *Talks at Google*. Accessed https://www.youtube.com/watch?v=pPn-xuifKFg on September 29, 2017.
34. 34. '"Villeneuve, 'Blade Runner 2049,'" *Talks at Google*.
35. "Blade Runner-2049-shooting-script. pdf," *docdroid*. Accessed https://www.docdroid.net/WWXneXj/blade-runner-2049-shooting-script.pdf#page=47, 46 on August 3, 2018.
36. Hampton Fancher, *Jois*, in *Blade Runner 101*, Warner Bros. Home Entertainment, 2018.
37. Fancher, *Jois*.
38. Mackenzie Davis, *The Replicant Evolution* in *Blade Runner 101*, Warner Bros. Home Entertainment, 2018.
39. "Blade Runner-2049-shooting-script," 29.
40. 40. "Blade Runner-2049-shooting-script,."70.
41. "Blade Runner-2049-shooting-script," 25.
42. "Blade Runner-2049-shooting-script," 104.
43. Plotinus, The Ethical Treatises, being the Treatises of the First Ennead [253], 2004–2018. Accessible at http://oll.libertyfund.org/titles/plotinus-the-ethical-treatises-being-the-treatises-of-the-first-ennead--5.
44. In Book I of John Milton's *Paradise Lost*, Satan is hurled "to bottomless perdition, there to dwell in adamantine chains and penal fire" (ll. 47–48).
45. In Book I of John Milton's *Paradise Lost*, when speaking about Hell to his fellow devils, Satan says, "Is this the Region, this the Soil, the Clime, / Said then the lost Arch-Angel, this the

seat / That we must change for Heav'n, this mournful gloom / for that celestial light?" (ll. 242–245).

46. In Book VI of John Milton's *Paradise Lost*, Satan joins the battle against God in Heaven "arm'd in Adamant and Gold" (l. 110).

47. "Blade Runner-2049-shooting-script, 34.

48. Anne Thompson, "*Blade Runner 2049*: Dennis Villeneuve on the Challenges of Three-Way Sex Scenes and His Very Real Need for A Nap," *IndieWire*. Accessed https://www.indiewire.com/2017/10/blade-runner-2049-denis-villeneuve-ryan-gosling-roger-deakins-1201885049/ on October 12, 2017.

49. See the reference to Satan in Book I of John Milton's *Paradise Lost*, l. 63.

50. In "*Blade Runner 2049*," Anne Thompson points out that Villeneuve encouraged his cinematographer Roger Deakins to extend *Blade Runner*'s *film noir* motif of slatted Venetian blinds in production and "go wild with Wallace's massive tower headquarters, with its dramatic bands of yellow light."

51. See this reference to Hell as a "fiery Gulf" in Book I of John Milton's *Paradise Lost*, in l. 52. Also referencing Antonioni's *Red Desert*, Villeneuve's toxic and apocalyptic industrial landscapes outside the Wallace Tower take on this characteristic of Milton's Hell—as K searches for Deckard outside the ruins of a Las Vegas casino, the red, polluted fog outside shines with a poisonous golden hue transforming what is left of Las Vegas into a "fiery Gulf."

52. In Book I of John Milton's *Paradise Lost*, Satan's "business" is conducted in "Here in the Heart of Hell to work in fire" (l. 151).

53. John Keats, "Ode on a Grecian Urn," *Bartleby.com*, l. 49. Accessed https://www.bartleby.com/101/625.html on August 22, 2018.

54. .Plotinus, The Ethical Treatises, being the Treatises of the First Ennead [253], 2004–2018. Accessible at http://oll.libertyfund.org/titles/plotinus-the-ethical-treatises-being-the-treatises-of-the-first-ennead--5.

55. Ana de Armas, *Jois* in *Blade Runner 101* in Warner Bros. Home Entertainment, 2018.

56. Philip K. Dick, "The Android and The Man." Accessed https://sporastudios.org/mark/courses/articles/Dick_the_android.pdf on September 5, 2018.

57. "Denis Villeneuve: 'Blade Runner 2049,'" *Talks at Google*.

58. "Denis Villeneuve: 'Blade Runner 2049,'" *Talks at Google*.

59. Mircea Eliade, *Myths, Dreams and Mysteries: The Encounter between Contemporary Faiths and Archaic Realities* (New York: Harper Torchbooks, 1960), 62–63.

60. Eliade, *Myths*, 239.

61. Eliade, *Myths*, 240.

Chapter Eight

Feminism Reboot in *Mad Max: Fury Road* and Hulu's *The Handmaid's Tale*

Kate Waites

Throughout history, the feminist response to sex and gender disparity, albeit transformative, has been fraught with cultural and political hazards. As early as the fifteenth century, Christina de Pizan's *The Book of the City of Ladies* rocked her early Renaissance world with an alternative perspective that challenged the patriarchal status quo and emphasized the value of "women's spaces."

> By re-"constructing" the past, Christine builds a feminist framework for the future. She can be considered the founder of the modern woman's movement, making a bold statement in the *Querelle des Femmes*, a long continuous battle between authors who attacked and who defended women. [1]

Intending to counteract widely held misogynistic views of her male peers, de Pizan's *City of Ladies* set the template for feminism. More such landmark feminist tomes would follow: Wollstonecraft's *A Vindication of the Rights of Women* (1792), Woolf's *A Room of One's Own* (1929), de Beauvoir's *The Second Sex* (1949), Friedan's *The Feminine Mystique* (1963), and Germaine Greer's *The Female Eunuch* (1970), to name but a few. Using varied approaches, these texts constructed a viable, theory-based movement that dissected long-standing male dominance, while garnering the derision and condemnation of those who remained steeped in male hegemony. Despite the weighty political and cultural obstacles to women's equality, however, the movement of feminism(s) has marched on, defying women's allotted space in the domestic sphere and placing them on a public stage where they might stand on equal footing with men. This powerful act continues to be feminism's chief sin in the eyes of an intractable patriarchal order, one that is fortified by the excesses and amorality of unrestrained capitalism.

Feminism's fundamental transgression of traditional gender norms, which is reflected in its monumental political and social advances, has incurred furious backlashes against women, as argued by journalist Susan Faludi in *Backlash: The Undeclared War Against American Women*. Faludi confines her polemic to the United States until the early 1990; however, a glance around the world confirms that obstacles to women's education, including reproductive rights, claim to a political voice, and sexual objectification, are persistent, conspiring to keep women contained. For instance, since the 1980s in the United States the supposed bastion for individual liberty, a resurgence of legislative attacks against women's reproductive rights, along with governmental failure to support dual-burdened working women, are mechanisms for denying them bodily autonomy and full social and economic equality. Exacerbating this imbalance, third-wave postfeminism and consumer feminism have served only to dilute the feminist goal of sex and gender parity, according to feminist philosopher Lorna Finlayson and cultural critic Andi Zeisler.[2] Consequently, for all of feminism's rebranding and newfound celebrity in the new millennium, political equality remains elusive, and women's bodily autonomy is in severe peril. Ironically however, intensified and harshly regressive policies aimed at women,[3] together with climate-change denial and rollbacks in environmental protections of the Earth and its resources, have sparked a resurgence of social activism. This kind of collective feminist activism has not been seen since the 1960s and 1970s, pointing the way to a more hopeful future going forward. As CNN editor Jodi Enda puts it: "Donald Trump is bad for women, but there's no disputing this: He is great for the women's movement."[4] The striking display of intersectional feminism in the Women's March on Washington and demonstrations around the world that occurred on the day following the Trump inauguration, signifies this long overdue and much-needed feminist reboot.[5] And it is about time, because the fate of women, the disenfranchised, and the Earth is in jeopardy.

Nowhere are the dire consequences of this long-standing war against women and the environment clearer than in recent dystopic fiction. Two popular texts that place a spotlight on the consequences of patriarchy's long-standing stranglehold on women and its carelessly utilitarian attitude toward the Earth are George Miller's *Mad Max: Fury Road* (2016) and Hulu's (2017–) adaptation and updating of Margaret Atwood's *The Handmaid's Tale* for streaming television. Both tales rely on the camera and the power of the image to convey a shared thematic: the destructiveness of the traditional masculine ethos and the fragility of its ego, whose continued dominance relies on monopolizing resources—of which women's bodies are essential—to prop itself up. Mirroring today's sociopolitical reality, in these visual texts, feminism is presented as an antidote to the ills of white-supremacist-capitalist patriarchy. As these texts reveal and our sociopolitical world demonstrates, women and the Earth are increasingly imperiled and a radical feminist reboot is necessary for saving the day for women and indeed the world.

MAD MAX: FURY ROAD[6]

At first glance, Miller's furiously paced extravaganza hardly seems like the stuff of feminist dreams. Featuring multiple camera angles of striking images and a dizzying, yet fluid, barrage of center-framed shots to capture Immortan Joe and his army of war boys racing across the post-apocalyptic wasteland in their relentless pursuit of outlaw Imperator Furiosa, Miller's *Mad Max* seems tailor made for a *Fast and Furious* audience. Nonetheless, this thrilling visual ride in a dangerous postapocalyptic future is deceiving. Supported by a "cacophony of sound" and "wall-to-wall musical score that reflects the insanity and accelerating chaos unfolding on screen,"[7] the Tom Holkenberg (Junkie XL) soundtrack supports Miller's filmic narrative, which is an apt objective correlative for a ravaged and dysfunctional world resulting from the greed and destructive impulses of a masculinist ideology run amok. As with all postapocalyptic texts, by showing us the white-supremacist/capitalist/patriarchal road *not* to travel, the film offers a dire warning about humankind's fate. In voiceover, in the opening title frame, a third-person narrator asks: "Why are you hurting these people?" The "you" obviously refers to the wealthy and powerful of the land, and the dismissive reply comes immediately: "It's the oil, stupid."

From this barely audible remark, the audience can infer that fossil fuels, rather than alternative energies, drove the culture's failed economy and disastrous legislative decisions. The dialogue also implies that because of their greed, as well as the stubborn refusal to recognize the hazards and limit of fossil fuels and adapt accordingly, humans have ruined the air and stripped the Earth. In voiceover, a female narrator says, plaintively: "Our bones are poisoned. We have become half-life." Images of the ravished landscape underscore this observation.

Miller's film takes a feminist stance by imagining this nearly uninhabitable future wasteland as the logical outcome of masculinist hegemony wed unrestrained capitalism. In the opening sequence, the title character Max speaks in voiceover from outside the film, suggesting his alienation from life and describing the "world" he finds himself in as "fire and blood." Indeed. The Earth has been ravaged and nearly drained of its natural resources. Desperate gangs roam the desert landscape, fuel is scarce, and water is coveted. One major water source is horded by the ruthlessly self-serving Immortan Joe, his wart- and pustule-ridden torso, encased in plastic armor, a fitting symbol of his noxious organization. Except for the cold eyes peering out in extreme close-ups, Immortan Joe's *human* features are obscured or distorted, signaling his corrupted soul. The rest of his face is hidden behind an oxygen mask and oversized lion's teeth, his grotesque appearance symbolizing his inhumaneness, and augmenting the savagery with which he rules.

From high on his perch on a fortified mountain enclave, appropriately named the Citadel, Immortan Joe doles out the precious commodity of water in a cruel, arbitrary fashion to the begging detritus of humanity on the baked red-earth below him. A long establishing shot of the ruler, speaking from the mouth of his Citadel-kingdom beneath enlarged lions' teeth carved into the mountain, is followed by an over-the-shoulder bird's-eye shot: Immortan Joe gazes down at the parched multitude swarming like desperate ants below him. His arms spread, Christ-like, Immortan Joe proclaims, "I am your Redeemer. It is by my hand you will rise from the ashes of this world." The camera zooms in with a high-angle, medium-close-up of a ragged-looking, toothless old man, who is surrounded by a sea of similarly decrepit men and women, eying his purported "savior." In the subsequent subjective point-of-view long-shot, we view Immortan Joe through the lens of the man's binoculars, thus heightening audience awareness of the leader's godlike status. The camera then shifts back to a high-angle, medium close-up of the old man, surrounded by similarly dusty, aged bodies, their desperate eyes cast upward and their hands holding up tin containers to capture water as they advance toward the camera. Immortan Joe's hands silence the screaming crowd before he releases the magical levers in a medium-long, low-angle shot. This scene is followed by a high-angle shot from behind that sees Joe looking down at the swarms of thirsty people vying for the coveted water. In a series of dramatic, alternating high- and low-angle shots, the water surges from three vast metal cylinders protruding from the mountain. With the camera zooming toward the gushing water, a swell of hymn-like orchestral music reinforces the cynical allusion to a baptismal rite presided over by the high anti-priest.

Within the Citadel, Immortan Joe's followers fare little better. Hordes of albino war boys and pups, who have been bred and brainwashed into their supreme leader's service, live only to die for him in glory at the promised "gates of Valhalla." Confined to the mountain's gloomy innards, Immortan's minions, such as Nux, are reduced to little more than functioning cogs in the wheels of their leader's toxic system, as portrayed in scenes that depict them powering the elaborate wheels and pulleys operating inside the Citadel mountain. Desperate, they compete with one another to gain their cult-like leader's favor. Warrior-turned renegade, Nux, repeatedly exclaims: "I live. I die. I live again!" Ultimately and ironically, however, Nux's is a feminist baptism because he lives "again" not by virtue of sacrificing himself for Immortan Joe but instead to ensure the freedom of Joe's renegade wives.

The hierarchy is clear: Immortan Joe at the top, followed by male family members and "generals" that keep the war boys and pups in line by having them contend for a place in Joe's war parties, and ultimately the glory of battle. "I am your Redeemer," Joe bellows from his perch atop the Citadel. "It is by my hand that you will rise from the ashes of this world." What he neglects to say is that it is also by capitalist patriarchy's hands that the Earth has been reduced to rubble, ash, and authoritarianism. Even though Joe's "breeders," (wives) are sheltered and nurtured, their singular function is to produce milk or to provide him with a healthy male heir. In an early scene depicted in an eerie long-shot, we see the older, well-nourished breeders lined up in reclining chairs, evoking the image of milking-cows in a barn stall. They look out at their closeted world with vacant eyes, while their enormous breasts—the raison d'être of their existence—are tethered to tubes and their milk is caught in huge glass containers that await Immortan Joe's close inspection. In a pull-away medium-close-up shot, Joe is portrayed holding the precious milk aloft before handing it over to Rictus Erectus for examination. Though fleeting, the scene is a shocking reminder of women's dehumanized place in a masculinist system, where woman is reduced, not only to a body but also to the most serviceable life-sustaining part of her body. Governed by a regressive masculinist ideology, reminiscent of the misogynistic policies fostered by the far-right wing of Trump's Republican party, the woman's body is not her own to govern.

Reminiscent of the male-ruled clans of ancient times, Immortan Joe's authoritarian rule represents the logical extension of a Trumpian administration, one that is comprised of close-knit insiders—his sons and son-in-law and his daughter—and a band of staunch loyalists, the bulldog-ish Kelly Anne Conways, sycophantic Reince Priubu ses and Michel Cohens, and Darth Vadar-like Bannons and Millers. In Trump world, other branches of power—the legislature, the courts, intelligence agencies—are there not to serve the Constitution but Trump himself. His anti-democratic governance is evidenced in his belittling of judges, and most significantly, his derision of the free press.[8] *Fury Road* imagines a future in which greed and unchecked corporatist power, epitomized in Trumpian/Republican devaluation of women and the patent disregard for settled science and the nation's storied history of welcoming immigrants, has resulted in a ravaging of the Earth and an obliteration of the rule of law.

In his investigation of the history of clan rule, Mark S. Weiner explains how clans have flourished in the vacuum of the weakened "liberal state," using "institutions . . . to advance narrow group interests above the common good."[9] Moreover, Weiner explains, "When rulers feel weak, they resort to 'bluster and bombast' and 'exploit national symbols' to 'generate centripetal force' and increase their perceived authority."[10] We see echoes of this phenomenon in Trump's recent exploitation of the Confederate statue debate and his ham-fisted, white-nationalist-tinged remarks in the wake of the Charlottesville terrorist attack.[11] Weiner explains that, in an "antimodern world of diminished individual autonomy,"[12] like the one aptly illustrated in *Mad Max*, a tribal mentality fills the power vacuum. In such a posttruth era, facts are negated or dismissed, loyalty to the sovereign takes primacy, outsiders are potential enemies, and healthy checks and balances on the power and whims of the leader are negated.

One major "whim," and the driving force of *Fury*'s diegesis, involves the nubile brides that comprise Immortan Joe's harem. When Furiosa—a lieutenant in Immortan's ragtag army—hits the gas pedal on her war rig and escapes the Citadel with the runaway brides safely stashed in the belly of the war rig that is filled with "mothers" milk, it represents a feminist act. No longer commodities and currencies in the service of masculinist hegemony, the newly freed women are presenting feminism as a viable antidote to the disruptive tendencies of unchecked power. This point is expressed in the graffiti scrawled on the walls of the prison cage by the bride rebels in advance of their escape: "Who killed our world?"—and "You do not own our bodies!" In a dramatic bird's-eye shot that diminishes the stunned figure of Immortan Joe surveying the abandoned harem prison, the camera zooms in on the oversized chalked letters on the stone floor that proclaim: "OUR BABIES WILL NOT BE WARLORDS." This dramatic shot also serves to underscore the brides' feminist battle cry, whose revolutionary act is reinforced by Miss Giddy, teacher and mentor of the wives who aims a rifle at the head of the distraught leader, informing him: "They are not your property." She also takes pleasure in reporting that, far from being stolen, Joe's "wives" begged Furiosa to take them far away from "him."

Connecting the systemic rape of the environment with the bondage and rape of women strengthens the feminist message, signaling an ecofeminist-consciousness in the film, one that recognizes the damaging effects of a utilitarian worldview in which the dominant white majority exploits "others," including women, minorities, and nature, for the purpose of material and personal gain. As characterized by Karen J. Warren, this particular feminist methodology targets "male-gender bias" and "the twin dominations of women and nature."[13] She adds: "Ecofeminists . . . . have shown how the logic of domination is at work in both the domination of nature by humans and the domination of women by men under various forms of patriarchy."[14]

That the male characters greatly outnumber the female characters in the film is also beside *Fury Road's* feminist point, given co-hero Furiosa's (Charlize Theron) commanding presence on the screen. Indeed, the women's empowerment theme is amplified by the David-like might of her small band of young runaway wives and the tag-along Vuvalini, the aging matriarchs of the elusive, now-ravaged sanctuary, the Green Place. It is Furiosa, however, who leads the rebellion and single-handedly plots their escape through dangerous territory, having made a deal with desert outlaws in exchange for fuel and safe passage. A fearless war-rig driver and soldier, Furiosa evokes the Amazon warrior women of Greek mythology. Where the absence of their right breast made them better marksman with the bow and arrow,[15] the one-armed Furiosa is similarly more strengthened than hampered by her absent arm. She uses its mechanical replacement to steer the truck through the rugged, dusty terrain and, at times, wields it as a weapon, such as when Max, manacled to Nux, overtakes the rig and attempts to steal it to make his own escape. Max ultimately overtakes her, only to discover that Furiosa's clever engineering prevents him from operating the rig without her. As a result, Max relents and the two agree to team up, an act that portends the feminist way forward for freedom lovers and caretakers of the Earth. Moreover, despite that Max is the title character, Furiosa is the hero who drives both the war rig and the film narrative, her menace and preparedness clearly evidenced in her shaved head, war paint, and fierce glare.

Moreover, despite having lived as chattel in Immortan Joe's kingdom, under Furiosa's leadership, the wives prove to be competent and resourceful. Far from being damsels in distress, Furiosa's cohorts facilitate their own escape by helping Furiosa manage her arsenal of weapons and fend off attacks from pursuers. For example, after heroically stepping on the running board of the racing rig to unbolt the chain locked through the steering wheel, effectively saving Max's life and abetting the rebel escape, the pregnant Splendid Angharad, Immortan's favorite wife, falls to her death, crushed ironically by the war boys' Doof-wagon being driven by Joe himself. This scene begins with a long, wide-angle shot of the Doof-wagon bearing down on the war rig, as Immortan Joe demands the return of his "property." As the scene nears the end, a poignant exchange of close-ups between a grateful Max and a quietly triumphant Angharad cuts to a medium-close-up of Angharad's terrified face as her tenuous grip on the broken cab door slips and delivers her to the dusty wasteland. The "perfect brother" she was carrying, ripped from her body and held aloft by Immortan's son, is killed along with her, and the message is clear: the greed and destruction Immortan sows is, ultimately, unsustainable. In its ashes however, a Phoenix-like rebellion unfolds, and Miller's film imagines the birth of a more compassionate, egalitarian world governed by women and enlightened men in search of a restored mother earth. This moment serves as a turning point for Nux, who has boarded and stowed away on the war rig with the intention of returning Joe's brides to him. After Nux fails to blow himself up in glory, as initially planned, however, and having spent time with the runaways who tend to his wounds, Nux undergoes a conversion. Having finally found an honorable cause, his commitment to their cause is unwavering and ends in his heroic death.

If Max is "mad"—tortured by demon memories of his impotence and reduced to a state of survival of the fittest—then Furiosa is outraged, driven by a mission to save herself and Immortan Joe's prisoner wives from bondage. Intent on finding her childhood "Green Place," and a more humane, Earth-friendly female-centric world, Furiosa's goal recalls Christine de Pizan's vision of a "city of ladies" where women may flourish unencumbered by an oppressive masculinist system. Even though their history has been erased in the Citadel, *Fury*'s women commit a revolutionary act by attempting to create the world anew and write their own *her* story.

Ironically, when they encounter the Vuvalini who report that the Green Place is no more and all seems lost, it is Max who points out the better way forward to Furiosa. Upon realizing that the war rig will not survive endless miles of desert sand, he persuades her to turn the rig around and return to the Citadel and the certainty of water and community *sans* its authoritarian leader, which they succeed in doing after setting a trap that destroys Immortan Joe and the remains of his war party. This shift in Max—from loner survivalist to life-affirming human being connected to others—is illustrated in the scene where Max, fresh from battle, quenches his rabid thirst and cools his face with breast milk from the rig, signifying his baptism into female, life-affirming energy: "At least that way we might be able to. . . together. . . come across some kind of redemption," he tells Furiosa, who clenches his hand to seal the pact. In "Sweet Nectar of the Matriarchy . . .," Colleen Martell explains how she sees echoes of pioneer feminist Charlotte Perkins Gilman's utopian novel, *Herland*, and the promise of a new female-authored "economy."

> Furiosa, the "Wives," the Vulvalini, and Max's triumphant return to the Citadel finds the once chained-to-their-pumps milk mothers now opening the floodgates and pouring water down on the people below. It seems likely that our heroes and the milk mothers will move forward on the "plentitude model"—bathing in an abundance of sweet, thick human milk, sharing water access, and growing green things from heirloom seeds—rather than continue in the scarcity model exemplified by Immortan Joe.[16]

A previous scene had revealed the lush plant life, hidden within the Citadel, upon which the privileged feast, while the multitudes waste away: a clear allusion to the growing divide between rich and poor in the contemporary United States. Here, then, is the promise of a new world order based on community and the equitable distribution of resources that is suggested in the film's closing scenes. After announcing Immortan Joe's demise in those scenes, Furiosa and her band of renegades receive a rapturous reception at the Citadel, demonstrating the prospect of a more egalitarian, feminist future.

THE HANDMAID'S TALE

Hulu hit pay dirt at the 2017 Emmy Awards, garnering multiple nominations and eight wins for its updated adaptation of Margaret Atwood's 1985 dystopian novel.[17] Highlighting the show's social significance in *Wired*, Angela Watercutter notes: "*The Handmaid's Tale*, a show where the patriarchy literally rules all and women's only hope of survival is to topple it, won the Emmy for Outstanding Drama, becoming the first streaming service to do so."[18] According to Joe Otterson, the "show received widespread acclaim upon its release, and currently holds a 99% approval rating on Rotten Tomatoes."[19] Reimagining Margaret Atwood's preoccupation with alarming cultural trends in the 1980s, Hulu's *The Handmaid's Tale* seems to have hit a raw cultural nerve in the second decade of the new millennium, specifically anxiety associated with intensified threats to the environment and women's rights.

Clearly, in addition to triggering a feminist resurgence, the Trump phenomenon has also inspired pro-feminist television programming. Although Hulu's version is situated in the social media age, showrunner Bruce Miller remains loyal to Atwood's fiercely satirical critique of the unhealthy marriage between extremist Christianity and the federal government, one that ironically echoes an ISIS Caliphate governed by Sharia Law. Like *Mad Max: Fury Road*, the punch is in the *how*, or in the visual grammar—particularly evidenced in the production design and cinematography—by which Hulu's *The Handmaid's Tale* illustrates the drastic consequences of capitalist patriarchy fueled by religious zealots and carried to its logical, unconstitutional extreme. The case for feminism as a viable antidote to despotic rule is presented in the narrative's subtext in the first season, and in startling narrative developments of the show's second season, which, although surpassing the scope of Atwood's novel, remains "true to Atwood's world and Atwood's tone," and in which Atwood, according to pop-culture critic Leah Thomas, had a hand.[20] Where an emaciated land is left with primitive tribal governance in *Fury Road*, in *The Handmaid's Tale*, the United is reduced to a theocracy, aptly named the Republic of Gilead and consistent with Atwood's aim to portray a modern-day US society "built on a foundation of 17th-century Puritan roots."[21] And so it was. Scratch the surface of the United States's democratic republic and what appear are John Winthrop's biblically based fire and brimstone brand of leadership in the seventeenth-century New England wilderness,[22] and Jonathan Edwards's righteous sermons, including "Sinners in the Hands of an Angry God" that, almost a century later, nudged his wayward flock back into line and retethered to Puritan law.[23]

Based on a book "of voiceovers and flashbacks," *The Handmaid's Tale* posed a particular challenge to Reed Morano, director of its first three episodes, which create the ominous tone and establish the visual "roadmap" for the series.[24] Hulu's *Handmaid* is set in New England, home to Harvard University and close to the birthplace of the American Revolution, an irony that reverberates throughout the narrative given Gilead's anti-intellectual, tyrannical rule forbidding all but commanders access to pens, books, and letters. Echoing *Fury Road*, rampant greed and deregulation have resulted in serious environmental damage—although the effects here are less visible and the causes, according to Aunt Lydia in "Offred" (S1, Ep1),[25] are attributed to people having strayed from biblical values. The resulting toxicity has adversely impacted fertility in humans and placed a high premium on children and fertile women. The Sons of Jacob rule with an iron fist, its laws drawn from the Old Testament. For example, while the Martha with whom Emily/Ofglen1 was having sex is sentenced by the "common mercy of the state" to be hanged, cruelly from the arm of a slowly moving crane. Emily, spared because she is fertile, is instead subjected to genital mutilation (S1, Ep3).[26] In a scene that finds her waking up to an eerily white and empty hospital room, Emily processes this horror. After easing herself from bed, Emily stands, lifting the white gown to reveal the diaper-like bandage over her "wound," ironically a double-wounding since her genitalia already signify her biological difference and the basis of her "otherness." Stupefied, she looks down at the site of her mutilation as Aunt Lydia's words slice her yet again: "You can't want what you don't have." The scene ends with seventeen extreme close-up shots of Emily's pained face from varied angles, revealing the depth of her anguish and ending in her piercing scream to the Jay Reatard's hard-driving, "Waiting for Something" on the soundtrack.

Atwood's novel[27] is narrated entirely through interior monologue, a first-person point of view that puts us in the narrator-protagonist's head. Renamed Offred in Gilead, she is the handmaid (and property) *of* Commander Fred Waterford. Confined to the protagonist's consciousness, the reader is compelled to identify with Offred's terrifying imprisonment and isolation: not only is she cut off from the world but she is also alienated from her former self. Through cinematic flashbacks in the Hulu adaptation, and consistent with Atwood's novel, we learn that "Offred' is June, an editor in the publishing industry, wife of Luke, mother of Hannah, and daughter of a radical feminist mother condemned to the colonies to do toxic waste clean-up. Morano's close-ups and extreme close-ups of the protagonist, often using handheld camera, enhanced by nondiegetic first-person voiceover, effectively convey the protagonist's disorientation and interiority. It also establishes June's authority over the narrative that unfolds on the screen. It is, after all, *The* Handmaid's *Tale.* June may be Gilead's powerless prisoner, but she is also the author of her own story. This cinematic voiceover method is complemented by Morano's use of a Zeiss 24-mm (wide-angle) camera, not typically used for close-ups.[28] Besides intensifying June's facial expressions, the wide-angle close-up conveys the traumatized protagonist's trancelike state as she processes the loss of her husband and daughter and awakens to her new life as sex slave in Fred Waterford's household, one of Gilead's chief architects. With the additional benefit of the omniscient camera, the visual storyteller is also free to explore other dimensions of the dystopian world outside June's consciousness. These include the toxic landscape populated by the condemned Unwomen somewhere beyond the cityscape and background on other characters, including June's husband Luke; best friend Moira; fellow handmaid Emily (Ofglen); Nick, a Guardian (and an Eye) in Waterford's household, who becomes June's lover; and the Commander's wife, Serena Joy.

Drawing from Atwood's meticulously conceived novel, both males and females in the series are categorized according to their status and function, as signified in the color of their clothing. This cautionary tale makes it clear that Commanders are absolute rulers. Women remain subordinate, including the Commanders' Wives who, although they enjoy more authority *inside* the household, must obey their husbands and remain restricted to their domestic role. Ironically, we learn through flashbacks that the now-powerless Serena Joy was a driving force behind her husband and a leader in the Christian takeover. In Gilead's anti-feminist, extremist Christian world, women, reduced to utter subservience, are divided according to their social function. Their role is marked by the color of their clothing, reminiscent of how the Jews were marked with a yellow star and Hester Prynne by the scarlet letter "A," of which Atwood was surely cognizant. Book reviewer Andrew Kim highlights the uneasy connection between the religious rigidity of the United States's Puritan past, as represented in Hawthorne's mid-nineteenth-century novel and political developments in the present and reflected in Hulu's timely adaptation:

> Perhaps the way to read dystopian fiction in the age of Trump—and especially in the unholy alliance between Trump and Mike Pence—is not to deem the unwelcome present an aberration on reality, but to look to America's past and examine its intimacy with dystopian possibilities.[29]

Here, color coding, an effective means of dividing and conquering, is strikingly highlighted. Wives are infertile women married to high-level men (dark teal or blue). Daughters are young girls, like June's daughter Hannah, raised to be pure and obedient (white). Aunts, such as the sadistic Aunt Lydia, "reform" fertile, transgressive women into Handmaids at the Rachel and Leah Centre (drab brown). Econowives are married to poor, lower-level men (green or blue with stripes). Marthas are household servants (drab green). Jezebels are transgressive women, such as Moira, who entertain and "service" the Commanders (whorish outfits and garish make-up). Unwomen (drab gray) are consigned to clean-up duty in a toxic wasteland. These are comprised of feminists, postmenopausal women (June's mother), or gender traitors, such as Emily/Ofglen (lesbian) in the show's second season. The Handmaids, who are assigned to a Commander's household to procreate, stand out. Imprisoned in a floor-length red dress and cloak and a white, wing-like bonnet that shrouds the face. This palette of colors, and in particular, the shocking visual contrast of colors, comes alive in the talented hands of Morano,

> the cinematographer-turned director, who established . . . Atwood's color-coded dystopia with cinematographer Colin Watkinson and costume designer Ann Crabtree. Because of the gray, muted look of Gilead, the red of the handmaidens stood in sharp contrast to the teal of the Commanders' wives, who shamefully observe their husbands sexually using the Handmaidens.[30]

Males—Commanders; Eyes (spies for Gilead); Angels (soldiers that protect borders); Guardians (drivers, domestic police); Econohusbands (poor men)—are similarly divided according to their function and status, but their clothing is uniformly dark. As reported by *Vanity Fair*'s Jamie Lincoln, costume designer Ane Crabtree found inspiration in her research of "real life religious and military groups that have controlled societies en masse."[31] Moreover, the narrative's connection to the Trump era is evident, as Crabtree's "creative process was particularly emotional and charged because the show's filming schedule aligned with the results of the 2016 presidential election."[32] Notably, apart from the Commanders' elegant dark grey or black suits, men's clothing is not as distinctive as the women's. Evoking the military, their clothing tends to be gray, green, or brown, a visual reminder that males are not as rigidly demarcated as the females. Moreover, relative to the women, Gileadean men have more mobility in the public sphere and exercise authority over the women.

This gendered color scheme amplifies the fundamental disparity between male and female in patriarchal society; more importantly, it reinforces Gilead's distinctions among women, effectively encouraging women both to disidentify from one another and to compete with one another for male favor to ensure their survival. Explaining women's subservient place historically, art critic John Berger argued that because "women are born into the keeping of men," they develop a double consciousness whereby they come to view themselves not just as a "self" but also as men see and judge them.[33] Although Berger confines himself to the study of the representation of the female figure in visual art within Western culture, his observation speaks to the ways in which women have learned to identify with and perform for their male "keeper" (oftentimes, oppressor) over their connection with other women. Herein also lies the clue to their liberation, as Hulu's *The Handmaid's Tale* ultimately reveals.

So long as women remain divided against one another, men prevail. The stark contrast between the dark teal of the Wife's dress and the deep red of the Handmaid's costume signals their oppositional roles. However, the red, a shade artfully selected by Crabtree because "it resembles blood" and is "a metaphor for female menstruation,"[34] also signifies female "otherness" that, ironically, links the wife and handmaid. Their contrasting colors certify the oppositional spaces they occupy *in relation to* men in Gilead. This age-old duality in Judeo-Christian society originates in interpretations of Eve's inferiority to Adam and her essential corruptibility because she ate the "apple" and tempted Adam to do so. In her ground-breaking historical analysis, Simone de Beauvoir highlights the religious, theological, and legal justification for women's long-standing oppression under patriarchy:

> Lawmakers, priests, writers, and scholars have gone to great lengths to prove that women's subordinate condition was willed in heaven. . . . Religions forged by men reflect this will for domination: they found ammunition in the legends of Eve and Pandora.[35]

These are little more than "rationalizations," according to H. R. Hays, and "evidence of the . . . assumption that women's biological difference sets her apart, that she is essentially inferior, destined to be a willing slave, a domestic drudge, an incubator for her race."[36] At the root of course is misogyny and, as observed by *The New Yorker*'s Moira Weigel, who appreciates the timeliness of Hulu's *The Handmaid's Tale* in the Trump era, powerful men and legislators now "speak the language of overt misogyny."[37] Although Eve is the fallen woman (Handmaid), the "Virgin" Mary from the Catholic tradition came to represent the pure, submissive wife and mother (Wife).

A chaste spouse, because she is infertile and sexual relations are no longer permissible *except* for the purpose of bearing children, Serena Waterford is literally a (Virgin) Mary figure. She is placed on a pedestal *within* the home, whereas June/Offred, the handmaiden-whore (Eve), is shamed and reduced because she had an affair with and married a divorced man in her pre-Gilead life. Gilead's laws and customs draw heavily on the Old Testament. In a key Genesis story, for example, Rachel is jealous of her child-bearing sister Leah; unable to bear children herself, she offers her handmaid, Bilhah, to Jacob saying: "go in unto her; and she shall bear upon my knees, that I may also have children by her."[38] In this way, the Sons of Jacob justify the Red Centre and the appropriation of the Handmaid to produce children for the barren Wives. June's life hinges on her ability to procreate for Waterford, and the sexual act is abetted by his wife. This paradigmatic dynamic is narratively and visually illustrated in the shocking rape Ceremony (S1 Ep1; S2 Ep10).

In the first episode (S1), Serena Joy sits on the marital bed above June, her legs straddling the supine Handmaid while holding down her arms, household members compelled to stand and witness the ritual. After the Commander enters the room, he lifts the Bible from a locked box. In a low-angle shot emphasizing his authority, Fred begins reading the Rachel and Leah passage. Nondiegetic organ music and "Onward Christian Soldiers" fill the soundtrack, alongside the sound of Waterford's droning, paternalistic voice, diegetically at first, and then nondiegetically as the ritualized rape proceeds. Both his head and face disappear from the frame, shifting to a close-up of Serena and then an extreme, high-angle close-up of June's face, displaying her powerlessness and adding to the travesty of sexual victimization within a Christian context. In a series of alternating quick cuts and close-up and medium close-up shots, the camera cuts back and forth between June and Serena Joy, calling attention to the contrasting color of their clothing and stressing their opposing roles in Gilead. Although Handmaid and Wife are pitted against one another, they are also unacknowledged sisters, allied by oppression and menstruation, which suggests the formula for resistance and liberation. In other words, *were* women to identify their common plight and collaborate *with* one another, they might challenge the patriarch and upend the system. In so doing, women might reclaim their full humanity and free themselves from male definitions. Thus, although the Ceremony plays out diegetically, semiotically the camera conveys an alternative feminist "story."

As the Ceremony proceeds and Waterford penetrates June, the camera cuts to a high- angle close-up of June's face in the dimly lit bedroom. It focuses first on her vacant eyes, then on her head and red-clothed upper torso moving mechanically to Waterford's thrusting. The camera tilts upward, highlighting Serena's teal bosom framed in deep shadow, and ending in a high- angle close-up of Serena's tight face and sealed lips, her head also moving mechanically to Waterford's thrusting. The next shot is a high-angle long shot of Waterford from behind as he stands over the headless, helpless red clothed-body of June splayed between the thrusting couple. The camera cuts to a series of alternating close-ups of the faces of husband and wife, underscoring their complicity in this highly orchestrated rape. The subsequent shot visually identifies June as an alienated, dehumanized "body" in the service of the male/father/patriarchy. It is a high-angle close-up of her red-clothed torso, knees elevated in front of Waterford, shrouding the sexual violation that is occurring. This shot is followed by another high-angle shot from above and behind her prone body in the shadowy room, adding to the strangeness of the scene. The camera then cuts to close-ups of Waterford's arm, chest, and face, before settling on Serena's hands, which are pinioning June's arms to her sides, signifying the couple's de-humanizing alliance. A high-angle shot of June's expressionless face follows, before the camera cuts to a medium-close up of Serena's teal dress from the side. This shifting pattern of shots suggesting fragmentation continues, culminating in an over-the-shoulder high-angle long-shot of Waterford as he ejaculates, and interchanged with close-ups of his face, Serena's face, and June's head, now lost somewhere in the folds of Serena's teal dress. The scene ends in a high-angle close-up of June, her vacant eyes and the red of her dress/shoulder against Serena's teal lap. The iconography of this scene is clear: although Handmaid and Wife are divided against one another, June's and Serena Joy's fate are intimately linked through their own otherness and male power.

In imagining a second act (season) for *The Handmaid's Tale*, Bruce Miller builds on this central opposition between Wife and Handmaid, and by extension on the separation between and alternatively the connection among women. Although this trope is amplified in the show's second season, it is also alluded to in the first season's theatrical rendering of the Salvaging and Particicution scene (S1, Ep1). Prisoners of Gilead, Handmaids are compelled to punish a man falsely condemned for the rape of a Handmaid. The scene opens with a spectacular bird's eye (crane) shot of the Handmaids' red cloaks and white bonnets streaming in an orderly, almost balletic fashion through a lush verdant park. The camera cuts to an extreme, eye-level long shot of Handmaids, their heads bowed and surrounded by armed guardians, before dollying in on a medium close-up of June and her Handmaid-partner Emily. At this stage, June remains wary of Emily, unsure if she is the spy that Nick warned her about. (As June later learns, she is also part of the resistance, as is Nick.) The camera then shifts back to another dizzyingly high bird's-eye shot of the Handmaids' formal procession toward the stage where Aunt Lydia stands, microphone in hand, to open the ceremony.

The pageantry, accompanied by violins on the soundtrack, is off-putting. It belies the horror of the event, and the machinations by which the Gilead regime draws on the pent-up rage of Handmaids to do its evil bidding. This ploy is clearly evidenced as the Particicution unfolds. A low-angle long-shot reveals the red-draped stage with the Aunts filing onto it, evoking the Aunts' critical role in getting the Handmaids to fulfill Gileadean law. The Aunts whip the Handmaids into a "frenzy," and because they "are not permitted weapons" they "must use their bare hands" to beat the "condemned man" to death, fulfilling the meaning of Particicution, "a portmanteau of . . . 'participation' and 'execution.'"[39] A series of close-up and medium close-up shots takes us back to June. While finding her position in this church-like arrangement, she queries Alma concerning the status of her escaped friend Moira. Janine (Ofwarren), unhinged from the eye gouging she received for misbehavior at the Red Centre, overhears the conversation and reports, sardonically, that Moira is "dead." This piece of information is crucial for helping us to understand June's unexpected brutality as the scene unfolds. While Aunt Lydia blows the whistle, having ordered the Handmaids to remove their "wings" (white bonnets) and place them on a red pillow before encircling the prisoner, June becomes increasingly agitated. Close-ups reveal that she is clearly processing the (alleged, but ultimately inaccurate) news of the death of her best friend, whose escape represented hope. June's distress and growing fury fuel her crazed contribution, along with the other Handmaids, to the violent pummeling of the innocent, doomed prisoner. The scene draws to a close in a close-up of June's horrified face as she absorbs her part in the man's inhumane execution.

The operatic staging of the scene, combined with the dramatic shift from bird's-eye to close-up, is suggestive. The color display highlights the ironic juxtaposition of death with life in the Handmaids' misguided "revolution." The deep red stands out *because* of the rich greenery. Red evokes passion and, as mentioned previously, may be associated with the adulterous harlot in the US classic, *The Scarlet Letter*. In Gilead, red is a signifier of "sinfulness." Unwitting performers in a drama not of their own making, Handmaids are manipulated into attacking a member of the Mayday network. However, what June and the other Handmaids do not observe because of their containment and lack of perspective, the viewer does: the potential for their collective energy to be redirected against the oppressor and to obtain freedom through resistance and revolution. The white of their so-called 'wings"—however small in comparison to the sea of red—connotes both flight and the Handmaid's innocence under evil Gilead. Red is also associated with rage, and when combined with hope/life of the green foliage, we see the potential for a counternarrative—an incipient feminist revolution to upend tyranny. This promise is echoed in a similar Salvaging season in the season's final episode when Offred, refusing to attack Janine/Ofwarren for having absconded with her baby, offers a shocking rebuke when she and her fellow Handmaids defy Aunt Lydia and walk away instead; as June exclaims, "[t]hey should never have given us uniforms if they didn't want us to be an army" (S1, Ep10).[40]

The spectacle of the funeral for the thirty-one Handmaids killed in the prior episode's bombing of the newly minted Red Centre (S2, Ep7)[41] in which Fred Waterford is injured, ironically parallels the Particicution scene, offering more evidence of a feminist revolution in the making. In contrast to the Particicution's lush backdrop, "After" opens to a blurry eye-level shot of silent black figures in the midst of swirling snow against a wintry backdrop dotted by barren trees. After the credits briefly appear over the image, it cuts to a bird's eye shot of paired-Handmaids. Quiet piano music, and the mournful voice of Iris de Mint's "My life don't count for nothing" swells on the soundtrack as the camera cuts to an eye-level tracking shot of black-cloaked and bonneted Handmaids from behind, the red of their collars peeking out. Subsequent shots from the front feature a young male drummer leading the march, and Handmaids walking behind and toward the camera in slow motion, the operatic shot highlighting black cloaks against red sleeves, gloves and neck scarves, with red veils obscuring their faces. The movement back and forth from bird's-eye to medium-close-up to long-shot, and back to a bird's-eye shot of the thirty-one red caskets arranged in a circle in a sea of white as the Handmaids take their places is cinematically stunning and narratively significant. Although Aunt Lydia stands atop a red disk in the center leading the prayer and naming each dead Handmaid, it is clear she—and by extension, Gilead—is isolated and steeped in death. It is the sisterhood of mourners that command the stage, as they remove their veils and kiss them to each coffin in the circuit. Captive as they are in Gilead's black and red garb, their spirit will not be suffocated. For instance, while shopping in the supermarket later in the day, June instigates a quiet rebellion. High key lighting, rarely used in the show, creates a cheerful atmosphere, with sunlight streaming through the windows, as June asks for Ofglen's real name, identifies herself as June, and each of the Handmaids, in turn, smiles and "names-it-forward" by whispering her real name.

"I'll need a pen" June tells Serena Joy at the end of "After" (S2, Ep7) in a charged moment that builds on the trope of women's kinship. An extreme close-up of Serena fingering one of Fred's pens and handing it to June speaks both to this portentous moment and to the power of language. With Waterford unconscious in the hospital, Serena (temporarily) replaces him. She crafts new security orders calling for the arrest of Commander Cushing who is posing a threat to the Waterford household, and she puts an end to the retaliatory and random killings of those suspected of being associated with "terrorism." Depicted in long shot, Serena smugly sits behind Fred's desk, a blatant violation of Gileadean law. The mise en scène underscores the clandestine nature of their meeting. The scene is shot in low-key lighting, producing a shadowy atmosphere for the forbidden alignment of Handmaid and Wife, especially since it is *in place of* the oppressor. "You're an editor," Serena tells her, asking June to proofread the orders she drafted. In a previous scene June had warned Serena that Commander Cushing interrogated her and intimated that Waterford was involved in Offred's escape (at the end of season one), an obvious power play because he's angling to replace the security Commander Price who was killed in the explosion. When Serena says that Fred would never allow this, June reminds her that he's "not here, Serena," thereby encouraging her to act in Fred's place to protect them. Serena's forgery is not only treasonous, but it marks a shift in their vexing, adversarial relationship. It foreshadows the season finale when Serena, sensing that brutal Gilead—which had executed young Eden's marital infidelity by drowning her, and cut-off Serena's finger for the transgressive act of reciting a Bible verse to the tribunal—is no place for "her" precious daughter, and she allows June to escape with her infant child.

By reclaiming "language" and crucial aspects of their former identities—Serena as leader and June as editor—and by recognizing their shared peril, the women empower themselves and commit an act as revolutionary as the Handmaid's bombing of the Red Centre. Both instances put Gilead on notice that authoritarian rule and legalized misogyny will not go unchallenged and that a much-needed feminist reboot to counter patriarchy is underway.

The worlds of *Mad Max: Fury Road* and Hulu's *The Handmaid's Tale* serve as frightening cinematic depictions of the consequences of dangerous impulses that have accelerated in the age of Trump: a depleted world where deregulation is paramount, misogyny is normalized, and the rule of law is bent toward authoritarianism. They also show us the hazards of complacency. Feminism arose in response to untenable restraints on women's bodies and opportunities, resulting in major achievements, which, as these texts illustrate, should never be taken for granted. More than escapist entertainment, these visual texts expose the damages caused by unrestrained capitalism wed to patriarchy, offering us an opportunity to recalibrate and to employ an intersectional feminist praxis to counter the amoral and immoral excesses emblematic of the Trumpian age before it is too late.

NOTES

1. Jill E. Wagner, "Christine de Pizan's City of Ladies: A Monumental (Re)construction of, by, and for Women of All Time" in *Medieval Feminist Forum: A Journal of Gender and Sexuality* 44, no. 1 (2008): 69, 77. Accessed https://ir.uiowa.edu/mff/vol44/iss1/6/ on May 18, 2017.

2. Andi Zeisler explores the drawbacks of a fashionable, albeit individualized feminism in *We Were Feminists Once: From Riot Grrrl to Cover Girl®, the Buying and Selling of a Political Movement* (New York: PublicAffairs, 2017.) Lorna Finlayson's more studied and substantive description of the pros and cons of feminist major traditions draws a similar conclusion about the shortcomings of consumer and celebrity feminism in *An Introduction to Feminism* (Cambridge: Cambridge University Press, 2016).

3. Most recently, the state of Iowa adopted the "fetal heartbeat bill," the most drastic bill to date, banning abortion once the fetal heartbeat is detected, according to *The Washington Post*'s Kristine Phillips (May 4, 2018). Such restrictive strategies to curtail abortion, and women's access to abortion services, have proliferated in states around the country. At the federal level, Title X funds that largely support Planned Parenthood are in dire jeopardy. On May 18, 2018, *The New York Times*'s Julie Hirschfield Davis reported that the Trump administration intends to deprive Planned Parenthood of Title X monies if it continues to provide access to medical abortions, thus raising "complicated questions about the fate of Planned Parenthood and other reproductive health organizations that provide both family planning and abortion services"—and the potential health effects on women who depend on such providers for basic care.

4. Jodi Enda, "Donald Trump is the Best—and Worst—Thing That's Happened to Modern American Feminism" in *STATE—CNN Politics—CNN.com*, July 29, 2017: 29. Accessed http://www.cnn.com/interactive/2017/politics/state/womens-movement-donald-trump/ on August 3, 3017.

5. Such feminist activism has continued to strengthen in Trump's second year in office. *Time* magazine's Alix Langone notes how "the groundbreaking anti-sexual assault and women's empowerment movements #MeToo and Time's Up upended the public conversation about women's issues around the world, and elevated the global consciousness surrounding the obstacles women encounter in their daily lives, both personal and professional" (March 22, 2018). Accessed http://time.com/5189945/whats-the-difference-between-the-metoo-and-times-up-movements/= on May 16, 2018.

6. *Mad Max: Fury Road*, directed by George Miller, performed by Tom Hudson and Charlize Theron, IMDb, *Mad Max: Fury Road*. Accessed https://www.imdb.com/title/tt1392190/ on June 23, 2018.

7. Jeff Labrecque, "*Fury Road* soundtrack: How Junkie XL scored the madness of *Mad Max*, *Entertainment*, May 25, 2015. Accessed http://ew.com/article/2015/05/14/mad-max-fury-road-tom-holkenborg/ on August 20, 2017.

8. Steve Coll, "Donald Trump's Fake News Tactics," *The New Yorker*, December 11, 2017. Accessed https://www.newyorker.com/magazine/2017/12/11/donald-trumps-fake-news-tactics on June 23, 2018.

9. Matt Apuzo, Maggie Haberman, and Matthew Rosenberg, "Trump Told Russians that Firing 'Nut-Job' Comey Eased Pressure from Investigation," *The New York Times*, May 19, 2017. Accessed https://www.nytimes.com/2017/05/19/us/politics/trump-russia-comey.html?_r=0 on July 13, 2017.

10. Mark S. Weiner, *The Rule of the Clan: What an Ancient Form of Social Organization Reveals about The Future of Individual Freedom* (New York: Farrar, Strauss, and Giroux, 2013), 80.

11. Weiner, *The Rule of the Clan* 80.

12. Weiner, *The Rule of the Clan* 47.

13. Karen Warren, "Introduction," in *Ecological Feminism*, ed. Karen Warren (New York: Routledge, 1994), 1.

14. Warren, Introduction, 26.

15. Kate Waites, "Babes in Boots: Hollywood's Oxymoronic Woman Warrior" in *Chick Flicks: Contemporary Women at the Movies*, eds. Suzanne Ferris and Mallory Young. (New York: Routledge, 2008), 207.

16. Colleen Martell, "Sweet Nectar of the Matriarchy: Breastmilk in *Fury Road*," *Bitch Flicks*, June 16, 2015. Accessed http://www.btchflcks.com/2015/06/sweet-nectar-of-the-matriarchy-breastmilk-in-fury-road.html#.WwBWjC-ZOgQ on May 19, 2018.

17. "The Handmaid's Tale (2017) Awards." Accessed https://www.imdb.com/title/tt5834204/awards on July 13, 2017.

18. Angela Watercutter, "Hulu's *Handmaid's Tale* Win Heralds Television's New Big Three," *Wired*, September 18, 2017. Accessed https://www.wired.com/story/hulu-handmaids-tale-emmy-win/ on July 13, 2017/.

19. Joe Otterson, "Hulu Carried to Emmy Glory By Eight Wins," *Variety*, September 17, 2017. Accessed http://variety.com/2017/tv/news/emmys-2017-hulu-handmaids-tale-1202557512/ on July 13, 2017.

20. Leah Thomas, "Now That *The Handmaid's Tale* Has Moved Beyond the Book, Who's Actually Writing It?" *Popsugar*, April 29, 2018. Accessed https://www.popsugar.co.uk/entertainment/Who-Wrote-Handmaid-Tale-Season-2-44827636 on June 9, 2018.

21. Margaret Atwood, "Margaret Atwood in what *The Handmaid's Tale* Means in the Age of Trump," *The New York Times*, March 10, 2017. Accessed https://www.nytimes.com/2017/03/10/books/review/margaret-atwood-handmaids-tale-age-of-trump.html on July 13, 2017.

22. "John Winthrop, American Colonial Governor," *Encyclopedia Britannica*. Accessed https://www.britannica.com/biography/John-Winthrop-American-colonial-governor on June 15, 2018.

23. Jonathan Edwards, "Sinners in the Hands of an Angry God," Jonathan Edwards Center at Yale University. Accessed http://edwards.yale.edu/archive?path=aHR0cDovL2Vkd2FyZHMueWFsZS5lZHUvY2dpLWJpbi9uZXdwaGlsby9nZXRvYmplY3QucGw/Yy4yMTo0Ny53amVv on June 10, 2018.

24. Jada Yuan, "How Reed Created the Emmy-Look of *The Handmaid's Tale*," Vulture, September 21, 2017. Accessed http://www.vulture.com/2017/09/the-handmaids-tale-how-reed-morano-created-its-look.html on July 13, 2017.

25. Bruce Miller, writer, "*The Handmaid's Tale*: "Offred," in Hulu. *Hulu*, April 26, 2017. Accessed https://www.imdb.com/title/tt5834204/episodes?season=1 on June 26, 2018.

26. Bruce Miller, writer. "*The Handmaid's Tale*: "Late," in Hulu. *Hulu*, April 26, 2017. Accessed https://www.imdb.com/title/tt5931652/?ref_=ttep_ep3 on July 13, 2017.

27. Margaret Atwood, *The Handmaid's Tale* (New York: Anchor Books, 1998).

28. Jada Yuan, "How Reed Moreno Crafted the Emmy-Winning Look for *The Handmaid's Tale*," September 21, 2017. Accessed http://www.vulture.com/2017/09/the-handmaids-tale-how-reed-morano-created-its-look.html on June 19, 2018.

29. Andrew Kim, "Dystopian American History: Reading *The Handmaid's Tale in the Trump Age*," *Ethos*, February 28, 2017. Accessed http://www.ethosreview.org/intellectual-spaces/dystopian-american-history-reading-the-handmaids-tale-in-the-trump-age/ on June 25, 2017.

30. Bill Desowitz, "'*The Handmaid's* Tale': How a Classic Technicolor Technique Made the Color Red a Political Act," *Indie Wire* (May 25, 2017). Accessed http://www.indiewire.com/2017/05/the-handmaids-tale-technicolor-the-color-red-political-12018317 on June 16, 2018.

31. Jamie Lincoln, *The Handmaid's Tale: The Hidden Meaning Behind Those Eerie Costumes, Vanity Fair*, April 24, 2017. Accessed https://www.vanityfair.com/hollywood/2017/04/handmaids-tale-hulu-costumes-margaret-atwood on June 12, 2018.

32. Lincoln, *The Handmaid's Tale*.

33. John Berger, "Chapter Three," *Ways of Seeing* (London, British Broadcasting Company, 1972), 46.

34. Lincoln, *The Handmaid's Tale*.

35. Simone de Beauvoir, "Introduction," *The Second Sex* (New York: Vintage, 2011) xi.

36. J. R. Hays, *The Myth of the Dangerous Sex* (New York: G.P. Putnam's Sons, 1964).

37. Moira Weigel, "We Live in the Reproductive Dystopia of *The Handmaid's Tale*," *New Yorker*, April 26, 2017. Accessed https://www.newyorker.com/books/page-turner/we-live-in-the-reproductive-dystopia-of-the-handmaids-tale on June 26, 2018.

38. Genesis 30: 3, *Bible Gateway*. Accessed https://www.biblegateway.com/passage/?search=Genesis+30%3A1-3&version=KJV on June 24, 2018.

39. "*The Handmaid's Tale* Wiki." Accessed http://the-handmaids-tale.wikia.com/wiki/Particicution on July 28, 2018,.

40. Bruce Miller, writer. "*The Handmaid's Tale*: "Night," in Hulu. *Hulu*, June 14, 2017. Accessed https://www.imdb.com/title/tt5931656/?ref_=ttep_ep10 on June 12, 2018.

41. Lynn Renee Maxcy, writer, "*The Handmaid's Tale*: "After," in Hulu. *Hulu*, May 30, 2018. Accessed https://www.imdb.com/title/tt7435250/?ref_=ttep_ep7 on July 28, 2018.

Chapter Nine

Architectures of *Ustopia*

CDMX as Setting and Character in Mischa Rozema's Short Film Sundays

Raúl Rodríguez-Hernández and Claudia Schaefer

Sundays (2015), Dutch director Mischa Rozema's first film, is a fourteen-minute concept sci-fi short funded by Kickstarter to the tune of $50,000.[1] The setting—and arguably a protagonist as well—is Mexico City at a date sometime in the future. From a Google Earth-like sky shot we descend into the maelstrom of a postapocalyptic world presented from the point of view of Ben (Brian Petsos), one of the survivors of the catastrophe. Rozema's film takes on the philosophical concepts of time, fear, isolation, destruction, identity, and above all "truth" and "love" in a world once welcoming and recognizable that has become an alienating nightmare.

The speculative vision of a postapocalyptic megalopolis—recognizable as Mexico City in both topography and architectural bits and pieces throughout the production—sets a single human life amid the debris and destruction that a moment before had housed the eternal hope of a throbbing heartbeat. Taken for granted as part of "normal" life, the heart as an organ and as a traditional metaphor for love gets interrupted by a violent cataclysm. Margaret Atwood proposes the word "ustopia" as a term applicable to the penetration of these two worlds—the rhythmic pulse of an individual life and the silencing of it, the transition from a place of enjoyment and satisfaction to a place illustrating the failure of social projects. She writes of ustopia as "a word I made up by combining utopia and dystopia—the imagined perfect society and its opposite—because, in my view, each contains a latent version of the other."[2] Viewed from the perspective of the fringes and minorities of so-called earthly paradises, from the point of view of "people who don't fit in,"[3] utopias look more like ominous places rather than the perfect society. Imagining other worlds may not imply imagining better ones for all inhabitants.

As Ben wanders the urban streets in search of himself and of a past, he recovers a memory that he holds onto in case it can offer him an anchor in this new world. Her name is Isabelle (Sofia Sisniega). And his search recalls none other than Dante Alighieri's Beatriz, the inspiration for *La Vita Nuova* and *The Divine Comedy* and a woman as shrouded in mystery as Isabelle. Long debated by historians, philosophers, and literati, Beatriz's figure of exalted love guides Dante through the *Inferno* to the *Purgatorio* and on to *Paradise*. Beatriz's proximity to the divine, combined with her angelic human form, gave purpose to the existence of the Italian poet. A woman as critical as Beatriz at the heart of Dante's quest remains in Isabelle, the lost love of Ben amid the ruins. Or so he thinks in a present devoid of past or future certainty. In our increasingly globalized world, Dante's partition of existence into hell, purgatory, and paradise instead often coexists simultaneously, and when they don't, each is always on the verge of becoming something "other."

Narrated primarily in Ben's extradiegetic voice over, *Sundays* opens with an epigraph from cognitive scientist Daniel C. Dennett. As we spend a few brief moments in preapocalyptic space looking down at the blue planet, we read: "What you can imagine depends on what you know." Self-defined atheist and secularist, Dennett frames the film's narrative within the confines of a world devoid of a deity or any transcendence. The multiplicity of decisions a rational human being makes is the result of a constant flow of encounters between individual and phenomena. How Ben reads what occurs is inflected by "what he knows," what his experience has taught him. After this point, he lacks any understanding of what is occurring and can only ask an endless series of questions that structure the cinematic narrative.

When the film opens, we hear an angelic choir singing as Dennett's words appear floating in blackness, suggesting the void of outer space. In a flash, the screen is filled with fiery explosions and the flares of the sun's corona shooting outward. A small black dot, the Earth, appears in contrast to the enormous glowing threat of the incandescent sun. Made to look tiny and exposed, the Earth rotates to the right, disappearing into the blackness. As the name of the film's production company—PostPanic Productions—and of the director emerge from the flames, the dramatically menacing sound vibrations of the coronal loops contrasts with the chorus. Heaven and hell meet in a single space. The camera, inexplicably, enters the flares of the sun and takes us on a journey beneath them as if we were surfers in Purgatory. As we see them supposedly with the naked eye, the flares crackle and extend further out into space. Suddenly, a lens appears between the spectator and the sun, making us aware of a technological mediator between the human eye and all of the world's phenomena. Rozema's film alternates between allowing the spectator access to details of a scene and creating a distance from it that impedes total comprehension. The result is a familiar but alien-looking universe.

A sound similar to a projector running through film sprockets forms the transition from solar surface to a communications satellite that comes into view. The silver panels of the man-made object now reflect the force of the sun we have been observing. This is followed by a frame of the Earth as a dark planet at the center of the screen surrounded by a representation of the Earth's magnetic fields bending in symmetrical curves around the planet. The director juxtaposes the chaotic bursts of energy from the sun with screeching sounds and images of the surface of the Earth. Computer codes materialize on the left of the screen, but rather than keep science under control they announce the destruction of the satellite and an emerging sense of chaos and disintegration. Utopia—communications, scientific achievement, and high technology—morphs into dystopia in the blink of an eye. The promises of technological knowledge and supremacy fall to Earth in blazing red-hot fragments, creating white arcs as they reach the planet's atmosphere.

Standing in for spectators, and standing literally alone on the shores of what remains of Lake Texcoco on which Mexico City is constructed, a young boy is silhouetted against a setting sun and a rain of debris. As he looks up, mystified, we might recall the film's epigraph. He can only imagine what he knows, but it is not clear what he imagines as he witnesses the destruction of all that he has known up to now. In one of the most dramatic sequences of the film, the boy stands in the foreground as an enormous jet crashes to the ground behind him, lacking any guidance system for flight. Radar would have gone out with the satellite, and all air traffic would be incapacitated and brought down. The human figure is dwarfed by the failure of technology and the airliner looms monstrously.

The point of view shifts to encompass the rooftops of the city as red-hot debris lands on streets and houses, gas tanks and water cisterns, businesses, and markets. Objects shoot past, whizzing across a landscape that has just been transformed from utopia into dystopia. As Deborah Root examines the long history of this geographical space where Mexico City stands, she finds a continuum between past and present, utopia and dystopia, in the inhabitants' historical dreams of a perfect place. She studies the codices of Montezuma, finding narratives of hope and paradise even during eras of natural disaster and catastrophe: "In the distant past, the Mexica [people] had journeyed from Aztlan through the vast deserts of northern Mexico, triumphing over adversity and bad omens to found the imperial city of Tenochtitlan in the swamps of Lake Texcoco."[4] The trappings of empire, later the adornments of a capital city, keep the dream of Aztlan alive if in name only. Root establishes that the transition in the city from hopeful utopia to something less than perfect establishes utopia itself as "movement and flux . . . a temporal state rather than something that exists in geographical space."[5] Utopias do not last but, as Atwood underscores, carry the seeds of their own destruction.

Rozema adds a third moment to this flux in the land of the Mexica: Aztlan became Tenochtitlan in the fifteenth century when the Spanish arrived, which in turn in the twenty-first century became Lennox-land. Lennox Company—of skyscrapers, global commerce, security forces, and faceless armies of workers—has created satellites, giant company edifices, and lock-step obedient employees. Their vision of perfection breaks apart like its space technology, pitting individual against corporation and the one against the many. Far from the aspirations of earlier societies in Latin America, the city of the Lennox Corporation belies the nineteenth-century's faith in science and progress as "the supreme guarantor of truth."[6] Ben's questioning the concept of truth extracts from the science and technology embodied in Lennox their monopoly on the interpretation of real events and facts or any transcendent reality about the world. Yet he cannot affirm his own agency but only question theirs, leaving a void of ambiguity. The legitimacy of Lennox's control over most humans in this city—with few exceptions such as the desperate woman in the middle of the traffic-filled street warning about the unreality of everything around them—is confronted by Ben as he (and the woman mentioned) experience a personal displacement in space and time. Does she mean that the catastrophic events are not really happening or that they are all encased in a fabrication promoted by Lennox?

Kate Wagner studies the embodiment of evil in the corporate structures of sci-fi films that stand in for the values (or lack thereof) of the business that takes place there. Surprisingly unchanging across cinematic history, these imposing buildings are powerful and faceless, visually present but mysteriously and enigmatically working behind the scenes. The architecture metonymically represents the dehumanized environment in which Ben finds himself, referencing the dark mise-en-scènes of Fritz Lang's *Metropolis*, Michael Radford's *1984*, and Ridley Scott's neo-noir *Blade Runner*. There are recognizable elements in the modern facades but dark corridors inside that resist sunlight, human warmth, or explanation. Wagner's conclusion about the intimate relationship between mega corporations and speculative fictions holds true for the film *Sundays* as it perpetuates the idea that "dystopian capitalism is a staple of many films' most successful antagonists."[7] Utopian settings are ambiguous, even dual, "sometimes visions of good and possible attainable social systems and at other times fantasies of a desirable but unattainable perfection."[8] In this case, Lennox's utopia is not a future into which one might project oneself easily; it has obviously existed for a while, but it is unclear what it replaced. The brutality of the exterior of the steel and cement edifice, partially crumbing as a victim of its own projects, looks as dystopian as the economy to which it contributes and the society to which it belongs. The city is revealed as the contrary of a harbor of well-being, shelter, and even redemption. There is no redemption, economic or social, in this vision of the future.

The sky across the valley of Mexico goes from blue to ashen gray, the smoke blocking out what had been a radiant sun. In a darkened living room, a family is shown huddled around a television set watching the news and trying to make sense of what is happening. They are silent as they watch a future calamity take place on an antiquated television set from the past. The alternation between outside cataclysm and out-of-sync interior space with worn furniture, framed portraits, and family history is jarring. How can these people imagine what they know nothing about? What is their place in this utopia? At this point, *Sundays* brings to light the periphery of all utopias, the zones of exclusion and invisibility. The sun burns on menacingly and hieroglyphic symbols appear that then turn into the film title: *Sundays*. Given Dennett's framing words, the director could hardly be referring to Holy Scripture in which a Sabbath day of rest is observed after the deity's creation of the world. That would mark a sacred day, one of stillness and contemplation. It is more revealing that Rozema's full-length feature film project will have the symbolic title slightly changed to *SunDays* to indicate the link between the celestial bodies of the universe and their influence on one another.[9]

The strident music of the soundtrack shifts to the muted sound of a heartbeat as the close up of a human eye appears. We look into an iris and a widened pupil as we previously looked into the lens of the camera to witness the solar explosion. The trope of the eye is a familiar one from other sci-fi films. It invites an inward gaze as it simultaneously suggests the critical role of the spectator. As the camera pulls back, we see Ben's face completely for the first time and recognize the human being the eye belongs to. Placed behind Ben, we share with him the panorama of overwhelming destruction; he drops the glass he has been drinking from and it crashes to the floor. The slow-motion shattering of the glass parallels the fragmentation of the satellite as the shards morph into the Milky Way against the black floor. Ben's glass is a microcosm of the entire universe that has been disturbed and cannot be put back together. This event opens a series of fundamental questions and deep philosophical comments about life that the character poses in voice over as interior monologue. They increase in uncertainty and quantity as the film progresses.

The first statement, "When I close my eyes at night there is only darkness," is followed by "When I open my eyes in the morning . . . there is only this." Ben is traveling on a commuter train to work as part of a routine to which he might be referring—"only this"—but he seems introspectively to be thinking about much more abstract issues. The alternation of day and night, a given for most human beings, is the natural rhythm of life yet what is expected and natural has just been disturbed. He enumerates the elements at the heart of modern cities, discounting each: "Our world is not powered by oil, or money, or dreams, or God . . . our world is run on trust" as he gazes down at the briefcase with the logo of Lennox that he holds onto tightly. The irony of his statement is that Lennox *is* the creator of power, money, dreams, and trust as if it were a deity. Lennox is at the heart of everyday life and everyone's imagination; the company is the center of knowledge as Dennett has written we rely on. The consummate outsider from these events in Atwood's terms, Ben continues to think out loud: "We see the universe as a machine, everything in the right place, gears forever rotating, our world eternal, fixed like the sun." His appeal to reason and science as well as predictable norms and the laws of nature sets up a counterpoint to the destruction outside the window of all that has been known. Trust in Lennox and trust in the universe as a well-oiled machine have just been ruptured; no one knows what will follow. Is this a "good place" or a "bad place?" How "flawed a society"[10] can a utopia be and still remain desired and longed for?

In a flashback to a more ironically utopian time, wheat fields glow in the sun and an idyllic couple embraces. In a close-up shot, the camera captures the flickering images of Ben and Isabelle (he calls to her in his thoughts) who disappear in an instant as the reality of the present intrudes. Ben's voice is heard again: "Trains and people and clocks will be on time . . . time marches forward, never backwards, never standing still." For Ben, the reality is that there seems to be only the present, no certain past and no imaginable future except for the perfect world of progress and motion. How does the moment of destruction fit into the images he recalls? He cries out to Isabelle "please" as if to make her reappear or assure him he is truly remembering and not just fantasizing and that she is indeed real. In a sense, time does not move but is paralyzed by the cataclysm of the present in which automaton-like workers arrive in droves. Reviewing the cycle of biological life, Ben speaks of sons burying fathers and tries to hold on to the certainties of the "truth" preserved in whatever books have survived the apocalyptic moment. A digital clock indicates the hour as Ben walks into the Lennox building, inserts his digital ID card into a slot, is welcomed by a remote electronic voice, and traces the steps to his office. The bars on the offices create the feeling of a prison atmosphere rather than an ergonomic and comfortable space. He repeats that the truth "has made us the kings," an ambiguous statement that might refer to the workers in the company or to human beings who control the artificial intelligence at the heart of their technologies.

As he walks by surveillance cameras that adjust to keep him in view, Ben enters his office and instead of working on the company's tasks begins to piece together a collection of photographs on his desk. As he arranges them in a collage, he thinks: "we trust that our memories are real and our pictures speak a thousand words and what they say will be the truth." His monotone voice is filled with doubt even as he places images side by side. Echoing George Eastman's promise of a picture's value—taking the place of 1,000 words—Ben looks up in doubt as to the truth of the story told by the images. Shifting once again to the past of the photos, Ben's memories are triggered and he hears himself say to Isabelle "Do you feel like you were born in another time, like you belong to another place?' One of those who obviously "don't fit in," Ben is an outsider despite his apparent belonging to the world of Lennox. He murmurs the word "love" to Isabelle as the idyllic scene ends and he returns to the present to say: "we trust that when people say they love us they mean it, not just in their heads but in their hearts." Both concepts—trust and love, head and heart—have evolved from the past to the present. In an efficient corporate Lennox world where trust does not mean what it meant to the lovers Ben and Isabelle, Ben retains romantic notions he tries to resuscitate in the real world of the future. Every woman he sees on the streets or in the subway train he thinks is Isabelle, or he wants to be Isabelle. He runs after this phantom, calling her name in desperation. He utters the words: "love is forever, like death" as the scene cuts to the surveillance camera that embodies no love, no individuality, and no subjectivity. No love. The word seems out of place in the hostile and dehumanized environment promoted by Lennox. Even the sun appears eclipsed behind the surveillance camera in the street, reduced in size and light, and dominated by the constructs of technology.

From this point on, Ben makes no assertions but asks questions about the basic tenets of western society. He asks whether anything is true, or "just a made up story, an illusion, a lullaby, a bedtime fairy tale, a lie?" He watches as buildings crumble around him and he looks on in horror, unable to know what is happening. He looks at his hand as if to reassure himself he is still alive, but concludes he is still asleep. As he watches home movies on a screen, Ben's voice on an answering machine is heard saying: "I know what I saw and I know what I remember; she is out there, she is real." Has Isabelle left him? Is she alive or dead? Does she live on only in his photographs and memories? Where is she now? His personal memories have been subsumed by the ideology of the powerful forces of the Lennox Company. They make him doubt what he has experienced. In his philosophical quest to recover something inside that has disappeared, Ben recovers memories, Polaroid pictures, and assurances from life past. He does not even recognize himself as he looks into the mirrored windows of a building. If life is a dream, what does he see when he closes his eyes at night he asks? His heroic quest for truth, for love, and for trust in an increasingly uncertain cityscape ends in a question rather than an affirmation. We might conclude that Ben stands in for us all amid the ruins of everything that we have thought was secure, all that we inherited from the past. As Karl Marx described the radical change in the bourgeoisie's myth that the inherited world was eternal and unchanging, "all that is solid melts into air, all that is holy is profaned."[11] Ben's world does not melt but implodes before his eyes, crumbling structures and erasing human connections.

Drumbeats accompany panoramic shots of fallen buildings that look suspiciously like Mexico City after the 1985 earthquake. Despite this damage, the bureaucracy continues to function. This time, Ben's ID card is rejected, the electronic voice asks him to report to the authorities, and his doubts about the universe resurface: "What if it is not fixed?" A high-angle camera shot down the shaft of a defunct elevator makes Ben look totally alone in a building we know is occupied by many. He runs to the roof and screams out: "what if the universe is falling apart?" The black and white of the film turns to sepia and a reddish cast. Suddenly, he finds himself in a crowded market, wandering among people buying and selling goods. A woman cries out in Spanish about the reality of it all, about all being false as another woman stuffs raw eggs into her mouth. Ben throws his briefcase away as he climbs a utility pole and shouts in defiance to the cameras: stop looking at me. It is unnerving to note that he is now speaking Spanish as he yells, then retreats from the pole to vomit in the middle of the traffic streaming by. Graffiti reflects the state of anxiety of the few: NOTHING IS REAL ALL IS FALSE is painted on the wall. A man in flames walks by. The scene condenses the idea that Ben has just awakened from a dream and realizes all that he expects to happen is no longer part of a coherent world.

A rapid series of still images flashes in montage, combining past and present, hope and despair, Isabelle and Ben. All of a sudden, he is shown on a flat metal slab—like a mortuary table or morgue slab—sitting up and gasping for breath. Dressed all in white, has Ben really been resuscitated or is this a metaphor for his waking up to what is not real? He sits in contemplation of the forces of nature and the expectation of cause and effect, of life and death: "what if all the graves are empty, what if the dead come back?" These words appear as images of Isabelle both in an old home movie and on the screen of some sort of technological device come into view. Is she an implanted memory or is she a real woman? The camera cuts to a ferociously barking pit bull on the flat cement roof of a house intercut with images of Ben running through the dusty streets in the outskirts of the city, calling her name as she disappears in the distance. We see a woman with a hood placed over her head taken away by the Lennox police. Is this Isabelle? If so, Ben is left alone and abandoned. He cannot save Isabelle from what is implied to be a kidnapping, as he stands disheveled and unkempt in the dirt road. He is helpless; this is no utopia. He ponders his experience of alienation, finds solace if it is shared, if one man represents everyman. Is this the new normal?

As the imposing Lennox structure fills the screen, whirling machines that look like a combination of helicopter and eggbeater fly around it, and the van with the hooded captive in it approaches an entrance, Ben asks: "what if we are *not* the kings?" Human beings are at the top of the hierarchy of animals, so what might displace them from that position? Artificial intelligence created by humans but now in control? The building seems to be unoccupied but we have seen that it is teeming with life. Or is it life? He continues to think about the divisions between waking and sleeping: "what if *this* is the dream?" As Ben lies writhing on the sidewalk, a boy in a Mexican wrestler mask rides by and stares. One is as mysterious as the other as figures in a nightmare. There are no words spoken between them and beginning with this moment the internal monologue of the film dissipates and ends. Ben exits the building as a heavy metal plate closes behind him. In the street once again, he finds an army of robots and humanoid robots marching in precise order down the street. They follow a type of street-cleaning vehicle and are dressed in a combination of gas masks and orange reflective vests, carrying weapons. At first, Ben gazes perplexed, but then we see him join their ranks. He picks up the pace and walks in the middle of a group, now having a backpack just like theirs on.

The transition of office worker to member of a squadron of security-sanitation-military forces ends with Ben's giving up his previous quest. He wonders: "what if there is no love because there are no insides to show?" Automatons have no heart; his dream of love is broken as beings exhibit only exteriors and no "insides," no emotion or empathy. What he sees is what there is. From here on, an aerial view across endless city roof tops accompanies harsh, discordant music as if a chase were on, an animal was being hunted, or someone was trying to make an escape. Crosscuts between the armies on the ground and a panoramic view of the city encircled by mountains that prevent escape last two full minutes to the fade out at the end. Ben wanders amid the chaos, asking if darkness is all there is. Ahead of him an overpass is filled with stalled and demolished cars; strange futuristic vehicles hover overhead. A shipping yard full of containers to be loaded onto trucks lies still and paralyzed. Nothing but the camera moves as it pans across the vast expanse of the city toward the remote distance. The urban ruins become the surrounding mountains and the title of the film reappears.

The apocalypse that was presented in the first frames is the cause of the destruction of the world we find below us. We cannot judge by others, as the troops that march have no faces and do not speak. We are not even sure they are human. But Ben, a man of many words and haunted by the past, is the epitome of fear and loneliness in a destroyed landscape that once harbored great expectations. The conceivable promises of Lennox and its projects, dreams of a better life and a better society, lie in ashes. Were humans so motivated by hubris that they, like Icarus, tried to reach the sun? If this metaphor works, then the satellite at the opening of the film is evidence of overextension. As Ben asks, "what if we are *not* the kings?" Human beings may be at the mercy of their own dreams. The recurrence of the idea of the Latin American city as a utopian space of modernity has produced images of urban centers as housing both the "marvels and monsters."[12] of globalization. The monster that Rozema presents is a dark place inhabited by masses of individuals but also by "people who don't fit in" because they question, remember, or try to make sense of events and experiences.

The conflation of bureaucracy and the administration of society divided into the narrowest of groups and categories—the workers at Lennox—enable control and the abolition of difference. Ben seems quite invisible to the hordes on the street and is merely a number and an ID card to his employer. He is empathetic because we can put ourselves in his place easily; we share experiences that are similar even if not exactly the same. Does he—or do we—have the right to maintain hope? Up to the end, Ben does not lose his burning desire to answer the questions of reality, truth, love, and, most of all, Isabelle.

Hannah Arendt envisions the survival of our right to knowledge and comprehension even in the worst circumstances. She writes: "even in the darkest of times we have the right to expect some illumination, and that such illumination may well come less from theories and concepts than from the uncertain, flickering and often weak light that some men and women . . . will kindle."[13] Within the closed walls, crumbled buildings, and ruined relations of the short film *Sundays* spectators can find in the voice of Ben a faint but persistent glimmer of light in difficult times. Espen Hammer joins Arendt and reiterates that "the utopian imagination thrives on challenges,"[14] even ones that come from within as ustopia threatens. After all, modern societies are defined as looking forward—as Ben states about time—and not back. The uncertainties surrounding Ben and the future city of the film call for a radical renegotiation of our estrangement from the world and a reconsideration of how we might address its benefits and its evils. Jill Lepore has studied dystopian fiction at length and found a persistence of the internal social dialogue that Atwood calls ustopia. Lepore sums up her evidence in two sentences: "Dystopias follow utopias the way thunder follows lightning. This year [2017], the thunder is roaring."[15] In the Age of Trump, the flash of lightning that catches our attention, like the satellite burning up with solar radiation, requires attention to the more muffled thunder of the lingering effects around us.

NOTES

1. *Sundays*, directed by Mischa Rozema (Netherlands: PostPanic Pictures, 2015).
2. Margaret Atwood, *Dire Cartographies: The Roads to Ustopia and the Handmaid's Tale* (New York: Anchor/Penguin Random House, 2015). Ebook, https://www.penguinrandomhouse.com/books/537387/dire-cartographies-by-margaret-atwood, 1.
3. Atwood, *Dire*, 1.
4. Deborah Root, "From Aztlan to Tenochtitlan: The Transformation of Utopian Space," Public 12, Toronto (1995), 132.
5. Root, "From Aztlan," 133.
6. Rachel Haywood Ferreira, *The Emergence of Latin American Science Fiction* (Middletown, CT: Wesleyan University Press, 2011), 5.

7. Kate Wagner, "The Architecture of Evil: Dystopian Megacorps in Speculative Fiction Films." Accessible at https://99percentinvisible.org/article/architecture-evil-dystopian-mega-corps-speculative-fiction/.

8. Christophe Pourtois, "From the City of the Caesars to the Demystified City," in *Cruelty and Utopia: Cities and Landscapes of Latin America*, ed. Jean-Francois Lejeune (Princeton, NJ: Princeton Architectural Press, 2006), 11.

9. Mischa Rozema, *Art of the Title*. Accessed http://www.artofthetitle.com/designer/mischa-rozema/ on July 10, 2018.

10. Lyman Tower Sargent, *Utopianism: A Very Short Introduction* (Oxford: Oxford University Press, 2010), 32.

11. Karl Marx, "Chapter 1: Bourgeois and Proletarians," *The Communist Manifesto*. Accessed https://www.marxists.org/archive/marx/works/1848/communist-manifesto/ch01.htm on July 8, 2018.

12. Rebecca Biron, "Marvel, Monster, Myth: The Modern City in Latin American Literature," in *Cruelty and Utopia: Cities and Landscapes of Latin America*, ed. Jean-Francois Lejeune (Princeton, NJ: Princeton Architectural Press, 2006), 136.

13. Hannah Arendt, "Preface," *Men in Dark Times* (New York: Houghton Mifflin Harcourt, 1993), ix.

14. Espen Hammer, "A Utopia for a Dystopian Age," Opinion, *The New York Times*, June 26, 2017. Accessed https://www.nytimes.com/2017/06/26/opinion/a-utopia-for-a-dystopian-age.html on July 5, 2018.

15. Jill Lepore, "A Golden Age for Dystopian Fiction," *The New Yorker Magazine*. June 5, 2017. Accessed https://www.newyorker.com/magazine/2017/06/05/a-golden-age-for-dystopian-fiction on July 11, 2018.

Chapter Ten

X-Men Saga and the Dystopian "Otherness"

Race, Identity, Repression, and Inclusiveness in the Mutant World

Elisabetta Di Minico

Sociopolitical dystopias, and often sociopolitical negative utopias, proliferate by using control, illusion of continuity, and uniformity to survive, govern, and avoid rebellions. They need not only "useful and docile" bodies,[1] but also esthetically, ideologically, or sociopolitically similar individuals to lead. Before repressing the "different," the community must first produce the "homologated." Within this context, the bodies that represent "otherness" often come to be interpreted as "dangerous." Individuals who do not fit the racial, sexual, religious, or sociopolitical standards of power (generally human, white, male, Christian, and heterosexual) must be subdued or erased for the safekeeping of authority.

In many dystopian comics, superheroes, mutants, aliens, rebels, women, homosexuals, minorities, and every group potentially able to alter the status quo are seen as threats and persecuted. Often presenting themselves as utopian powers offering security and peace, and exploiting the necessity of "control," dystopian political and nonpolitical authorities, military, and media negatively stereotype diversity and spread alarming news and anxiety to justify the limitation of civil rights and the use of brutal force against their enemies. Because dystopia works on both the macro level represented by sociopolitical contexts and the micro level represented by personal relationships, people—generally influenced by propaganda—tend to go from fear to hatred to exploitation, and from there to violence. After all, the final aim of dystopia is not to protect but to control the population using stereotypes, a sense of alarm and a demonization of an enemy that is more social than biological.

But why are we frightened by otherness? Why do dystopian authorities need to transform diversity into an element of crisis, trauma and conflict? Nowadays more than ever, these questions are not simply about fiction. The destructive nightmares of dystopia, in most cases, expose an "evil" that is nothing but the transfiguration of real issues that are inspired by history and dramatically present in our world. They directly deal with the xenophobic, misogynist, and homophobic drifts in our society. Even if they do not completely undermine the progress of the postwar world, the last decades have witnessed a continuation or a restoration of racist, populist, patriarchal, nationalist, or even fascist discourses, themes, and actions in many Western countries against political or religious minorities, immigrants, refugees, the LGBTQ community and women, among others. Just in the last three years, the option "Leave" won at the Brexit referendum (2016), divisive businessman Donald Trump became president of the United States (2016), conservative Sebastian Kurz became Chancellor of Austria (2017), and autocratic Viktor Orbán was reelected as Prime Minister in Hungary (2018). Moreover, many populist, extreme, radical, or far-right parties are getting more support in elections,[2] and, according to the Organization for Security and Co-operation in Europe (OSCE), the numbers of hate crimes are higher than the preceding years in several nations, including in the United States, the UK, Italy, Austria, Poland, and Germany.[3]

These few examples clearly show the lingering crisis that endangers Western democracies, where attacking otherness and exalting the constructed enmity of particular racial, social, ideological, and religious groups is becoming a distinctive trait of the political narrative and of mass media. These approaches bring contemporary history closer to a dystopia.

Clearly, equating fiction to reality is a provocative exaggeration, but this chapter aims at enlightening some sociopolitical processes, thus stimulating thought-provoking dialogue and deep reflections on the fundamental themes of otherness, identity, and integration.

OTHERNESS, DYSTOPIA, AND MUTANTS

Presenting "a montage of both word and image" where reading is interpreted as "an act of both aesthetic perception and intellectual pursuit,"[4] comic books are a powerful medium to provocatively analyze and clarify the prejudices, the dangerous rhetoric and the methods that contribute to the demonization of otherness, and to the perpetuation of hate crimes and racial and social tension, both in fiction and in history. Reshaping ancient myths and folklore[5], comics constantly tell stories with superheroes, outcasts, rebels, and trans- and post-human figures, and we often read about discrimination, segregation, and violence against weak or "discordant" bodies and about opposition between "good" and "evil."

On the one hand, comics make popular and normalized archetypes, ideas, and representations of otherness, promoting inclusion and tolerance. On the other hand, they maximize the fears and the devastating impulses of regular, conservative, or heinous characters, often portraying villains or evil powers ready to annihilate innocent people, upon whom they impose their insane and sacralized vision of the world.

In comic book worlds, there are countless works with a strong social stance (e.g., *V for Vendetta*, *Avengers*, *Wonder Woman*, *Persepolis*, etc.). The *X-Men* saga appears to be one of the most significant because it excellently depicts the violence against otherness and the repercussions of discriminatory actions on society. Created by Stan Lee and Jack Kirby in 1963 and relaunched by Chris Claremont and John Byrne in the 1970s, the *X-Men* comics relate the story of humans born with superhuman abilities or characteristics (e.g., flight, speed, extra strength, telepathy, telekinesis, shapeshifting, etc.) that are activated by a particular gene, called the "X gene." So whereas many superheroes and villains obtain their abilities because of accidents, experiments, and magical or sci-fi objects, mutants are different by birth.

In a ruthless world dominated by anti-mutant bigotry, repression, confinement and bias, the X-Men oppose hatred and fear, trying to create a peaceful and fair society, free of prejudice, for their "kind," and for humans.

The *X-Men* world is really complex and wide, hardly able to be summarized in these pages. The superhero team is guided by Charles Xavier, aka Professor X, one of the most powerful and intelligent characters of the Marvel universe, with extraordinary telepathic and mental-manipulation abilities. The first five members of X-Men, as they appear in issue #1 (September 1963), are also students of the Xavier's School for Gifted Youngsters: Angel (Warren Kenneth Worthington III, later Archangel), a flying mutant with majestic wings; Cyclops (Scott Summers), a mutant with archetypal positive heroic characteristics and the ability to emit red and destructive beams from his eyes; Beast (Hank McCoy), a brainy and tough mutant with animalistic features (blue fur, fangs, etc.); Iceman (Bobby Drake), a mutant who can manipulate ice and cold temperature, and Marvel Girl (Jean Grey, later Phoenix), the first and only woman of the group, with really strong telekinetic and telepathic powers. Despite being white and mostly from middle-upper class, they end up representing a feared and rejected minority, opposed to the traditional and prevailing society. In the following years, many other characters have joined and sometimes left the team. They come from different nations, racial and ethnic groups, and economic backgrounds, and they perfectly embody the idea of otherness not only conceptually but also visually and historically, promoting alternative models of superheroes. Just to quote a few examples, sonic "screamer" Banshee is Irish, steel-strong Colossus is Russian, and Thunderbird is an Apache with overdeveloped senses and strength that pay homage to American Indian culture and folklore. Wolverine is a Canadian mutant with extra-powerful agility, reflexes and combat skills, retractable claws, and adamantium skeleton. Characterized by an antiheroic attitude, internal contrasts, and a tormented past, he is an outlaw with addictions (e.g., alcohol, tobacco, etc.) and psychological issues, but he is also bighearted, loyal, and brave. Nightcrawler is a religious German mutant with irreversible and evident physical mutations (i.e., indigo skin, yellow eyes, tail, hands with three fingers, etc.), teleportation power and extra-agility, flexibility and speed. Storm is a mighty Kenyan American mutant with great leadership capacities who can control and manipulate weather. She is one of the strongest female and black figures in comic history and a strong anti-patriarchal and anti-racist symbol. She incarnates African countries coming to independence and also reflects the fight to protect the environment. Kitty Pryde, aka Sprite, Ariel, and Shadowcat is a young Jewish girl with phasing and intangibility powers who represents both an often-tormented minority and an activist and politically engaged youth trying to find her place in the world. The list of mutant superheroes contains many more members, all of them incredibly interesting and inspiring, and I'm sorry not to mention them.

The X-Men fight against several human and superhuman villains, such as their archenemy Magneto, a mutant who creates and manipulates magnetic fields, and his followers of The Brotherhood of Evil Mutants, a group that promote mutant superiority. Partially recalling the opposing philosophies and activism of Martin Luther King and Malcolm X, Professor X and Magneto have antagonistic views regarding the relationship between mutants and humans. Xavier believes in pacific and constructive approaches to build a tolerant community of humans and mutants, whereas Magneto, a concentration camp survivor who also suffered persecution for being a mutant, chooses a violent path and prefers to fights against humans "by any means necessary"—a quote from a Malcolm X's speech given in 1964.[6] "In a very real sense, they [Professor X and Magneto] have identical goals—the safety of mutantkind—but Xavier chooses the arduous, slower, path of cooperation, whereas Magneto's plans would result in *Homo superior* ruling the earth and replacing *Homo sapiens* with Magneto ruling over the mutants."[7] Shapeshifter and bisexual Mystique is another of the most notable villains of the *X-Men* universe. She is an ally of Magneto, and in the 1980s, she recreates and leads a new Brotherhood of Mutants, committing several crimes, including terrorist attacks and murders of anti-mutant personalities. However, the boundaries between X-Men and the Brotherhood are not fixed, and sometimes they join forces to defeat major threats, as, for example, Apocalypse, possibly the first mutant. Similarly, Magneto is not solely a villain with a terroristic attitude and dictatorial aspirations, and, mostly when he cooperates with the X-Men, he reveals antiheroic or superheroic traits and attempts toward redemption. In the *X-Men* stories, other parallel "good" or "evil," mutant or human characters, projects, and organizations appear. For example, the Hellfire Club is a group of privileged mutants who plot to control the world; the Friends of Humanity is a populist anti-mutant group that evokes white supremacy, neo-Nazis, and Ku Klux Klan groups; and Project Wideawake is a covert CIA research task force with paramilitary autonomy that studies mutants and identifies them.

The X-Men were created in the 1960s, when Western society was shaken by protests for the rights of disadvantaged groups (e.g., African Americans, women, etc.), demanding integration, emancipation, civil rights, and gender equality, among others. The well-known saga can be interpreted as a long allegory for intolerance, injustice, and violence against minorities, and it shows an iconic influence on contemporary times as well, popularizing stories that invite readers to resist against discriminating powers, to defend civil and human rights, to respect and support differences, and to stand up for freedom, understanding, and equality. It resists the suspicion, the fear, and the hate that authorities advocate, that humans feel toward "others," and that mutants face during their entire life. Mutants have mostly turbulent interpersonal relationships with humans as a result of prejudice and concern, and they suffer from marginalization, verbal and physical abuses, and often, plans of extermination. This traumatic treatment generates a debasement of mutant subjectivity, permanently affecting their social behavior, personal development, and civil participation. Many mutants, for example, are forced to "keep their status hidden, hoping to blend or pass into mainstream society."[8] The risk of mutants' exclusion from society is especially illustrated by the Morlocks, a group of mutants whose grotesque appearance make them feel they are safer living underground in New York's hidden tunnels, with no chance of ever going back to human society.

TRUMP VERSUS OTHERNESS

The leitmotifs of the *X-Men* stories are quite similar to the ones of Trumpian rhetoric and propaganda, which promote discriminations based on racial, ethnic, sexual, religious, economic, or ideological factors; employ distorted, incorrect, or fake news; and uphold the production and the propagation of fear and social, racial, and sexual stereotypes. Hate speech, the use of war propaganda clichés, such as demonization and dehumanization of "enemies" and otherness, in daily political propaganda and the standardization and normalization of prejudicial themes sharpen social conflicts between the self-styled "right" people and powers and the "others." This narrative of hate and dismay legitimate, both for militants and ordinary citizens, discriminatory behaviors and claims (previously generally considered illicit and amoral), violent actions against minorities, and incivility. These processes are not completely new in US society, but their consequences and dangers should not be underestimated. Quoting Giroux, "the United States has lived through a number of historical periods that tested the ideals of democracy including the genocide of Native Americans, slavery, and Jim Crow in its historical and current versions. American society now faces a new threat to the ideals and promise of a viable democracy and that threat is one of an incipient authoritarianism."[9] As a matter of fact, according to many studies,[10] also based on hate crime data from the FBI, there is a strong possibility that Trump's election and presidency go hand in hand with a statistically relevant increase in reported hate crimes, one of the most serious of the last century, second only to the spike in hate crimes registered after 9/11.

Trump perfectly understands "the power of spectacle, shock, and performance."[11] As many charismatic leaders before him, including Adolf Hitler and Benito Mussolini, he unifies revolutionary faith with reactionary and nationalist principles, leading an ideological attack against "corrupted" liberal and democratic politics. He is dramatizing the myth (only valid for the imaginary "true" Americans) of "a lost era of industrial might, shared prosperity and social cohesion" and inserting it into a new political liturgy, stimulating a "harsh contempt for the establishment—the media, Wall Street and global economic elites," and a "racial resentment among the white working class."[12] The polarization of political discourse and the resulting paranoia and discontent foster the depiction of common and menacing enemies against which he addresses fear and debasement. When Mosse analyzed the processes of trivialization and sacralization of war during the First and the Second World War, he also focused on the double standard that enemies represent for propaganda: they have to be not only dreadful and dangerous but also treacherous, grotesque, and risible, opposed to the honorable and virtuous side that produce the message.[13]

Dystopian fictions, as well as real political systems, need a nemesis to act against. Identifying hostile forces is fundamental for the creation of a state and a community because, as philosopher Carl Schmitt suggested, without an opponent, political dimension and actions would not exist. Enmity has a structuring power in the creation of society and its norms because "the distinction of friend and enemy denotes the utmost degree of intensity of a union or separation, of an association or dissociation."[14] Schmitt continued, "[t]he political enemy need not be morally evil or aesthetically ugly; he need not appear as an economic competitor. . . . But he is, nevertheless, the other, the stranger; and it is sufficient for his nature that he is, in a specially intense way, existentially something different and alien, so that in the extreme case conflicts with him are possible."[15] Thus, the internal and external enemies are, by definition, something "other" and antithetic that oppose the idea of right and threaten order and security. According to Hannah Arendt, enemies do not even need to reject common ideals or try to overthrow the government: the objective enemies are simply "carriers of tendencies" that authorities can transform into suitable and plausible targets, justifying repression and control.[16] In addition to exacerbating the role and the representation of the enemy, Trump is disempowering the rational opposition to his work in favor of post-truths and insults, also "elevating trolling, both online and off, into a mainstream political practice."[17]

DISCORDANT BODIES IN FICTION AND REALITY

Let us analyze a few examples from the *X-Men* universe, mostly from comic books, but also taking into consideration film and television series and comparing them with the history of the United States.

In *Days of Future Past*, a storyline presented in *Uncanny X-Men* #141–142 (1981), the protagonists have to deal with a dystopian future in which the Sentinels, mutant-hunting robots, govern the United States and the mutants are tracked down, killed, and incarcerated in internment camps. In 2013, after decades of repression started with the Mutant Control Act of 1988, the population is divided into three classes: "H," humans without mutant genes, "A," anomalous humans with mutant genetic potential (forbidden to have children), and M, mutants, "the bottom of the heap, made pariahs and outcasts."[18] The way mutants are depicted in this story arch visually and theoretically evokes Jewish persecution by Nazis. At the beginning of this story, millions of mutants have already died, and millions live in atrocious conditions.

With the help of telepath Rachel Summers (daughter of Scott Summers and Jean Grey from an alternate future), an adult Kitty Pryde (who calls herself Kate) transfers her mind into her younger self of 1980, hoping that the X-Men of the past will avoid the assassination of Senator Robert Kelly by Mystique and the (new) Brotherhood, composed of Blob, Pyro, Avalanche, and Destiny. This murder precipitated anti-mutant hysteria that led to the approval of the Mutant Control Act. Even though the mission to the past is successful, and the X-Men save Kelly, dystopia still remains a possibility, mostly because a strong racist propaganda is already enforced.

Senator Robert Kelly is an iconic character; created by Claremont and Byrne for *Uncanny X-Men* #135 (1980), he is a rigid anti-mutant speaker who supports actions against mutants because he deeply believes that they represent a threat to "real" humans. Treating otherness as a collective and doomed bio-social disease that needs to be controlled and restricted, Kelly is an impressive metaphorical incarnation of bigotry and hate.

However, one of the most shocking characters in the *X-Men* stories is Reverend William Stryker. In the graphic novel *X-Men. God Loves, Man Kills* (*Marvel Graphic Novel* #5, 1982), Stryker kidnaps Xavier and the X-Men have to team up with Magneto to save him and bring the bloodthirsty reverend to justice. Stryker presents himself to the public as a devoted and passionate preacher who promotes a crusade against "devils," and therefore advocates for the genocide of mutantkind on religious claims: mutants are abominations in the eyes of God. In a context in which the Purifiers, a human supremacist group, patrol the streets to register, assault, and even murder these "despicable" creatures, the reverend, a war hero who killed his wife and his mutant newborn son and staged a car accident to cover the assassinations, opposes the idea of mutation as a natural process of evolution (also attacking science and supporting creationist views). Invoking God's will and pretending to protect the Christian roots of humanity, he compares mutation to sin: "We are as God made us! Any deviation from that sacred template—any mutation—comes not from Heaven, but from Hell."

The propaganda depicted in *Days of Future Past* and *God Loves, Man Kills* is rough and merciless. It insists on the dangerous nature of mutants and exploits stereotypes and prejudices to spread rejection, fear, and insecurity in the nonmutant population. This narrative of hatred starts with the repetition of negative words and images attributed to mutants: they are evil abominations; they are dangerous; they represent a risk for society; and they can easily hurt, manipulate, or subjugate people with their powers, etc. Linguistically, even the offensive slurs used against them (e.g., "muties") support the identification, the categorization, and the further separation between outcasts and the righteous population. Words and labels have a devastating influence on society and on individuals, as Professor X reminds us in *Uncanny X-Men* #294: "Freak, flatscan, deadend, genejoke, mutie. Words, powerful words meant to distance, to demean, to destroy the havens of self-respect we each carry and nurture within us. . . . Those words carry us away from the light and lead us marching, no—charging—into a darkness where prejudice and bigotry reign."

Moreover, supporters of mutant rights are derided and criminalized, accused of betraying humanity in favor of an enemy species, thus undermining any attempt at moderate and peaceful opposition, and promoting the use of speeches that, instead of objectively present arguments, aim at frightening, angering, or unsettling their recipients. This system calls for a purification of society in which mutants have "no right to have rights."[19] Kelly, Stryker, and their supporters refuse to see mutants as human beings and attack them as if, quoting Charles Xavier, they were a "monolithic group, possessing one set of attitudes or goals."[20]

A similar social, political, and religious denial of otherness and individuality is present in Trump's speeches. Presidential propaganda refuses to see otherness as a positive and constructive element of society, divides society into antagonistic groups, and depicts minorities and opponents as an indivisible group of dangerous or disgraceful elements. It is fiercely offensive to immigrants, women, gays, transsexuals, and other potentially "questionable" (from a racist, patriarchal, and conservative point of view) categories in the process.

In *X-Men* (2000), first of the *X-Men* film series, Senator Kelly has no qualms saying that mutants are naturally dangerous, criminalizing their own essence, and that "American people deserve the right to decide if they want their children to be in school with mutants." He also adds that mutants "are among us. We must know who they are, and above all, what they can do." To know who mutants are and what they do, as seen in several *X-Men* comics and films, some kind of registration is proposed or enforced, such as the aforementioned Mutant Control Act. Similarly and on many occasions, Trump has described "otherness" as a critical problem and has addressed entire communities as dangerous or not worthy of support or humanitarian assistance, decrying the crimes committed by "blacks and Hispanics," equating Muslims with terrorists and denigrating history, religion, traditions, and dramatic realities of foreign poorer countries. When he announced his candidacy for president, part of his speech was dedicated to insulting Mexican immigrants: "When Mexico sends its people, they're not sending their best. . . . They're bringing drugs. They're bringing crime. They're rapists. And some, I assume, are good people."[21] At the end of 2015, Trump suggested the possibility of a Muslim registration system and compared Islam with a "sickness." During a CNN interview in 2016, he affirmed that "Islam hates us," and a few days later, he added that it is difficult to separate radical Islam from Islam because "you don't know who's who."[22] In November 2015, he retweeted crime statistics about murders that displayed completely false data, including that 81 percent of "whites" are killed by "blacks." Actually, according to the FBI data for 2014, the real number is 15 percent. The image of the tweet showed a menacing face-covered black man with a gun.[23] In January 2018, he hoped for the end of immigration to the United States from "shithole countries" like Haiti, El Salvador and some African nations.[24] His populist, autarchic, and reactionary politics also include the project for the construction of a fortified wall at the border with Mexico to stop illegal immigration, as well as the so-called Muslim Ban, enforcement of executive orders titled "Protecting the Nation from Foreign Terrorist Entry into the United States," that prevent citizens from several Muslim-majority countries (e.g., Iran, Libya, Sudan, Syria, etc.) from entering in the United States. At the same time, Trump did not condemn, or did so without the fury he generally shows when talking about minorities and immigrants, violent actions and hate crimes perpetrated by harmful groups like white supremacists, neo-Nazis, neo-Confederates, and Ku Klux Klan members, among others. This was particularly clear after the "Unite the Right" rally on August 11–12, 2017, in Charlottesville, Virginia. This neo-fascist and supremacist protest was organized after the decision was made to remove Confederate monuments from public spaces. Counterprotesters from several religious, democratic, leftist, anti-racist, and civil rights groups opposed the rally. There were clashes that resulted in dozens of injured people and a car attack against counterprotesters perpetrated by a neo-Nazi domestic terrorist who attended the "Unite the Right." One woman was killed and another nineteen people were wounded. Trump failed to denounce the far-right groups for the violence. In the following statements, he declared that there were "hatred, bigotry, and violence on many sides,, as well as "very fine people on both sides," and he also defended the reason for the rally, comparing the removal of the confederate statue to an attempt to "change" US history and culture.[25] Instead of speaking "to people's ideals," hopes, and positive feelings, Trump, as Kelly and Stryker point out, "speaks to people's fear" and he "knows the audience and appears nice with a damn scary message."[26] This debasement of "discordant" subjects helps to strengthen public prejudices and fears, forcing the population to perceive otherness and differences as traumatic elements, thus legitimating hate crimes, bullying, and bias, while at the same time ensuring freedom of action to the government. This narrative does not support nor guarantee anyone's safety, and, in terms of human and civil rights, the actions encouraged by these discourses do not make America great again. They end up hurting innocent people, like the thousands of traumatized children separated from their families caught illegally crossing the US–Mexico border during spring 2018.[27]

In the same way that mutants' struggle for integration is depicted, some sections of the US population, including citizens and residents, want to be part of society but do not know where they belong or where to stand. These constant attacks against otherness destroy the image, the individuality, and even the self-perception of those labeled as "others," making them feel wrong, excluded, and persecuted. Although it is not a recent problem in US history, it is clear that discriminatory actions increase social conflicts and that, in extreme cases, they can be used by real terrorist groups to reinforce their anti-western propaganda.

> Separating themselves from humankind, Magneto and the Brotherhood of Evil Mutants use the oppression of mutants at the hands of average humans as a rallying cry and a reason to harm, even kill, humans as they see fit. One of their implicit arguments is: if mutants do not deserve the same degree of moral consideration that we afford to average human beings, then mutants are justified in placing humans outside of mutants' moral consideration.[28]

This comic book analysis could be applied to Terrorism Studies as wells: from the fictional Magneto's Brotherhood of Evil Mutants to the real and treacherous Islamic State and others, terrorist groups often persuade and attract people who live on the margins of society and exploit their need to belong and lack of integration and inclusion to bring them closer to their cause, stimulating empathy toward the criminal organizations by depicting the marginalized as victims of persecution by society as a whole.[29]

FROM DYSTOPIAN WORDS TO DYSTOPIAN ACTIONS

The distance between the debasement and the criminalization of otherness is unfortunately too short, with consequences that range from limitation of rights to worse types of exclusion and violence, like segregation, imprisonment, slavery, summary executions, and genocide. This is summarized by the reaction of Dr. Moira MacTaggert, a geneticist close to Charles Xavier, to an anti-mutant speech of Senator Kelly in *Uncanny X-Men* #141: "Registration of mutants today, gas chambers tomorrow."

Two storylines in X-*Men* that remind readers of this fine line concern the Sentinels and Genosha. Created by Lee and Kirby for *The X-Men* #14 (1965), Sentinels are constantly used in the *X-Men* universe. As mentioned previously, they are robots (or human-machine hybrids) programmed to capture or kill mutants. Sentinels were invented by military scientist Bolivar Trasks and employed by many other human and superhuman villains such as Larry Trask, Steven Lang, Sebastian Shaw, and Cassandra Nova. They are the perpetrators of several massacres, as in *Operation: Zero Tolerance* (1997) and *Ultimate X-Men* (2001–2009), and are also responsible for the genocide of 16 million mutants in the story *E is for Extinction* (*New X-Men* #114–116, 2001). Sentinels punish and exterminate mutants for no other reason than their natural essence. Instead of integrating, recognizing and valorizing diversity—and building bridges between different groups—dystopic entities like the Sentinels choose to separate, annihilate, and build walls, sometimes literally.

In *Uncanny X-Men* #235 (1988), readers discover Genosha, one of the richest countries in the world, where mutants are exploited as slaves, making the comparison with US history caustic and painful. The government tests their citizens at birth, and the ones with the X gene[30] (offensively called "genejokes") are stripped of freedom, rights, and consciousness, literally becoming the brainwashed property of the state. Thanks to this exploitation, Genosha presented itself as a "green and pleasant land of hope and opportunity where the watchword is freedom,"[31] where there is no poverty or hardship, and where people are not discriminated against for the color of their skin. "The irony of a nation that enslaves mutants pointing out that it doesn't discriminate on the basis of skin color is very effective in communicating that what's going on in Genosha is similar to what's far too often happened along racial lines. Indeed, mutants, like some racial minorities, are not even thought of as people."[32] They are "organic machines"[33] that suffer for psycho-physical conditioning, who lose their identity, forget their names, and consider themselves numbers, as the ones they are assigned when they enter into the slavery system. Their memories, aspirations, feelings, and dreams are erased and replaced by the wish to serve their human bosses, and to obey. The younger of them are directly "bred to serve."[34] They are made easily recognizable for the uniforms they have to wear and deeply isolated, because "if no one befriends them, no one can feel sorry for them."[35] While non-mutant Genoshans happily live their lives without knowing (or pretending not to know) the legalized crimes committed to guarantee their standard of living, the treatment of mutants recalls some of the darkest pages of real history, such as slavery in the United States, the Shoah, and Apartheid in South Africa. As in the aforementioned cases, the law in Genosha allows discrimination, segregation, exploitation, humiliation, and assassination. Mutant identity is criminalized and ferociously repressed and manipulated, until resistance is not even conceivable because slaves are programmed to not rebel.

As shown in the comic book series *Astonishing X-Men* (vol 3 #1–6, 2004) and in the film *X-Men: The Last Stand* (2006)—two of the few *X-Men* episodes that are less violent, though still oppressive—the solution deemed most effective for dealing with the mutant problem is a cure that can suppress the X gene and "relieve" mutants of their abilities, a cure "designed to heal what was never broken."[36] Mutants, as many other undesirable groups, are "the object of institutional prejudice, at best, and the targets of a potentially genocidal program, at worst,"[37] but it is also possible to "eradicate differences through assimilation."[38] The never faded "white man's burden"[39] that characterized colonialism and imperialism becomes, in this case, humanity's antidote to mutant "barbarism;" but the process is the same: a dominant part of society decides that the essence (e.g., culture, traditions, practices, language, religion, esthetic, etc.) of a well-defined community judged "inferior," "uncivilized," or "threatening" must be erased and substituted with more appropriate and orthodox forms. Otherness must be classified, ordered, and cured, as an illness.

Of course, we are not there yet, and hopefully we will not arrive at these brutal points; but, still, the symptoms of dystopia are already present in our world: beginning with the normalization of hate, violence, and abuses; the division of society into groups and the debasing of "others;" and the reinforcement of speeches that rest more on instinctive sentiments than rational reasoning and concrete evidences. Quoting Arendt, "after murder of the moral person and annihilation of the juridical person, the destruction of the individuality is almost always successful."[40] Repression does not start immediately, but, once authorities clear the way, no one is safe anymore.

As Magneto says in *X-Men: The Last Stand*: "No one ever talks about it. They just do it. And you'll go on with your lives ignoring the signs all around you. And then one day, they come for you. Then you realize, while you're talking about organizing and committees, the extermination has already begun."

What the X-Men teach us is about the mutability of the fight and the victimization. Everyone can be persecuted for a reason: mutants have unstoppable abilities that can threaten and harm humans, Muslims can be terrorists, immigrants can be criminals, women can reject the patriarchal system and undermine the cult of masculinity, homosexuals can weaken traditional and conservative values, and so on. Dystopian authorities only need a suitable excuse to transform otherness into a menace and a sin.

MUTANTS TODAY AND TOMORROW, BETWEEN UTOPIA AND DYSTOPIA

The issues of *X-Men* published during the Trump presidency keep reflecting on otherness with provocative storylines and clear references to contemporary political situations. In *X-Men Gold* #9 (2017), for example, Kitty Pride has to speak in front of the Congress about mutant rights, trying to defend her kind and to reject a new bill on mutant deportations, directly dealing with a tough question Trump raised many times about illegal immigrants. Her speech easily adapts to modern US politics. She attacks the constant and degraded depiction of mutants as "others" and opposes the discriminatory proposal of the government, pointing to the contradictions between such a project and the values of freedom, tolerance and justice upon which the United States was built: "This is about human rights, American rights. To single a minority out for deportation or special treatment is about the most un-American thing I can imagine." As examples of previous prejudicial episodes in the United States, she mentions the segregation of African Americans and the internment of Japanese Americans during the Second World War, and she expresses her hope that those in powers will not choose to stay on "the wrong side of history" again. Although her words are touching and compassionate, Congressman Baker answers with overused Conservative clichés and incorrect information—often adopted in today's political debates—insisting on safety issues, stating that "the vast majority of mutants are walking weapons," and citing economic problems related to the expensive cost to normal citizens of mutants' activities and incidents. He, of course, forgets to mention or diminishes the suffering caused to mutants by Conservative propaganda and avoids the mention of any positive outcomes that could arise from integration.

One of the most relevant works of the latest *X-Men* stories is *X-Men Red* (2018), that directly opens with Jean Grey and her crew (Nightcrawler, Gentle, Namor, Trinary, Honey Badger, and Wolverine) saving a little mutant girl named Heather from anti-mutant vigilantes. Jean, one of the most powerful telepaths, perceives the pain, the dread, the rage, and the anxiety in society, as she never felt them before. Thus, the story revolves around her desire to "heal the world" from hate, violence, and fear, to save it from a "divisive path that will lead to more fear, more violence."[41] Issue #5 is, in my opinion, one of the most emotional of all the *X-Men* sagas. While Polish soldiers are ready to attack innocent mutants, Jean avoids a violent escalation by using her powers to merge the minds of the two groups. She shows them "the other side," and "instead of monsters, each soldier experiences another person standing in front of them, with hopes and faults and fears and dreams." In *X-Men Red*, hate and fear of otherness becomes physically invasive when a dark villain starts to infect people's amygdalae with nanite sentinels (with mutant detection ability) and leads them to become mutant hunters and to commit atrocious crimes. These manipulated haters embody a powerful metaphor and fictionally show how irresponsible and "evil" propaganda can turn even ordinary citizens into brutal militants of a violent and repressive doctrine.

As Jean believes in humanity, she knows that "whoever is trying to breed hate" is responsible for the world's sickness. Like Professor X, she affirms that people are "simply protective, misinformed and scared," and that the X-Men are "going to crush the lies" and "weaponize the truth."[42] Here, the truth is that we should try to empathize with "others" and embrace diversity. This simple idea is revolutionary and particularly powerful, especially in a post-truth society, where sociopolitical narrative can rely more on emotion, subjectivity, and prejudice than on verified facts and objective data.

Many references to Trump and the climate of hatred he has generated are present in a recent and socially engaged Fox series based on X-Men comics: *The Gifted* (2107–2018). *The Gifted* tells the story of the Strucker family. District attorney Reed Strucker and his wife Caitlin discover that their teenage children, Lauren and Andy, have powers and are forced to run from authorities and join the underground mutant community, where they meet rebel fighters. In the society depicted, mutant rights are no longer guaranteed. Mutants are treated as terrorists, ruthlessly hunted down, and exterminated like "cockroaches," as anti-mutant activist Franklin Bennett says in episode 12. Many are imprisoned in Mutant Detention Centers. Tortured, drugged, and conditioned, some of them are used for the Hound Program, in which they are transformed into "hunters" of other mutants. Most of the humans seem to reject mutants and support the anti-mutant hysteria promoted by the government, as is shown in episode 3, when a group of "concerned citizens" with weapons threatens Caitlin and her children, evoking images of villagers with flames and pitchforks that attack Frankenstein's monster. The character of Senator Matthew Montez seems to explicitly refer to Trump. His hate speech against mutants in episode 12 is filled with themes used many times by the president: Montez wants "to take our country back" from mutants; he proposes restrictive laws that will violate mutants' fundamental rights; and, because the enemy is "trying to destroy our way of life," he proclaims the right for humans to "defend themselves" and the end of political correctness.

The X-Men are a strong metaphor for discrimination, racism, and prejudice.[43] They stand up "for any other 'other', whether racial, ethnic, sexual, or foreign,"[44] while, according to Claremont, one of the most important *X-Men* writers, "they are hated, feared, and despised collectively by humanity for no other reason than that they are mutants."[45] Dystopian wisdom insists on the X-Men's innate dangerousness, on the impossibility of their integration, and on the need to protect from them the worthy part of the population. By using the most common and trite types of propaganda, politicians, and instigators constantly repeat that "humans come first," that mutants put society, security, and the future in danger, that they are a menace to families and to the natural order, and so on. Otherness is scary, and by injecting population with fear and insecurity against diversity, the self-proclaimed "healthy body" of society can impose its command, protect its authority, and ensure its safety and privileges, while the "sick bodies" can be easily removed or annihilated. In a real world where families can be torn apart, where women and LGBTQ communities' rights can be questioned, where violence against minorities can be justified, where immigrants can be left to die in the sea, where people can become illegals, we all can be mutants. If we want to build a utopian future, we should face the abyss of dystopia and peacefully fight against racist discourses, myths, and actions through education, culture, and tolerance. The only way to relate to otherness is through dialogue, integration, and respect, recognizing, and protecting the uniqueness of our lives. It may seem strange, but comics can support this resistance. As Xavier says in *Uncanny X-Men* #294, the X-Men fight to valorize diversity: "Seeing past their differences, humans and mutants share a common unbreakable bond. No amount of words—derision, distrust, or disinformation—can change the truth that each of us, man, woman, black, Hispanic, Jew, Asian, Native American, homosexuals, mutant, everyone . . . underneath all the words, we are related. We are all family." In utopia and in dystopia, what unites us is and will be stronger than what divides us.

NOTES

1. Michel Foucault, *Discipline and Punish: The Birth of the Prison* (New York: Vintage Books, 1995), 305.

2. Just to quote few examples, in Italy, Lega (before Lega Nord) has increased from 4 percent (2013 general election) to 17 percent (2018 general election), while Neo-Fascist Casapound went from 0.14 percent (2013 general election) to 0.90 percent (2018 general election). German AfD went from 4.7 percent (2013 Federal Parliament election) to 12.6 percent (2017

Federal Parliament election). Le Pen's Front National gained almost 34 percent at the ballot against Macron for the 2017 French presidential election. Neo-Nazi Golden Dawn is currently the third party in Greece.

3. According to Organization for Security and Co-operation in Europe (OSCE), in 2012 reported hate crimes were 71 in Italy, and in 2016 they were 763. In Austria, they passed from 91 in 2012 to 425 in 2016. In Germany, 2016 hate crimes were 3,598, more than 550 more that 2015. In the UK, they went from 62.518 in 2015 to 80.763 in 2016. In the United States, the recorded hate crimes in 2015 were 6,885, whereas in 2016, the number reaches 7,321.

4. Will Eisner, *Comics and Sequential Art* (Tamarac: Poorhouse Press, 2000), 8.

5. Chris Gavaler, *Superhero Comics* (London: Bloomsbury Academic, 2018), 15.

6. The Malcolm X quote is a translation of a phrase used by French philosopher Jean-Paul Sartre in his 1948 play *Les Mains sales* (*Dirty Hands*).

7. Peter Coogan, *Superhero: The Secret Origin of a Genre* (Austin: MonkeyBrain Books, 2006), 98.

8. Mikhail Lyubansky, "Prejudice Lessons from the Xavier Institute," in *The Psychology of Superheroes. An Unauthorized Exploration*, eds. Robin S. Rosenberg and Jennifer Canzonieri (Dallas: BenBella Books, 2008), 84.

9. Henry Giroux, *The Public in Peril: Trump and the Menace of American Authoritarianism* (New York: Routledge, 2017), 141.

10. Karsten Müller and Carlo Schwarz, "Making America Hate Again? Twitter and Hate Crime Under Trump," *SSRN Electronic Journal*, March 30, 2018. Accessed https://papers.ssrn.com/sol3/papers.cfm?abstract_id=3149103 on July 27, 2018; Stephen Rushin and Griffin Sims Edwards, "The Effect of President Trump's Election on Hate Crimes," *SSRN Electronic Journal*, January 14, 2018. Accessed https://papers.ssrn.com/sol3/papers.cfm?abstract_id=3102652 on July 27, 2018.

11. Giroux, *The Public*, 144.

12. Robert Lieberman et al., "Trumpism and American Democracy: History, Comparison, and the Predicament of Liberal Democracy in the United States," *SSRN Electronic Journal*, August 31, 2017, 6. Accessed https://papers.ssrn.com/sol3/papers.cfm?abstract_id=3028990 on July 27, 2018,=.

13. George Mosse, *Fallen Soldiers. Reshaping the Memory of the World Wars* (Oxford: Oxford University Press, 1990).

14. Carl Schmitt, *The Concept of the Political. Expanded Edition* (Chicago: University of Chicago Press, 2007), 26.

15. Schmitt., *The Concept*, 27.

16. Hannah Arendt, *The Origins of Totalitarianism* (Cleveland: Meridian Books, 1962), 423–24.

17. . Jason Hannan, "Truth and Trolling," in America's Post-Truth Phenomenon. When Feelings and Opinions Trump Facts and Evidence, ed. C. G. Prado (Santa Barbara: ABC-CLIO, 2018), 139.

18. Chris Claremont and John Byrne, *Uncanny X-Men* Vol 1 #141 (New York: Marvel, 1981).

19. Chris Claremont and Brent Anderson, *Marvel Graphic Novel* Vol 1 #5 (New York: Marvel, 1982).

20. Clarement and Anderson, *Marvel Graphic*. .

21. Donald Trump, "Presidential announcement," New York, June 16, 2015.

22. Jenna Johnson and Abigail Hauslohner, "'I think Islam hates us': A Timeline of Trump's comments about Islam and Muslims," *The Washington Post*, May 20, 2017. Accessed https://www.washingtonpost.com/gdpr-consent/?destination=%2fnews%2fpost-politics%2fwp%2f2017%2f05%2f20%2fi-think-islam-hates-us-a-timeline-of-trumps-comments-about-islam-and-muslims%2f%3f&utm_term=.db1a82b79254 on August 6, 2018.

23. Eric Bradner, "Trump Retweets Fake, Racially Charged Crime Data from Non-existent Group," *CNN*, November 23, 2015. Accessed https://edition.cnn.com/2015/11/22/politics/donald-trump-black-crime-police-retweet/ on August 5, 2018.

24. Davis Hirschfeld et al., "Trump Alarms Lawmakers with Disparaging Words for Haiti and Africa," *New York Times*, January 11, 2018. Accessed https://www.nytimes.com/2018/01/11/us/politics/trump-shithole-countries.html on August 3, 2018.

25. Michael D. Shear and Maggie Haberman, "Trump Defends Initial Remarks on Charlottesville; Again Blames Both Sides," *The New York Times*, August 15, 2017. Accessed https://www.nytimes.com/2017/08/15/us/politics/trump-press-conference-charlottesville.html on August 13, 2018.

26. Chris Claremont and Brent Anderson, *Marvel Graphic*.

27. William Wan, "What separation from parents does to children: 'The effect is catastrophic,'" *The Washington Post*, June 18, 2018. Accessed https://www.washingtonpost.com/national/health-science/what-separation-from-parents-does-to-children-the-effect-is-catastrophic/2018/06/18/c00c30ec-732c-11e8-805c-4b67019fcfe4_story.html?utm_term=.60052a4f4421 on August 1, 2018.

28. Cynthia McWilliams, "Mutants Rights, Torture, and X-perimentation," in *X-Men and Philosophy. Astonishing Insight and Uncanny Argument in the Mutant X-verse*, eds. Rebecca Housel and J. Jeremy Wisnewski (Hoboken, NJ: John Wiley & Sons, Inc., 2009), 103.

29. Roger Griffin, *Terrorist's Creed: Fanatical Violence and the Human Need for Meaning* (Basingstoke, UK: Palgrave Macmillan, 2012).

30. The marginalization of Genosha mutants, which become almost invisible to "regular" people and are avoided for their X gene, also "parallels the negative treatment of people who are HIV-positive," see Jeremy Pierce, "Mutants and the Metaphysics of Race," in *X-Men and Philosophy: Astonishing Insight and Uncanny Argument in the Mutant X-verse*, eds. Rebecca Housel and J. Jeremy Wisnewski (Hoboken, NJ: John Wiley & Sons, Inc., 2009).191. In the *X-Men* stories, there are several references to HIV and AIDS as forms of otherness, such as, for example, the Legacy Virus, a virus with degenerative effects that initially infect only mutants and that, according to Ramzi Fawaz (*The New Mutants: Superheroes and the Radical Imagination of American Comics*. [New York: New York University Press, 2016]), is "not simply a disease but a powerful material expression of the mutant race's ugly inheritance: a legacy of xenophobia and violence" (267–68). Also Rogue (a villain that joins X-Men in the 1980s) can be partially interpreted as a metaphor for HIV and AIDS. Because she can absorb powers, memories and personalities by touching, Rogue has really limited personal interactions and perceives her mutation as a curse.

31. Chris Claremont and Rick Leonardi, *Uncanny X-Men* Vol 1 #235 (New York: Marvel, 1988).

32. Jeremy Pierce, "Mutants and the Metaphysics of Race," in *X-Men and Philosophy,* 191.

33. Chris Claremont and Marc Silvestri, *Uncanny X-Men* Vol 1 #238 (New York: Marvel, 1988).

34. Chris Claremont and Rick Leonardi, *Uncanny X-Men* Vol 1 #237 (New York: Marvel, 1988).

35. Chris Claremont and Marc Silvestri, *Uncanny X-Men* Vol 1 #238 (New York: Marvel, 1988).

36. Simon Spurrier and Paul Davidson, *X-Men. Blind Science* Vol 1 #1 (New York: Marvel, 2010).

37. Christopher Robichaud, "Professor X Wants You," in *X-Men and Philosophy*, 148.

38. Katherine Kirby, "War and Peace, Power and Faith," in *X-Men and Philosophy*, 212.

39. *The White Man's Burden* is an 1899 poem about the Philippine American War (1899–1902) written by Rudyard Kipling.

40. Arendt, *The Origins*, 455.

41. Tom Taylor and Mahmud Asrar, *X-Men Red* Vol 1 #1 (New York: Marvel, 2018).

42. Tom Taylor and Mahmud Asrar, *X-Men Red* Vol 1 #5 (New York: Marvel, 2018).

43. Mutants generally start to develop their powers during adolescence. Thus, according to many studies, teenagers easily identify with them. P. Andrew Miller ("Mutants, Metaphor, and Marginalism: What X-actly Do the X-Men Stand For?" *Journal of the Fantastic in the Arts* 3, no. 51 [2003]) says: "Mutants are just like everyone else until they reach puberty.[. . .] They are genetically, and often emotionally, alienated from their parents. They find comfort with

others who are alienated and get together and save the world. They find the control over their lives that many adolescents feel they lack" (282).

44. Peter Coogan, *Superhero*, 15.

45. Chris Claremont, qtd. in P. Andrew Miller, "Mutants, Metaphor, and Marginalism, 283.

Chapter Eleven

Hang the DJ

Black Mirror *in the Age of Trump*

Matthew Paproth

At 10:28 p.m. on November 8, 2016, the night that Donald Trump was elected Forty-Fifth President of the United States, the official Twitter account for *Black Mirror* (@blackmirror) tweeted: "This isn't an episode. This isn't marketing. This is reality." The tweet, which has been retweeted more than Trump's election, alludes to *Black Mirror*'s prescience regarding the possibility of a Trump-like figure rising to political prominence in the current cultural moment.[1]

From 2011 to 2017, across four seasons and nineteen episodes, *Black Mirror* explores the potential pitfalls of our fascination with technology in a range of possible dystopian scenarios. Its first two seasons, which were produced by Channel 4 in England and aired from 2011 to 2014, present seven distinct dystopian visions, with each episode exploring a different world in which some sort of technology has run amok: the premiere episode, for example, presents a relatively familiar world in which the British Prime Minister is compelled via social media to have sex with a pig on national television. In contrast, the second episode, "Fifteen Million Merits," constructs a far more elaborate diegetic world, seemingly set far in the future, in which citizens are forced to ride stationary bicycles to receive merits, which they can exchange for various benefits. The final episode of the first season, "The Entire History of You," explores the ramifications of a particularly compelling bit of technology—a searchable recording of every moment of your life, embedded in your brain, and viewable by anyone you choose to let see it. Throughout its first season, then, series creators Charlie Brooker and Annabel Jones show us the range of possible scenarios that the anthology structure of their series will allow them to engage while exploring different angles of their primary theme, which is how technology allows us to give in to our worst impulses.

The second season unfolds similarly. One episode, "The Waldo Moment," presents the story of a wise-cracking cartoon bear who makes an improbable bid to be the next Prime Minister. Although the episode focuses primarily on Jamie Salter, who operates Waldo and eventually encourages people not to vote for him, its message, about how social media can be weaponized to take advantage of the general public's feelings about politicians, and overall ignorance about political matters, resonates when we look at the rise of populism in the form of politicians like Boris Johnson and Donald Trump.[2]

Although the first two seasons take a determinedly scattershot look at a series of "what if" scenarios, the third season marks an important shift in approach. In 2014, Netflix acquired rights to the existing episodes, and in 2015 Brooker and Jones began producing the series for Netflix rather than Channel 4. They signed a contract for two six-episode seasons, which premiered in late 2016 and late 2017. The production of season three coincided with the US presidential election and saw a notably lighter tone in several of its episodes. Regarding this shift, Brooker states:

> This season, the writing of it started in July 2016, so there were episodes being written all through the American election . . . and everything was looking horrible. I genuinely thought, I don't know what state the world's going to be in by the time these [episodes] appear, and I don't know how much appetite there will be for nothing but bleak nihilism. . . . If you're living in a dystopia, you don't necessarily want to look at another one.[3]

The episodes "Nosedive" and "San Junipero," in particular, featured determinedly upbeat endings unlike anything in the first two seasons. Season four continued this trend, allowing viewers to spend more time with sympathetic characters who were finding ways out of their dystopian conditions.

The evolution of *Black Mirror* reads like a determined, deliberate response to England's Brexit vote and the US presidential election, and it plays out most clearly in two seemingly opposing shifts. The first is the increasing presence of figures who resist the toxic narcissism that allows the technological breakthroughs to spiral out of control in most episodes. Although early seasons were populated by, and often asked us to sympathize with, characters who gave in to their worst impulses, several episodes from season three and nearly all the episodes from season four put figures of resistance front and center, at least some of whom are successful in their acts of resistance. Paradoxically, the second facet of *Black Mirror*'s evolution where we see Brooker and Jones responding to Trumpism is in the confirmation that these episodes take place in a shared diegetic world. On the surface, this makes the entire *Black Mirror* enterprise significantly darker; instead of exploring a series of what-if scenarios, the series now asks viewers to piece together retroactively the various moments and eras in a single unified timeline. Instead of allowing each episode to reboot the whole system and start fresh, we are encouraged to imagine the transitions between episodes and situations. And, although some of the season three and four episodes are lighter in tone, we now know that the bleakest, darkest episodes, such as "Fifteen Million Merits" and "Metalhead," are the inevitable endpoint of the worlds we encounter in lighter episodes like "San Junipero" and "Hang the DJ."

What these two changes have in common is their creation of an engaged, active fandom. The episodes from seasons one and two are punishing, exhausting affairs, suffocating in their bleakness and uniformly downbeat in their conclusions; they present closed, individualized dystopian spaces that resist active fan participation. Throughout the closing credits, Brooker and Jones continue twisting the knife further, with additional scenes that eliminate any possibility of escape for their characters or ambiguity in the reading of their plots.[4] And although there are a few Easter eggs hidden throughout these early episodes, Brooker clearly and repeatedly refuted the notion that the episodes were taking place in the same timeline in many interviews. He actively discouraged engagement and participation from fan communities and downplayed the notion that he was constructing a unified diegetic world across various episodes. However, in seasons three and especially four, Brooker and Jones changed their approach within the episodes, in their comments about the series, and in the advertisements for it. Through the shift in tone and perspective and through the increased presence of concrete connections among the episodes, they recalibrate their audience to become active, engaged participants in the *Black Mirror* experience and, by extension, in resisting cultural and political forces in the real world.

In the introduction to *Utopia/Dystopia: Conditions of Historical Possibility*, Michael D. Gordin, Helen Tilley, and Gyan Prakash discuss the complicated relationship between utopia and dystopia:

> Every utopia always comes with its implied dystopia—whether the dystopia of the status quo, which the utopia is engineered to address, or a dystopia found in the way this specific utopia corrupts itself in practice. Yet a dystopia does not have to be exactly a utopia inverted. . . . We confront, therefore, something of a puzzle, almost mathematical in nature: the opposite of a dystopia seems to be a utopia, but the converse does not hold. There is rather a triangle here—a nexus between the perfectly planned and beneficial, the perfectly planned and unjust, and the perfectly unplanned.[5]

At the beginning of *Black Mirror*, Brooker and Jones envisioned each episode as a representation of a particular dystopia. Jones describes the goal in these seasons: "The technology we use is nearly always enabling. What we explore is what can go wrong when human frailty comes into the equation."[6]

This human frailty is the subject of exploration across the majority of these seven episodes, each of which results in "the perfectly planned and unjust" dystopian space hypothesized by Gordin, Tilley, and Prakash. The "human frailty" they explore throughout these early episodes manifests itself in characters like Liam, the protagonist of "The Entire History of You," who repeatedly gives in to the impulse to self-sabotage that a memory implant allows him to access. The episode posits the question of what sorts of ways we would find to corrupt a seemingly utopian technology that would allow us perfect, complete control of and access to our individual and shared experiences with our loved ones. The same can be said for Bing, the protagonist of "Fifteen Million Merits," who navigates himself to the brink of revolution against a corrupt system before ultimately leveraging his authenticity into a key to the easiest room in this particular hell. Furthermore, this human frailty can be seen in both the men at the heart of "White Christmas," who both at times appear quite sympathetic, due to some selective withholding by the script. The charm of actors Rafe Spall and especially Jon Hamm, and the temptation of the technologies that lead to their undoing and imprisonment are softening effects.

Taken as a group, the seven episodes that comprise *Black Mirror*'s first two seasons routinely ask viewers to occupy complicated positions and to empathize with the characters who display this "human frailty" by actively abusing the focal technology of the particular episodes. In their essay "British Satire, Everyday Politics: Chris Morris, Armando Iannucci and Charlie Brooker," James Brassett and Alex Sutton describe the complicated position in which viewers of early episodes of *Black Mirror* find themselves: "On this view, it can be argued that the person who watches Charlie Brooker is performatively inscribed as both the recipient and the instigator of the satire. Beyond questions of getting the joke or not, liking it or not, a performative instability is presented at the centre."[7] But the engagement described here stops at the conclusion of each hermetically sealed episode. These isolated dystopic visions enact the "perfectly planned and unjust" corner of Gordon and Tilley's paradigmatic triangle. However, they argue that our understanding of both utopia and dystopia becomes more fruitful when we consider the spaces and tensions opened up in the center of that triangle, when we do not simply limit ourselves to the single precise opposite of the utopia. They conclude that, "utopias and dystopias by definition seek to alter the social order on a fundamental, systemic level. They address root causes and revolutionary solutions. . . . Utopia, dystopia, chaos: these are not just ways of imagining the future (or the past) but can also be understood as concrete practices through which historically situated actors seek to reimagine their present and transform it into a plausible future."[8]

The "chaos" of the third corner of this triangle, and the exploration of the volatile spaces between the poles, rings truer to the *Black Mirror* that viewers encounter in the third and fourth seasons. It certainly rings truer of the real world following Brexit and Trump's election. The tweet from @blackmirror on election night serves as a wakeup call for its audience and a Rubicon being crossed by the series in its willingness to entertain and even engage its fans within its texts and paratexts, including its social-media posts, advertisements, and interviews with Brooker and Jones. Thus, we can see a deliberate shift in tone and perspective, starting in the third season in episodes like "Nosedive" and "San Junipero," which are lighter than anything we encounter previously and allow us to sympathize with their episodes' protagonists in ways unfamiliar to the *Black Mirror* viewer. Lacie Pounds's journey in "Nosedive" is the first of season three, and it immediately subverts expectation both in tone and in its progression across the episode. Like so many episodes, "Nosedive" is grounded in a technology that could feasibly generate either a utopia or a dystopia, with the 1-to 5-ranking system of every social interaction feeling like a realistic possible creation of our current technological landscape. As usual, the horrific elements of the episode quickly propel Lacie into the titular nosedive; but unlike most episodes, Brooker and Jones offer her a reprieve. Through the chance meeting with the truck-driving Susan, Lacie encounters a true, thriving figure of resistance. More importantly, she learns from it and mounts a resistance of her own, beginning with her drunken toast and concluding with a meet-cute when she lands in jail. The closing sequence unfolds with a previously unseen joyousness for the world of *Black Mirror*.

The point here is that, as the world was growing ever closer to the type of dystopian visions that they had prophesied in the first seven episodes, the vision for the series was lightening, offering avenues for hope and resistance to viewers. These shifts are even more pronounced in the fourth season, in "USS Callister," "Hang the DJ," and "Black Museum," where we encounter more sympathetic protagonists revolting against technological systems designed to exert their will over them. In an interview given just before the 2016 presidential election, Brooker describes his fundamental outlook on the world:

> I think most people are inherently good. . . . When they throw themselves behind some ugly cause, it's usually out of fear or because they're not availed of all the facts. The show generally reflects that. It's usually just people with a weakness who end up fucking up. We don't have many mustache-twirling villains. But I am a worrier and I do think things are going to go horribly wrong by accident.[9]

Season four, however, which was written and filmed after the election, is bookended by episodes featuring mustache-twirling villains, in addition to featuring female protagonists in all six episodes. Both "USS Callister" and "Black Museum" break new ground in that they spend a significant amount of their respective runtimes letting us witness the actions of overtly villainous male characters from the perspectives of sympathetic female characters, both of whom are able to rebel and escape from their situations in unambiguously upbeat fashion.

The moral universe of *Black Mirror* is relatively straightforward and can best be understood by the preceding quote from Brooker, in that he often explores that space between the inherent goodness that he believes is within most people and the corruption of that goodness as a result of technological developments that allow us to do things we are not mentally prepared to do. Particularly in the first two seasons, the source of the toxicity is typically located above the individual spaces where the drama plays out, in the form of business or government interests. However, Robert Daly and Rolo Haynes, the toxic figures driving the action in "USS Callister" and "Black Museum," respectively, mark a significant shift in the perspective through which we engage this moral universe, and the episodes are strikingly different from anything we encounter before them. For its first twenty minutes, "USS Callister" functions like an episode from the earlier seasons, as we are with Daly as he goes to work, experiences various humiliations there, and retreats to the virtual world where he reigns freely. He appears to be a flawed, sympathetic protagonist in the vein of Liam, Bing, and Jamie Salter. Then, as his tyrannical behavior in the virtual *USS Callister* spaceship becomes increasingly unsympathetic, our perspective switches, and we spend the rest of the episode with Nanette Cole, a new employee at Daly's company, who he soon renders as a virtual "cookie" (a digital replication of someone) and uploads to his virtual kingdom. Along with the sudden shift in perspective, the various acts of emotional, physical, and sexual abuse that Daly commits soon after realign viewers' sympathies in a way that Brooker and Jones had never done before in an episode. While there are episodes the twisted endings of which force us to question the morality of the protagonists with whom we have spent the episode sympathizing ("White Bear," "White Christmas," and "Shut Up and Dance," to be specific), this shift in perspective happens with an hour left in the episode, which Brooker and Jones spend chronicling Cole's suspenseful and ultimately successful rebellion and escape from Daly's virtual prison.

The male power fantasy that Daly enacts in "USS Callister" reflects the escalation of toxic masculinity in the real world, in various real and virtual spaces. Brooker admits the ways in which this atmosphere affected the creation of the episode: "It was written in November last year, so certainly when we came to film it in January 2017, it was around the time of the inauguration. There was a certain mood among a lot of the cast that we were dealing with a new regime coming in. . . . Really 'USS Callister' is about someone who is wielding absolute power who shouldn't be, and people overthrowing him."[10] Trump's "America First" worldview (along with his business practices, his views on minorities, and his abuse of women, for starters) clearly marks him as the ultimate mustache-twirling villain in *Black Mirror*'s moral universe.[11] At various times, Brooker has described Trump as a demolition derby car, a Chicago mob man, and "a cling-filmed parcel of frankfurter meat that's been kicked through a yellow cobweb," so it's no stretch that the episodes created post election would feature more overtly abusive and tyrannical characters.[12] At one point, Cole's cookie discovers that she has been created without any sexual anatomy; this pushes her over the edge, as she declares, "[s]tealing my pussy is a red fucking line." The scene clearly evokes Trump's infamous *Access Hollywood* tape, in which he can be heard bragging about his propensity to approach women and "grab them by the pussy." What is ultimately most striking, though, is the empowering nature of the episode and the potential that it shows for rebellion against the toxic, pussy-stealing misogyny embodied by Daly and Trump. The episode ends with Daly alone, trapped in a virtual prison, and Cole occupying the captain's chair and navigating her way free of his clutches.

In the introduction to their book *Fandom: Identities and Communities*, Jonathan Gray and Cornel Sandvoss discuss the proliferation of fandom studies in the past decade, particularly in relation to the rise of streaming methods of viewing. They argue that "the coproduction and the utilization of user-generated content has changed production regimes and business models"—namely, from traditional television viewing to computers—and has "allow[ed] enunciatively and textually active fans to post, repost, remix, and embed content in their commentary or other paratexts, thus constructing, amending, or reinforcing the boundaries of their fan object."[13] The reddit community (r/blackmirror boasts more than 178,000 subscribers) is especially active in unpacking episodes, in exploring connections between existing technologies and the speculative technologies explored in the series, and in providing a hub for the many other existing fan communities working to engage in the series in the new ways that fans are being invited to. The thread "Master List of Episode Connections / Easter Eggs" has more than four hundred comments and five thousand upvotes.

Brooker's statements about the possibility of the *Black Mirror* shared universe is frequently cited by redditors in comment threads presenting, analyzing, and defending various theories about connections among the episodes. In a 2011 essay for *The Guardian*, Brooker describes the creation of the series, explaining its relationship to *The Twilight Zone* and concluding: "for me the joy of shows like *The Twilight Zone* . . . was precisely that you hadn't already seen it. Every week you were plunged into a slightly different world. . . . That's what we're aiming for with *Black Mirror*: each episode has a different cast, a different setting, even a different reality."[14] In the early years of the series, Brooker and Jones clearly downplayed any sense of intentional connection between the episodes and the worlds portrayed in them.

The third season marks a turning point in this evolution because every one of its episodes contain references to characters and technologies from the first two seasons. In an interview with Thrillist in October 2016, in anticipation of the upcoming third season premiering on Netflix, Brooker acknowledges the growing sense of connection among the episodes: "I've read a couple things where people have tried to work out whether this whole thing is set in one coherent universe, and my view is, if they want to believe that, that's fine. But I don't approach it that way, any more than *The Twilight Zone* was set in one coherent universe. It's probably all in the same psychological universe. . . . So it is deliberate, but it's not part of some grand unveiling that this is all set in the year 2030 or something."[15] These new responses to questions about the connectedness of the universe fit with the increased presence of Easter eggs that pop up in the episodes of season three, most of which suggest this sort of shared universe but stop short of providing references that would allow viewers to piece together any sort of deliberate, coherent timeline. Finally, in preparation for the release of the fourth season, Brooker admitted that he and Jones had consciously decided to embrace the idea of the episodes existing within the same universe:

> We are definitely tonally expanding what this show is. . . . Hopefully that means that you're constantly on your toes as a viewer. . . . As time has gone on, we've put more and more of these nods to those other stories and certainly this season for the first time . . . one of our episodes "Black Museum," has got very specific references to previous stories we've done, and it is sort of filling in a bit of backstory there. . . . It does actually sort of seem to imply that it is all a shared universe, which is the opposite of the answer I used to give to this question.[16]

Brooker here admits that both the change in tone and the concrete linking of the worlds are attempts to keep viewers actively engaged in the experience, and this interview is quoted constantly on reddit and many of the sites where intrepid viewers post their thoughts and theories. Thus, we can look at the changing responses of Brooker and Jones to the question of whether or not the episodes of *Black Mirror* are intended to be connected as a litmus test of their desire for active participation from fans from year to year, season to season, and particularly before and after Trump's election.

Furthermore, many of the Easter eggs throughout seasons three and four are directed at the type of active, engaged fans that Gray and Sandvoss describe as prevalent in the streaming era. These connections are visible primarily by users willing to actively engage the text, poring over it frame by frame, using screengrabs to confirm theories and decode messages, many of which are written specifically for them. The Easter eggs fall into two broad categories—references to textual objects (characters, businesses, and technological artifacts) from other episodes, and messages that communicate information directly to real-world cult fans. In his book *Fan Cultures*, Matt Hills defines cult texts through a number of common characteristics, including the creation of *hyperdiegesis*, "the creation of a vast and detailed narrative space, only a fraction of which is ever directly seen or encountered within the text, but which nevertheless appears to operate according to principles of internal logic and extension."[17]

The first category of Easter egg found in the later seasons of *Black Mirror* is largely intended to suggest (and ultimately confirm) the existence of this type of "vast and detailed narrative space." For example, the song "Anyone Who Knows What Love Is (Will Understand)," originally sung in the season one episode "Fifteen Million Merits," recurs in "White Christmas," "Men Against Fire," and "Crocodile." Companies like UKN (a fictional news channel), National Allied Bank, and TCKR (the company responsible for the technology in San Junipero) recur in various episodes, as does the logo seen throughout White Bear. Character-related references are both more overt and more useful to viewers trying to piece together the hyperdiegetic world of *Black Mirror*. At one point in "Nosedive," Lacie is scrolling through her feed; a careful viewer can see that one of the "highest rated posts" is from Prime Minister Michael Callow, reporting that he "Got thrown out of the zoo again." In other episodes, Easter eggs proclaim that he is still trending on Twitter, and that he is set to divorce. Victoria Skillane, the protagonist from "White Bear" who is eventually revealed to be a convicted felon being tortured in a theme park, also reappears in various news items (in "White Christmas," "Shut Up and Dance," and "Hated in the Nation"); her picture is prominently displayed in "Black Museum." These character recurrences have the added benefit of allowing dedicated viewers to piece together cohesive timelines using them as concrete reference points orienting episodes with one another.

The second type of Easter egg is aimed directly at real-world fans who are actively searching for hidden connections and meanings, and usually they can only be spotted by pausing the episodes and zooming in to read newspaper headlines, TV news crawls, and other objects in the diegetic space. In "Hated in the Nation," a newspaper headline reads "What If Phones, But Too Much," which was a viral description of the typical *Black Mirror* episode from a 2015 tweet (and Toast article) by Daniel Mallory Ortberg. More pointedly, a screengrab of a moment in "Metalhead" shows a list of files that includes "LOADED: \BMS1E1.drivers.tna.pigpoke," a reference to "The National Anthem" (TNA) which was in season 1, episode 1 (S1E1) and featured the Prime Minister having sex with a pig. The list has six more similarly structured entries (such as "LOADED:\BMS1E2.drivers.15mm.bing.abi"), before concluding with "LOADED:\WHY.did.you.bother" and "LOADED:\PAUSING.this.you.freak."

Finally, in season four's "Crocodile," Reddit-user AFellowofLimitedJest found the following text visible in a newspaper article being read by one of the characters: "'Of course the real question is why anyone would pause what they're watching just to read a sentence in a printed out newspaper article,' says a voice in your head—before advising you to go and share this finding on Reddit." This type of authorial intrusion is interesting mostly because of the implied assumption that members of the audience will pore over every frame of the text seeking additional clues and meanings that the average viewer would miss. In different ways but toward the same goal, both types of Easter eggs work to cultivate a passionate, engaged fandom interested in extending the experience from the screen out into the real world.

"Black Museum," then, marks the apotheosis of not only the fourth season but also many of the ways in which Brooker and Jones respond to the Trump era. As mentioned, it is the episode that leads Brooker finally to use the phrase "shared universe," and it neatly fuses together the two types of Easter eggs that the series uses to engage fans. Furthermore, like "USS Callister" and "Hang the DJ," it makes clear that the appropriate response to tyranny is violent revolution, this time in the form of eye-for-an-eye vengeance. Structurally modeled after "White Christmas," "Black Museum" is comprised of three vignettes presented as part of a conversation between two characters. The titular "Black Museum" is owned and operated by Rolo Haynes, a mustache-twirling villain who delights in horrifying visitors with his artifacts and stories. These artifacts include objects linking to every other *Black Mirror* episode, some of which are impossible to miss and feature directly in the plot, whereas others require careful pausing and detective-work. Unlike "White Christmas," which slow-plays the villainous nature of its characters, "Black Museum" is upfront about Haynes, the most overtly Trump-like figure in the *Black Mirror* universe; like Trump (but unlike so many of its flawed characters), Haynes is a showman, a gregarious braggart who loves to be the center of attention, a loud and sweaty American with bad hair. Several moments in the episode foreground this connection, such as Haynes's reference to the "gut full of security shit" that he assumes the episode's British protagonist, Nish, must have encountered at the airport; his anecdote about a US Senator who was poisoned by a Russian as part of "that whole thing"; and his response of "fake news" (one of Trump's favorite phrases) to Nish's question about the supposed innocence of convicted murderer Clayton Leigh, whose digital consciousness resides in Haynes's museum.[18] These direct evocations of Trump function both as winks to the audience and as implications that Brooker and Jones just might be in the process of changing their answer that the episodes are "not part of some grand unveiling that this is all set in the year 2030 or something." The episode's upbeat ending, in which Haynes gets exactly what is coming to him, throws into sharp relief just how far the series has evolved in its willingness encourage its viewers to engage and participate in actively consuming the series and to provide its characters with a way out of the darkness.

In addition to planting various types of connections within the episodes and to confirming fans' shared universe theories in interviews, Brooker and Jones have also used advertising as a method of provoking viewers into various types of action. Since Trump's election, the advertising on various media platforms has gotten increasingly provocative. In October 2016, in conjunction with the release of the third season, Netflix advertised the series using a controversial ad specifically targeting users with ad blockers enabled on their browsers. Users without the ad blockers would see a traditional ad for the series, but if a user had ad blockers installed, they would see an ad reading "HELLO AD BLOCKER USER. YOU CANNOT SEE THE AD. BUT THE AD CAN SEE YOU. WHAT'S ON THE OTHER SIDE OF YOUR BLACK MIRROR?" Although only a few websites agreed to run the ad, it sparked a flurry of content discussing its intrusive nature and debating its merits and its ethics.

In "Interactive Audiences?" Henry Jenkins discusses the relationship fostered between media and its audience with advertisements like these: "Transmedia promotion presumes a more active spectator who can and will follow these media flows. Such marketing strategies promote a sense of affiliation with and immersion in fictional worlds."[19] In his essay, "Culture Jamming: Hacking, Slashing, and Sniping in the Empire of Signs," Mark Dery pushes even further with the concept of culture jamming, which is useful to consider in relation to *Black Mirror*'s post-Trump marketing techniques. Dery defines the concept of culture jamming: "'Jamming' is CB slang for the illegal practice of interrupting radio broadcasts or conversations between fellow hams with lip farts, obscenities, and other equally jejune hi-jinx. Culture jamming, by contrast, is directed against an ever more intrusive, instrumental technoculture whose operant mode is the manufacture of consent through the manipulation of symbols." He goes on to describe the action of a culture jammer: "Part artistic terrorists, part vernacular critics, culture jammers, like Eco's 'communications guerrillas,' introduce noise into the signal as it passes from transmitter to receiver, encouraging idiosyncratic, unintended interpretations. Intruding on the intruders, they invest ads, newscasts, and other media artifacts with subversive meanings."[20] This description certainly fits the type of advertisements being created for *Black Mirror* in the Age of Trump, and the culture jammer would be the ideal audience member for both the ads and the episodes themselves.

On November 18, 2016, ten days after Trump's election, @blackmirror tweeted a link to a video advertising Netflix Vista.[21] The video advertises a (still-fictional) technology that allows users to stream Netflix directly into their heads via a chip-and-lens system similar to the one in "The Entire History of You." The provocative clip alternates personal, probing questions like "What do you love most in life" and "What if the things you love could always be with you?," with shots of Netflix menus and viewers mesmerized by streaming content, oblivious to the equally mesmerized other people around them. It concludes with a shot of a couple at dinner, both staring blankly at their content, followed by "Your life is a story" and finally "Get out and watch it." The ad is ambiguous in both the form (it is presented as a legitimate advertisement, only really tipping its hand in the final seconds as an ad for the show) and the content (as a company, Netflix surely would love viewers to have and to use this technology, if it existed). Like the Ad Blocker ad, the ad for Netflix Vista provides fodder for think pieces, reddit threads, and other active spaces for viewers to create their own content.

These provocative advertisements continued in 2017, as @blackmirror highlighted various moments throughout the year when technologies from the series manifested in the real world, with links to articles about an automated pizza delivery van (a collaboration between Toyota and Pizza Hut) like the one in season four's "Crocodile." Brooker and Jones also continued to blur the lines and complicate matters through the creation of real-life versions of apps featured in seasons three episodes "Nosedive" and "Hang the DJ," in the form of RateMe.Social and Coach.Dating. Users can actually engage these apps and, while they pretty quickly redirect users to Netflix's page for *Black Mirror*, they are another way in which Brooker and Jones create meta-texts that complicate a passive viewing experience for post-Trump *Black Mirror* viewers.

Other 2017 advertisements similarly push at boundaries and force viewers to engage in uncomfortable ways. In Turkey, an account named "Iamwaldo" began sending users direct messages reading "We know what you're up to. Watch and see what we will do." Like the ads targeting ad blockers, these posts were incredibly successful in generating discourse about their legality and ethics. Finally, in a video titled "*Black Mirror*: Happy New Year," posted to Youtube on December 29, 2017, they present clips from the series alongside real and staged news stories, in an attempt to highlight the series' general prescience regarding technological advances and their impact on contemporary society. Like the Netflix Vista advertisement, here again viewers are being asked to navigate complicated questions about authorship and messaging, with the interweaving of real-world and fictional artifacts making for a complicated viewing experience.

It's unclear the extent to which Brooker and Jones are directly involved in the advertisements since Netflix acquired rights to the series, but the approach of these meta-texts echoes the increasingly provocative episodes themselves, as they confront and engage viewers in uncomfortable ways. The proper way to engage these texts is active response because they violate spaces and cross boundaries usually respected by companies advertising a product they wish viewers to consume. In his discussion of the "iamwaldo" ad stunt, Rhett Jones argues that it "illustrates the precarious nature of a tech giant getting in on the dystopian themes that *Black Mirror* attempts to warn the public about. The show started out on the BBC, a publicly funded television network. Its move to Netflix, a private media company with world domination on its mind, gives *Black Mirror* an extra hint of subversive mischief."[22] Although the ethics of the ad are certainly debatable, what is undeniable is the success of these marketing techniques in keeping the series in the public eye as a vocal source of concern about the direction of contemporary political, technological, and social discourse. Ultimately, the various paratexts surrounding *Black Mirror* have evolved along with episodes themselves, to create a fandom that is actively engaged in reading, deciphering, and culture jamming before, during, and after the viewing experience.

Throughout seasons three and four of *Black Mirror*, creators Brooker and Jones alter their original plan to present distinct dystopian visions, a *Twilight Zone*-inspired look at how technology can make good people do terrible things. They have demonstrated this shift both within the episodes—through a marked shift in tone and perspective, through multiple types of Easter eggs, and through the building of a vast, connected, hyperdiegetic world—and in the various paratexts surrounding those episodes, through their interview responses and through confrontational advertisements. As a result, they are creating an active fandom willing to engage their series in ways beyond the traditional viewing experience. By moving away from the bleak nihilism of the first two seasons and the positioning of the viewer alongside the sympathetic male narcissists causing the problems, toward female protagonists who fight back and escape from their situations, they suggest a path forward for viewers frustrated with the many ways in which the real world is beginning to resemble the dystopian visions presented in their black mirrors.

NOTES

1. Regarding Trump's election, Brooker says: "As soon as Trump was running for the Republican candidacy I remember thinking he is going to win and he will become president. . . . I thought people would vote for him because he is a vandal and enough people want to throw a brick through a window, just because. So it felt to me there was a grim inevitability to all the stages" in Alastair Campbell, "Charlie Brooker on *Black Mirror* Season 4: 'It's like We Are Curating a Little Film Festival'," *GQ*. December 29, 2017. Accessed http://www.gq-magazine.co.uk/article/charlie-brooker-interview-black-mirror-season-4 on September 7, 2018.

2. Regarding this episode, Brooker says: "At the time, I thought that was one episode that I didn't really nail, didn't get the stakes right. But if you look at that now, it's really quite terrifying. . . . It's more prescient than I realized. He's an anti-politics candidate who's raucous and defensive, and that's all he is, and he offers nothing. He insults everyone and they lap it up because they're so sick of the status quo. And then you look at Trump," in "Charlie Brooker's 2016 Wipe HD," filmed [December 2016]. Youtube video, 1:00:16, posted [January 2017], https://www.youtube.com/watch?v=mN9SiMLM3nw.

3. Morgan Jeffery, "Black Mirror S4 'explicitly' Confirms Shared Universe," Digital Spy, December 21, 2017. Accessed http://www.digitalspy.com/tv/black-mirror/news/a845932/black-mirror-shared-universe-confirmed-Easter-eggs/ on September 7, 2018.

4. Although every episode of the first two seasons extends into the credits in one way or another, none of the Netflix episodes do. Netflix, in fact, discourages us from even viewing the closing credits by ushering the next episode in within seconds of the cut to black.

5. Michael D. Gordin, Helen Tilley, and Gyan Prakash, introduction to *Utopia/Dystopia: Conditions of Historical Possibility* (Princeton: Princeton University Press, 2010), 2.

6. Gerard Gilbert, "Without Annabel Jones, Black Mirror Wouldn't Exist," INews. December 28, 2017. Accessed https://inews.co.uk/culture/television/without-annabel-jones-black-mirror-wouldnt-exist/ on September 7, 2018.

7. James Brassett and Alex Sutton. "British Satire, Everyday Politics: Chris Morris, Armando Iannucci and Charlie Brooker," *The British Journal of Politics and International Relations* 19, no. 2 (March 17, 2017), 259.

8. Gordin, Tilley, and Prakash, Introduction, 2.

9. Giles Harvey. "The Speculative Dread of *Black Mirror*," *The New Yorker*, June 19, 2017. Accessed https://www.newyorker.com/magazine/2016/11/28/the-speculative-dread-of-black-mirror on September 7, 2018.

10. James Hibberd, "*Black Mirror* Season 4, Your Burning Questions Answered," EW.com, January 2, 2018. Accessed https://ew.com/tv/2018/01/02/black-mirror-season-4-interviews/ on September 7, 2018.

11. When asked what "The National Anthem" would look like with Trump in the position of the Prime Minister forced to have sex with a pig: "If that was Trump, he'd say, 'Show me the pig! I'm gonna make that pig come!' . . . . And then, as it was happening, he'd be shouting, 'This isn't happening! This never happened and you all know it didn't happen!'" (Hibberd).

12. Charlie Brooker, "Charlie Brooker's 2016 Wipe HD," filmed [December 2016]. These comments are from Brooker's annual year-in-review comedy show.

13. Jonathan Gray, Cornell Sandvoss, and C. Lee Harrington, introduction to *Fandom, Second Edition: Identities and Communities in a Mediated World* (New York: New York University Press, 2017), 12.

14. Charlie Brooker. "Charlie Brooker: The Dark Side of Our Gadget Addiction," *The Guardian*, December 1, 2011.

15. Sean Fitz-Gerald, "*Black Mirror* Creator Charlie Brooker Explains Season 3 and Reveals Easter Eggs," *Thrillist*, October 23, 2016. Accessed https://www.thrillist.com/entertainment/nation/black-mirror-netflix-season-3-charlie-brooker-interview on September 7, 2018.

16. Jeffery, "*Black Mirror* S4."

17. Hills, Matt. *Fan Cultures* (New York: Routledge, 2002), 137.

18. Two excellent essays, by Hari Ziyard and Ashley Nkadi, discuss the episode's complicated racial dynamics. In short, Nish's blackness speaks directly to the history of the United States commodifying black pain, and her overcoming her white oppressor is particularly significant. Additionally, the racial component of the episode links it to Trump and his long history of racism and racist dog-whistling. See Hari Ziyad, "Black Mirror's 'Black Museum': The Slave Revolt Fantasy Hollywood Never Intended to Make?" *The Black Youth Project*, January 3, 2018. Accessedhttps://blackyouthproject.com/black-mirrors-black-museum-slave-revolt-fantasy-hollywood-never-intended-make/on September 10, 2018, and Ashley Nkadi, "Black Mirror: 'Black Museum' Reckons with America's History of Commodifying Black Pain," *The Root*, January 9, 2018. Accessed https://www.theroot.com/black-mirror-black-museum-reckons-with-america-s-histo-1821814356 on September 10, 2018.

19. Henry Jenkins. *Fans, Bloggers, and Gamers: Exploring Participatory Culture* (New York: New York University Press, 2006), 147.

20. Mark Dery. ""Culture Jamming: Hacking, Slashing, and Sniping in the Empire of Signs," in *Culture Jamming: Activism and the Art of Cultural Resistance*, ed. Marilyn DeLaure and Moritz Fink (New York: New York University Press, 2017), 46.

21. Netflix, "Introducting Netflix Vista," YouTube video, 2:11, posted [November 2016].

22. He concludes that: "Its creators can feel like they're kind of getting away with something. But when the big corporate entity attempts to get in on the satire, it leaves a bad aftertaste."

Chapter Twelve

Through the Eyes of the Wardens

Rethinking Judge Dredd *in the Age of Trump*

Tom Shapira

It is a striking image. A group of heavily armed men, all wearing bulky and sinister-looking black armor, advance upon the center of power of the US government; flames erupt in the background as the symbol of democracy is destroyed; and the following words are uttered: "Take the White House!"[1]

The destruction, or takeover, of the White House by hostile forces has long been a focal point of many fantastic texts, a signifier that the grimmest had occurred. In *Independence Day* (1996), the building is destroyed by an alien vessel; in *G.I. Joe: Retaliation* (2013) the flag of terrorist organization Cobra flies over the White House to signify a stealth-takeover of the country is complete; in the Avengers comic book storyline, *The Kang Dynasty* (2001–2002), the entire city of Washington is leveled by futuristic invaders with the president escaping from the White House in the last second.

All these images provoke a scene of horror. However, in *Judge Dredd: Origins* the scene carries a different tone. The visuals are clear, the attackers are dressed in black armor that conceals their faces and erases their individuality, like the disposable Storm Troopers who populate the various *Star Wars* movies, existing simply to provide killable bodies for our heroes. But by the time we see these attackers, the story has taken a more ambiguous turn: The Judges, the invading forces, are a proto-militarist, brutalist police force who treat all civilians as potential criminals who cannot be trusted to govern themselves. The White House they attack is under the control of fictional president, "Bad" Bob Booth, a violent lunatic who cheated his way into the presidency, the first person to launch the nuclear attack that started the atomic wars. Thus, the taking of the White House becomes an event colored in shades of grey—something that feels both necessary and wrong at the same time.

Created in 1977, for publication in a then fledgling British comics anthology, *2000AD*, *Judge Dredd* is the story of the United States in the twenty-second century. In the world after the atomic wars, surviving humans are crowded into gigantic Mega Cities, hosting hundreds of millions each, with most of the land outside the walls being given up as irradiated wastelands. To preserve order, regular police forces and the entire system of justice have been replaced by "judges," armored lawmen given full authority to arrest, judge and punish criminals on the spot, as quickly and as harshly as possible. In this world, the idea of "democracy" is something between heresy and a crime, and the Judges are in full control of city life, the citizens having long ago relinquished their rights in the name of security. From these humble beginnings—just one strip among many in a sea of British comic anthologies—arose one of the greatest icons of modern comics: *Judge Dredd* is still in constant weekly publication more than forty years later, and the strip has many spin-offs and adaptations for various media (from novels to computer games to cinema).

The leading question throughout the *Origins* storyline, and indeed throughout much of *Judge Dredd* in general, is at what point is one willing to renounce essential freedoms for the sake of safety. "Those who would give up essential Liberty, to purchase a little temporary Safety, deserve neither Liberty nor Safety" is one of those long-held maxims in the United States; something that is easy to believe in the abstract but is quite difficult to adhere to when one's security is truly threatened. Reading the story for the first time in 2013, I found it easy to be repulsed by the Judges' ascendency to power; no matter how terrible Booth was, their ascension still signified the death of democracy. They offer people a sense of security, but for the price of "every essential freedom."

Then comes the year 2016 and suddenly that primal image, "Take the White House!" takes on a different meaning. Suddenly there sits a man who seems impervious not only to the conventions of the rule of law but to any norms at all. With news in the first few weeks of heated arguments between leaders of formerly allied states, with the president of the United States boasting online and warning others of possible nuclear retaliation, the storyline of *Judge Dredd* seemed to carry new relevance.

The *Judge Dredd* comic strip was created in the 1970s, when the Cold War was still threatening to go hot, by people who knew for a fact that there was a chance that they could all die at the push of a button and that the buttons were not necessarily given to the most rational and humane individuals. Though futuristic in setting, the first strip takes place in the year 2099 and advances in comic book time with each year in the real world, *Judge Dredd* still reflected these fears. The fear of nuclear conflict reached its seeming zenith in the 1982 storyline, *The Apocalypse War*, which saw East Meg One (the futuristic descendent of the Soviet Union) attacking Mega City One (its US counterpart) with nuclear missiles before occupying it. East Meg One killed half the population of Mega City One, more than four hundred million people, before being annihilated in turn by Judge Dredd himself who turned their own arsenal against them. After this stark moment, one which would forever shape the strip itself, innumerable plots arose as various factions attempted revenge against Dredd for this act of genocide, and it left its impact on readers as well. Comics writer Garth Ennis, who was twelve years old when the story came out and would later become a regular contributor to the strip, summed it up:

> Even now I don't know if Dredd was right or if he was wrong. It was the only way to win, to avoid the further slaughter and enslavement of his own people—but it was genocide. It was moral courage on an almost unimaginable level—but it was appalling. In the end, it was a dilemma not unlike those faced by a number of good and bad men in our own history, and if I had to sum it up in one line, I'd say this: what are you prepared to do when there isn't any easy way out?[2]

This was a comic book about consequences, about actions and reactions. US -style superhero comics are written more in terms of myth than science fiction, with characters forced to forever assume the same architypes. In these stories crisis moments like the end of *The Apocalypse War* would be rewritten to allow new writers to avoid dealing with their implications. There is no such escape for Judge Dredd; his history remains fixed; and he must always carry the weight. Many stories were written either about survivors seeking revenge or about Dredd himself coming slowly to terms with what he has wrought—the past cannot be changed; it must be dealt with.

Yet Dredd's past, the pre-strip history, itself was something to be mostly avoided. The first story takes place in medias res, with the judges' system already in place for decades and Dredd himself as a hardened and celebrated veteran. For the first thirty years of the strip information came in short drips: how the world fell into the first nuclear wars, how the judges took over the Mega Cities that were left of the old world, how Dredd was part of a cloning program to create the ultimate judges. Stories introduced back matter if relevant to the plots in the present but never simply indulged in it for its own sake. *Origins* changed this unofficial policy: it went back to the past of its characters to show the reader how easy it is to give in to despair (both personal and national) and engages with the way (mostly) US media taught us to expect a savior and to refuse to question him.

AN AMERICAN (SUPER) HERO

In the months leading up to the 2016 U.S. election, the FBI seemed to take the antagonist's role in the left-wing narrative: a role that was cemented when then head of the FBI, James Comey, announced the reopening of the Hillary Clinton e-mail investigation just days before the ballot casting began.[3] The scandal, which involved the possible misuse of personal e-mail servers to conduct government business, dogged the Hillary campaign from day one, and its reopening was considered by many to be the final push that cost her some critical votes—even though the investigation ceased on November 6 with Comey announcing to Congress that the investigation was closed without criminal charges.

After the 2016 election, Comey found himself suddenly supported by the same people who despised him just short months before, as the FBI announced an investigation into a possible collusion between the Trump campaign and various Russian nationals with suspicion of election tampering. It was, however, another former FBI head, Robert Mueller, who served before Comey, who found himself in a new starring role as the possible savior of the Republic.

The hosts of popular late night comedy TV shows, such as Stephen Colbert of *The Late Show*, made regular use of Mueller as a crusading fighter for justice, standing up to the immerse powers of a corrupt presidency. On October 31, 2017, Colbert opened a pre-holiday monologue with "it's almost Halloween, and this year it's going to be super-spooky—for Donald Trump."[4] A June 16th segment from the same year was titled "Robert Mueller's Dream Team Is Giving Trump Nightmares." He referred to Mueller as nothing less than Batman[5] —directly utilizing the comic book–inspired images of super teams such as The Avengers or the Justice League of America taking on another evil overlord.

The July 3, 2017 issue of *Time* magazine used Mueller on the cover: a stark black-and-white-tinted image with the man looking directly at the reader with a hint of a smile (he knows something neither we, nor Trump, know) captioned as "The Lie Detector." It was as fine a sobriquet as that of any caped crusader: Batman is "The Dark Knight," Superman is "The Man of Steel," Captain America is "The Sentinel of Liberty," and Robert Mueller is "The Lie Detector."

The Internet, as expected, took on the idea of Mueller as a superhero. For a short while, images of Mueller from his time as a soldier were contrasted with those of Donald Trump who avoided the draft during the Vietnam War. One was awarded a bronze star and a purple heart for his service, the other was "Cadet Bone Spurs"—a name given to Trump by US senator and former Lieutenant Colonel Tammy Duckworth, a name alluding to the seemingly unmanly manner by which Trump avoided the service.[6]

Thus, arose an image of Mueller as the one who would cure the nation's ills. Despite knowing full well that such investigations can take months and even years, TV hosts, newspaper columnists, and Internet commenters were all begging him to work faster to produce the results needed to hunt down the liars and traitors and stop them with the full force of law; in short: "Take the White House!"

A CBS news survey, from July 29, 2018, found that Democrats had more trust in both the FBI and US Intelligence Services than did Republicans.[7] After years during which the opposite was true, with both the failure of intelligence before the second Iraq War and growing publication of law-enforcement mistreatment of African Americans and other minorities (most of whom belonging to groups that traditionally voted for the Democratic Party), there seemed to be rising support for law enforcement—as long as it led the fight against Trump.

COWBOYS AND INDIANS

The celebration of Mueller brings to mind an old tradition in US fiction, made especially popular and knowable in the cinema of the 1970s but with roots all the way back to the foundation of the nation. That is the solitary justice figure, bucking the rules and trends of the system, going out to enforce his own will upon the world: he "does what it takes" by "any means necessary." He is the lone cowboy, the superhero, the renegade cop on the streets. It is his job to save civilization, which he does by ignoring the same rules that hold that civilization together: "[Batman] genuinely desires a safer social order in which both the individual and communal values can flourish. Yet in the service of these goals, he is willing not only to commit crimes, but also to wield authoritarian power, and his sympathies for the innocent are much less evident than his determination to prevent wrongdoing (other than his own)."[8]

In their *American Monomyth* authors Robert Jewett and John Shelton Lawrence claim the foundational pop-culture idea behind much US fiction is characterized as a mix between sexless puritanism and salvation by force of arms. They describe the prototypical male US heroes of pop culture thusly: "[T]hey are selfless, sexually unattached, and committed to justice though not to the restraints of due process."[9] It is quite easy to see the characteristics they describe in Mueller—not so much the man himself but the public image that has been fashioned around him. To those hoping for him to bring down Trump he is Paul Kreasy; he is The Lone Ranger; he is Harry Callahan.

These are also the qualities of Judge Dredd, in whom these qualities are taken to the nth degree and beyond. Dredd is not merely "selfless." He has no personal life outside of serving the law (which he does more than twenty-three hours per day, thanks to a futuristic sleep machine). He is not just "sexless." By law the judges are forbidden from any type of personal liaison. And as for being "committed to justice without the constraint of due process," as Dredd's oft-used catch phrase "I am the law" shows, there is hardly any authority that can oppose him. This makes him not into a man, but into something a hair's-breadth away from a machine (indeed, his character greatly influenced the creators of the cyborg protagonist of the film *Robocop*[10]).

In the end of the film *Dirty Harry*, the protagonist, tough-as-nails cop Harry Callahan, having disposed of his enemy, the serial killer Scorpio, stands gazing over a lake before tossing his badge into it. Finding it impossible to square his own sense of morality with due process, Harry, who went against direct orders in confronting the killer, quits the force. Writing of the film, critic Paulina Kael noted that "it's about a right-wing fantasy of that police force as a group helplessly emasculated by unrealistic liberals. The conceit of this movie is that for one brief, glorious period the police have a realist in their midst—and drive him out."[11] Calling it a "deeply immoral movie," Kael spends the review on the one-sided presentation of the film which has no room for shades of grey—only the moral absolutism of the gun.

One could have pointed to the final scene as at least an attempt at moral ambiguity: does Callahan reject the badge or feel that he is no longer worthy of wearing it? But the siren call of big box-office numbers was impossible to ignore and Harry Callahan returned to a series of financially successful sequels, which either ignore the last minute of the first film or invent an alternative continuation to it in which Harry decides to wade into water and reclaim his badge. Whatever the case may be, the sequels play within the same murky milieu of other post-1960s action films, which Kael identified in her review. In that type of film the main problem of US policing is that the cops are too softhearted and too hidebound by various regulations to actually deal with the violent criminals who infect the streets.

In *The American Monomyth*, the authors note that the process of turning a novel into a film, of translating it into the language of the mass medium, is also the process by which meaning is subtracted and ideas are simplified. Their main subject of study is the 1974 film *Death Wish*, an adaptation of the 1972 novel of the same name by Brian Garfield. The film was a contemporary of *Dirty Harry* not only in terms of release time but also in terms of success (spawning several sequels) and place in the US cultural milieu:

> [*Death Wish*] is archetypical in the way that is adapts the dominant American myth of the western vigilante to the modern urban situation. Moreover, the transformation of Brian Garfield's novel *Death Wish* into this monomythic film points towards an equally significant process. It indicates how a traditional paradigm becomes a mythic prism through which both the story and the audience response are refracted, through a golden aura onto the path of violence.[12]

Though the hero of *Death Wish* is a citizen instead of a renegade cop, the basic themes are similar—one man must rise above to enforce justice when society is unwilling to defend itself. In an interview, Garfield, said: "The point of the novel *Death Wish* is that vigilantism is an attractive fantasy but it only makes things worse in reality. By the end of the novel, the character (Paul) is gunning down unarmed teenagers because he doesn't like their looks."[13] The fundamental point of the story was changed when it moved to the big screen: vigilantism was now seen as an untarnished public good and the only people objecting to it are the criminals being killed or the police who are being "shown up" by a more efficient form of justice.

It is interesting to note that, like the original novel upon which the *Death Wish* film is based, the *Judge Dredd* comics also received a cinematic adaptation from Hollywood that is noted among fans of the original for the way it perverted the messaging of the source material. The 1995, US-produced *Judge Dredd* movie dispensed with any notions that judges are anything but heroic. Sylvester Stallone, one of the biggest action stars in the United States at the time, was cast as the lead figure. Stallone was, at this point, known for playing unabashed heroes and so the grey morality that is at the center of the comics was ignored, continuing a trend for Stallone that began with the transformation of the novel *First Blood* into the jingoistic film series *Rambo* (in which the hero is allowed to go back to Vietnam and win the war single-handedly). His expensive visage was also deemed wasted if the public could not gaze upon it and so the character of Judge Dredd, infamously a faceless representation of impersonal law-keeping (never once in the comics have we seen his face), quickly removed his helmet and spent most of the film with the star's multimillion-dollar face clear to the audience.

There is a flattening effect involved in mass culture: complex social situations, the poverty, racism, and other society-wide ailments that can often lead to crime, are ignored in favor of morally simplified stories of good and evil. This is nothing new. The authors of *The American Monomyth* believe the yearning for this type of hero predates the mass media of television and cinema (though they certainly spread it more efficiently) and has its roots in the puritan ideals that led to the foundation of the nation. This notion is also explored in Pamela Haag's book, *The Gunning of America*, a chapter of which is dedicated to the methods various gun companies have used to publicize the efficiency of their products.

Taking on legends and rumors about the actions of real-life lawmen and gunslingers and amplifying them via the US version of the British penny dreadful—the dime novel: "One dime-novelist writer recalled that in a 'little den on the upper floor' of the 'worm-eaten old building' of Publisher Beadle & Adams, he would 'grind out dime novels day after day with the steadiness of a machine.'"[14] Beadle & Adams published 3,512 novels over the course of a single year, most of which follow the same narrative thrust of violent gunplay solving the problems of civilization. Edmund Pearson, who studied the pulps, summed them up thusly: “In their pages, during the next four decades, tons of gunpowder were to be burned; human blood was to flow in rivers; and the list of dead men was to mount to the sky. They dealt in violent action, in sudden death and its terrors.”[15]

With these novels, US gun companies were mass producing not only guns but also the stories that show why guns were necessary—and how they could be wielded by “good men,” in the same way Excalibur was wielded by King Arthur. Harry Callahan, waving his .44 Magnum, which he dubs “the most powerful handgun in the world” in much as the same manner as a mythic hero might describe the name and history of his sword, signifies the same things King Arthur does: lawlessness abounds, and only one person may restore it by bringing his own law.

Judge Dredd’s own handgun might not be as personalized, but his “lawgiver,” a futuristic pistol capable of firing different kinds of ammunition and booby-trapped so that only a judge may wield it (just as Excalibur could only be wielded by the rightful king of Britain), gets the same fetishized treatment as Harry Callahan’s cannon. Character designer Carlos Ezquerra recalls thinking up the lawgiver: “I wanted it to be a big, long handgun, something that gets noticed and instantly commands respect.”[16]

The idea of a “good man with a gun,” endlessly used by representatives of the National Rifle Association (NRA) whenever a mass shooting event galvanizes anti-gun legislation, remains vital for these types of stories: the man might appear “bad” to other civilized folks, who by their nature renounce violence and do not understand the necessity of it, but he saves them nonetheless. This notion is rooted in real-life cases as well; no less of an authority than future US President Theodore Roosevelt explained how important the gun slingers of his time had been to expansion of the country: “The ‘bad men,’ or professional fighters and man-killers, are of a different stamp [from regular criminals], quite a number of them being, according to their light, perfectly honest. These are the men who do most of the killing in frontier communities; yet it is a noteworthy fact that the men who are killed generally deserve their fate.”[17]

John Sanders, one of the initial managing publishers of *2000AD*, explained the appeal of Judge Dredd in similar terms: “He could be as violent as hell and no one could say a thing because his victims were hideous people who didn’t deserve to be alive.”[18] It’s important to remember that *2000AD* came right on the heels of *Action*—another comics magazine containing many of the same creators, which was censored, and then pretty much cancelled, due to its violent content. Sanders’s point was that the success and long shelf-life of Judge Dredd showed that the protest of public groups was less about the violence itself than about who was perpetrating it.

Though the tales of these gun-wielding mavericks, in films, comics, and pulps, are rooted in the real world, often presented in a "gritty" type of storytelling for added verisimilitude, they are based on fantasy as strong as that of any superhero. Dirty Harry will never shoot a fleeing suspect who turns out to have been an innocent bystander, nor will the car chases of detective Popeye Doyle (*The French Connection*) end up with the mass of injuries one would expect from a speeding car going through a busy thoroughfare unheeded. Writing for *The Comics Journal*, critic Tegan O'Neill recognizes that the basic premise of vigilante characters like The Punisher is just as fantastic as that behind Superman:

> The Punisher's great super power, and it is a super power, is that he never misses. He's never wrong. He never shoots a bystander by accident. He never mistakenly blows up a school bus full of kids. And that's why he can exist as an absolute exception, because the premise—that he is the world's greatest mass murderer, but only ever kills people who completely and unambiguously deserve it—is as much gossamer as a man from Krypton who can leap tall buildings in a single bound.[19]

That is the basic illusion: the authority that can never be wrong, and thus should not be bound by regulations. In defending his character, actor Clint Eastwood later claimed in an interview that "Harry is a fantasy character. Nobody does what Harry does."[20] This is wrong. Many cops do what Harry does; that is, ignore regulations and take the law into their own hands. But when real cops do it the result is often harm to innocents rather than to guilty people, evidence is planted, violence is delivered to already surrendered suspects, then hidden, etc. Cops in the real world do not enjoy the defense of narrative convenience.

It is here that we return to *Judge Dredd*, a character whose creation was inspired by Dirty Harry and his ilk, as many British characters at the time were riffs on popular US cinema.[21] *Jaws* became *Hookjaw* and *The Dirty Dozen* was transformed into *The Rat Pack*. *Judge Dredd*, however, ended up being a deconstruction of the idea rather than a repurposing of it. The strength of *Judge Dredd*, as a concept, is that it forces the reader to contend with the notion of a cowboy-cop type who might come after them. In Judge Dredd's eyes, in the eyes of most of the judges, all citizens are criminals just waiting to be discovered; the streets are a battleground.

Dredd has all the qualities that we admire in Harry Callahan: he is relentless, honorable (in his own twisted way) and extremely capable; but the fictional shield that allows Harry to only target "bad guys" has been dropped. Dredd does kill "people who deserve it," but he also puts away the people who usually cheer on such antics, the middle-class crowd whose fears of savage criminals lurking at every corner are stoked by the likes of *Death Wish*. The seminal *Judge Dredd* story, "Letter from a Democrat," features a team of judges coldly blasting away at the future version of a suburban housewife, white, well-groomed and seemingly middle class, for daring to hijack a TV broadcast for a pro-democracy group. After this he goes to her house and berates her law-abiding husband and children lest they think of following her path: "Let that be a lesson to you, citizen. Democracy's not for the people."[22] This moment blasts away at the illusion that you would want someone like Harry Callahan enforcing laws with the point of a gun—it's easy to enjoy that thought until the gun is pointed at you. Thanks to the strict continuity of the strip this moment cannot be undone—Dredd will always be the man who killed a mother and then shouted at her grieving children.

It is vital, in storytelling terms, that Dredd is a not a villain figure; he is good at his job, he genuinely defends his city and the world from various apocalyptic threats. To make Dredd a villain would be the easy choice. It would make the work no different than hundreds of other pieces of dystopic fiction with nameless, faceless storm troopers enforcing an evil order which the reader and character can easily oppose. John Wagner and Carlos Ezquerra's vision of that character is what Douglas Wolk called a "useful monster"[23] : we need him to make these tough choices—but only because we set up the social conditions that demand his type.

Writing in *The Nation* magazine Chase Mader explored the way twenty-first-century US policing encroaches more and more into fields once left to civilian administration, making the futuristic world of Judge Dredd closer to reality every day: "Wall-to-wall criminal law encroaches ever more on everyday life as police power is applied in ways that would have been unthinkable just a generation ago."[24] If all problems, from Internet piracy to childhood misbehavior, are thought about in terms of crimes, then the solution to all of these problems must involve the police—a force that becomes ever more militarized. Mader's words seem to echo those of Dredd himself. In a story published more than twenty years earlier, the judge began to develop doubts about the nature of existence and work. Talking to a rookie on the street he asks "[Do you know] that we keep a greater proportion of our citizens locked away than any other Mega City on this Earth?"[25]

Radley Balko's *The Rise of the Warrior Cop* explores the transformation of police in the United States, and how the use of SWAT teams became a more common response to possible threats, especially after 9/11 budget changes allocated anti-terrorism equipment and training even in the rural small-town departments. An article in *The New Yorker* mentioned how "local governments have received approximately thirty-four billion dollars in grants from the Department of Homeland Security to buy their own military equipment from private suppliers."[26] In 2013 the legislators of Jefferson County, New York (population 120,000), authorized the deployment of a twenty-ton Mine Resistant Ambush Protected vehicle—a tool meant for the field of battle now patrolled the streets of a county that experienced, in the same year, a total of 122 "violent felonies."[27]

When all you have is a hammer, everything starts to look like a nail. And when your police force has a bunch of scary tactical uniforms and weapons meant for counterinsurgency, they might soon be tempted to use them—even if the targets are local drunks and small-time drug dealers. In fact, the SWAT teams, with their body- and face-concealing uniforms, their quick-on-the-trigger methodology and reputation for martial prowess evoke exactly the kind of feeling of judges in *Judge Dredd*. SWAT teams are not meant to be approachable or communal, they are meant to scare. In his book, Balko quotes an officer who was aghast at latest trends in policing: "[Officer] Pastore told the *New York Times* that outfitting cops in battle garb 'feeds a mind-set that you're not a police officer serving a community, you're a soldier at war. I had some tough-guy cops in my department pushing for bigger and more hardware.'"[28] This account brings to mind a moment from the celebrated story *Judge Dredd: America* in which a young child gives her view on the judges: "Adults, they'd tell us the Judges were there for our good, to protect and make our streets safe. But we'd hear the tremor in their voices when they talked about them and see their furtive expressions whenever a judge caught their eye—and we'd know they were afraid."[29]

Fear response is good if you imagine the cop confronting a violent offender bent on committing assault, but most of police duty involves nonviolent crimes. Dirty Harry is only necessary in world fiction because said fiction, the US monomyth, imagines a reality in which violence lurks behind every corner. You would not want to deal with Dirty Harry if you were simply looking for guidance on the street, or if he caught you committing jaywalking. The uniqueness of *Judge Dredd* is that it shows the protagonist dealing both with violent crime and with everyday misdemeanors—and he deals with both with the same degree of harshness: because he is a hammer and the citizens are nails.

FROM THE OTHER SIDE

Discussing the ethos of the *Judge Dredd* stories writer Josie Campbell noted that they offer a rarely seen angle on dystopian science fiction stories: "[Judge Dredd is] a dystopia told from the position of power. That's not something you see in most science fiction. Dystopias are things to rebel against (*Hunger Games*, *Star Wars*) or escape (*Logan's Run*, *Fahrenheit 451*) or tragically perish from (*1984*, *Brave New World*). In these worlds, there are no terrorists, only revolutionaries."[30]

Anti-judge organizations have been part of the strip since early on. Other than the previously mentioned "Letter from a Democrat," stories such as

"Revolution" and "Terror" featured various facets of the pro-democracy movement, from pacifists to nuclear bombers. In 1991 a pair of stories called "The Devil You Know" and "Twilight's Last Gleaming" featured Dredd advocating for a democratic referendum, allowing the citizens of the city, for the first time in their lives, to decide whether they want to live under the boots of the justice system or to abolish it. Given the titles of the stories it is little surprise to learn that the judges "won," mostly by the public being too apathetic to vote. This itself, as Dredd notes, is a choice—a choice against change.

It was easy, before the year 2016, to lambast the choice the citizens of Mega City One made: to declare that one would never surrender essential freedom in the name of security. It was especially easy to left-leaning liberals, the critical crowd to which Paulina Kael and the authors of *The American Monomyth* belong, who did see the theoretical danger posed in stories like *Death Wish* or *Walking Tall*. As long as there had been quasi-fascistic entertainment there were those who warned of it. With the election of Trump, the shoe was suddenly on the other foot.

The Bulletin of the Atomic Scientists, an academic journal that covers threats of a nuclear nature, famously publishes announcements regarding the moving of the "Doomsday Clock"—the closer the clock gets to midnight the closer humanity is to nuclear war (and total destruction). In January 2018, one year into the presidency of Donald Trump, it was announced that the clock is now at two minutes to midnight—the closest it has ever been since the height of the Cold War: "The year just past proved perilous and chaotic. . . . we saw reckless language in the nuclear realm heat up already dangerous situations and re-learned that minimizing evidence-based assessments regarding climate and other global challenges does not lead to better public policies."[31] The Bulletin of the Atomic Scientists might not have named Trump himself but their mentioning of "reckless language" left little doubt as to whom they were referring (Trump being well known, by both supporters and detractors, for his belligerent tone and verbiage).

It is here that *Judge Dredd: Origins* and Mueller collide. The side that for long resisted the ideas behind *The American Monomyth*—that criticized the militarization and violence offered by police forces, that tangled with the FBI and CIA over their hawkish policies—now found itself wholly dependent on exactly that kind of hero for salvation: an authoritarian figure, a straight and narrow professional, stern of gaze and relentless in his task.

There is, more often than not, a large number of people who disagree with a sitting president; who might consider his policies unethical or even criminal. But under US President Donald Trump a large chunk of the left, and apparently a growing chunk on the right as well, seem to feel not simply unrepresented but genuinely unsafe. It is with this notion in mind that a revisit of *Origins* produced a different, and far more radical response, to the image of the burning White House. John Wagner noted the seducing effect of Judge Dredd as an idea: "A man with that kind of power appeals to the bad guy in everyone—and believe me, it's there in everyone, even if it's buried deeply."[32] It is a sober reminder that surrendering to the easy solution is not singularly a "right wing fantasy," in Paulina Kael's terminology.

Writing in the *LA Times* Virginia Heffernan noted that "I know there's a move among liberal women to romanticize Mueller, and make kitsch of him as a savior. That seems wrong; we're a democracy, and any kind of worship too closely mirrors the cult of Trump."[33] Yet, as the article continues, she admits she will fall in line behind him because "[Robert Mueller] belongs to the informal political party I most admire: the disciplined." This is what Judge Dredd is, not a man you like, not a man you love, but a man you admire; you admire him for all of the right qualities and thus forgive all the bad ones. He even sounds the same: "I stand four-square for justice. I stand for discipline, good order and the rigid application of the law[.]"[34]

Particularly because everyone's favorite fantasy is being the underdog, the lone rebel fighting against superior forces, even in films like *Dirty Harry*, in which the hero is a cop with the theoretical backing of an entire system hunting down a single man, reality must be reimagined so that the system is against him, that he goes at it alone. Judge Dredd neutralizes this fantasy by giving us the world not through the eyes of the rebels but through the eyes of the wardens: Dredd is not only physically powerful but socially powerful as well, able to mobilize large forces and operate with little to no boundaries on his authority.

As *Origins* closes, Judge Dredd gets to have a final conversation with his "father" (the man from whom he was cloned) who was also the creator of the judges' system. As the old man nears death, he delivers one final line: "it was never meant to . . . be forever, Joe. We created a monster—we, us, we're the monster!"[35]

President Booth ended up causing even more harm than he intended—by his actions the judges took power, by his actions they adopted the justifications to safeguard the people from their own mistakes; for if they allowed someone like him to govern, then surely, they did not possess the proper ability to govern themselves.

Origins, and *Judge Dredd* in general, is not a narrative about Donald Trump: it is narrative about social reactions to a Trump-like figure. It is not about the damage a figure like this causes by his actions but about the damage he might cause when citizens do not take action to stop him and about the way he corrupts even beyond his own end.

NOTES

1. John Wagner and Carlos Ezquerra, *Judge Dredd: Origins* (London, England: Hachette. 2015).

2. Garth Ennis, "When 2000AD was the Future," *Bleeding Cool,* August 24, 2009. Accessed https://www.bleedingcool.com/2009/08/24/garth-ennis-when-2000ad-was-the-future/ on August 14, 2018.

3. Stephen Dinan, "FBI reopens Clinton email investigation," *Washington Times*, October 28, 2016. Accessed https://www.washingtontimes.com/news/2016/oct/28/james-comey-fbi-director-reopens-clinton-email-inv/ on August 15, 2018,=.

4. "'Tis the Season for Treason: a Very Mueller Christmas," *The Late Show*, hosted by Stephen Colbert, directed by Jim Hoskinson, written by Jay Katsir and Opus Moreschi, June 16, 2017. Accessed https://www.youtube.com/watch?v=ZQc5yNUyLvc on August 1, 2018.

5. "Robert Mueller's Dream Team is Giving Trump Nightmares," *The Late Show*, hosted by Stephen Colbert, directed by Jim Hoskinson, written by Jay Katsir and Opus Moreschi, June 16, 2017. Accessed https://www.youtube.com/watch?v=ZQc5yNUyLvc August 1, 2018.

6. Maegan Vazquez. "Duckworth calls out 'Cadet Bone Spurs' after Trump's 'treasonous' remark," *CNN.com*, February 6, 2018. Accessed https://edition.cnn.com/2018/02/06/politics/tammy-duckworth-cadet-bone-spurs/index.html on August 12, 2018.

7. Anthony Salvanto et al., "Americans wary of Trump tariffs' impact, but support plan to aid farmers," *CBS News*, July 29, 2018. Accessible at https://www.cbsnews.com/news/americans-wary-of-trump-tariffs-impact-but-support-plan-to-aid-farmers-cbs-poll/.

8. Christopher Pizzino. *Arresting Development* (Austin: University of Texas Press, 2016), 83.

9. Robert Jewett and John Shelton Lawrence. *The American Monomyth* (Garden City, NY: Anchor Press, 1977), 44.

10. Sven Gerrets, "Terug naar Kuifje: een interview met Paul Verhoeven," *Xi Online*, August 6, 2002. Accessed https://web.archive.org/web/20020806134046/http://www.xi-online.nl/feature/28 on August 12, 2018.

11. Paulina Kael, "Dirty Harry: Saint Cop—Review," *The New Yorker*, January 15, 1972. Accessed https://scrapsfromtheloft.com/2017/12/28/dirty-harry-saint-cop-review-by-pauline-kael/ on August 12, 2018.

12. Robert Jewett and John Shelton Lawrence, *The American Monomyth* (Garden City, NY: Anchor Press, 1977), 77.

13. Nicky Turner, "Historian: Interview with Brian Garfield," *PopMatters*, March 4, 2008. Accessed https://www.popmatters.com/historian-interview-with-brian-garfield-2496171202.html on August 12, 2018.

14. Pamela Hagg, *The Gunning of America: Business and the Making of American Gun Culture* [Audio version] (Oregon: Blackstone Audio, 2016).

15. Edmund Pearson, *Dime novels; or, Following an old trail in popular literature* (Boston: Little, Brown and Company, 1929), 5. Accessible at https://www.scribd.com/document/53105910/Pearson-Edmund-Dime-Novels-Or-Following-an-Old-Trail-in-Popular-Literature-1929.

16. Colin M. Jarman and Peter Acton, *Judge Dredd: The Mega-History* (Mackerye End, Harpenden: Lennard Publishing, 1995), 22.

17. Theodore Roosevelt, *Ranch Life and the Hunting Trail*, 1986. Accessed https://www.pbs.org/weta/thewest/resources/archives/seven/w67trmem/w67tr01.htm on August 12, 2018.

18. David Bishop, *Thrill-Power Overload: 2000AD—The First Thirty Years* (Riverside House, Oxford: Rebellion, 2009), 22.

19. Tegan O'Neill, "Jerk City, USA," *The Comics Journal*, February 2, 2018. Accessed http://www.tcj.com/jerk-city-usa/ on August 13, 2018.

20. Paul Smith, *Clint Eastwood: A Cultural Production* (Minneapolis: University of Minnesota Press, 1993), 92.

21. American Comics, *The Rise of the American Comics Artist: Creators and Contexts*, eds. Paul Williams and James Lyones (Mississippi: University of Mississippi Press, 2013), 33.

22. John Wagner, Alan Grant and John Higgins, "Letter from a Democrat," *2000AD #460*, March 8, 1986.
23. Douglas Wolk, "Case Files 16," *Dredd Reckoning*, January 15, 2012. Accessed https://dreddreviews.blogspot.com/2012/01/complete-case-files-16.html on August 13, 2018.
24. Cahse Mader, "Everyone Is a Criminal: On the Over-policing of America," *The Nation*, December 9, 2013. Accessed https://www.thenation.com/article/everyone-criminal-over-policing-america/ on August 10, 2018.
25. John Wagner, Will Simpson, and Jeff Anderson, "Tale of the Dead Man," *Judge Dredd: The Complete Case Files* 14 (Riverside House, Osney Mead, Oxford: Rebellion, 2013), 3–51.
26. Dexter Filkins, "'Do Not Resist' and the Crisis of Police Militarization," *The New Yorker*, May 13, 2016. Accessed https://www.newyorker.com/news/news-desk/do-not-resist-and-the-crisis-of-police-militarization on August 11, 2018.
27. *Division of Criminal Justice Services*, "Adult Arrests: 2008–2017," New York State. Accessed http://www.criminaljustice.ny.gov/crimnet/ojsa/arrests/Jefferson.pdf on August 10, 2018.
28. Radley Balko, *Rise of the Warrior Cop* [Audio version] (Oregon: Blackstone Audio, 2013).
29. John Wagner and Colin McNeil, *Judge Dredd: America* (Jordan House, London: Hachette Partworks Ltd., 2015).
30. Josie Campbell, "Total War," *Dredd Reckoning*, November 11, 2012. Accessed http://dreddreviews.blogspot.com/2012/11/total-war.html on August 2, 2018.
31. Kiona N. Smith, "What is the Doomsday Clock," *Forbes*, January 25, 2018. Accessed https://www.forbes.com/sites/kionasmith/2018/01/25/what-is-the-doomsday-clock/#3f7b85a8618a on August 1, 2018.
32. Colin M. Jarman and Peter Acton, *Judge Dredd: The Mega-History* (Mackerye End, Harpenden: Lennard Publishing, 1995), 17.
33. Virginia Heffernan, "How Donald Trump made me love privileged men," *LA Times*, August 19, 2018. Accessible at http://www.latimes.com/opinion/op-ed/la-oe-heffernan-mueller-20180819-story.html.
34. John Wagner and Colin McNeil. *Judge Dredd: America* (Jordan House, London: Hachette Partworks Ltd., 2015).
35. Wagner and Ezquerra, *Judge Dredd: Origins.*

Chapter Thirteen

Grab 'em by the Seeds

The Regressive Utopianism of Trumpism and Katherine Burdekin's Swastika Night

Ryan Farrar

Many observers around the world will likely not equate the faultless rhetoric dispatched by the Trump administration, which includes the president's blathering on Twitter, with the actual effects the White House's policies manifest on the United States and world stage. It would be difficult to encounter a pluralistic citizen who regards President Trump and his associates as bearing the Midas touch when it comes to transforming the United States to a revived golden beacon of liberty and justice. Based on poll numbers, most Americans readily doubt the administration's declarations that they are keeping up their promise to liberate white, working-class Americans from the so-called gutter of gang-ridden cities and emancipating them from the so-called clutches of drug-dealing, immigrant rapists.[1] Yet, enough voters do believe that Trump is taking the country in a justifiable direction, and though the state of the union has yet to reach the apex of a crazed fascism run amok, the beat of the Trumpist drum certainly reverberates at levels that should give pause and conjure images of past authoritarian nationalisms. Trump's nostalgic motto "Make America Great Again" rings for a state that has been lost, a kind of paradise that must be regained. Many defenders of Trumpism see his policies as insulating US jobs and Anglo/European culture from the expansion of multicultural, globalized forces. According to Daniel Bessner and Matthew Sparke, Trump has capitalized on

> reactionary anger against globalism . . . unconsciously with the deployment of a vulgarian [*sic*] style that appeals symbolically—and often sexistly and racistly—to the "common man" who despises cosmopolitan political correctness

> and the corporate multiculturalism of multinationals (note that "globalist" and "cosmopolitan" have long been coded anti-Semitic slurs).[2]

As Bessner and Sparke imply, the reality contradicts the message that Trumpists advocate. Although they labor to manufacture a vision of a United States of the past, they wager their hopes on a figure who is more of a Godot than a messiah. Exposing the president as a mendacious champion of grassroots nativism, Henry Giroux characterizes Trump and his cabinet members as unsophisticated machiavellians, observing that "Trump's contempt of democratic processes is matched by his commitment to the market and economic policies that favor the financial elite."[3] The president may perorate about bolstering working-class interests, but his actions favor the 1 percent. Although profit functions as Trump's endgame, his nationalist and dictatorial bearing emboldens groups such as the alt-right, and the violence and chauvinism espoused by their platform elicits images beyond the Pacific and Atlantic shores of the United States and recalls the hypermasculine, hypernationalist mania of fascist states, such as Nazi Germany. Yet, Trump's demagoguery and pandering to the alt-right is ultimately a false flag for reestablishing a feudalistic privilege predicated on a plutocratic exceptionalism.

Despite Trump's neoliberalist motives, his shift toward a privileged elitism still warrants considerations of fascism's past. As Giroux claims, "[u]nder President Trump, the scourge of twentieth-century fascism has returned as neo-fascism, not only in the menacing plague of populist rallies, fear-mongering, hate, and humiliation, but also in an emboldened culture of war, militarization, and violence that looms over society like a rising storm."[4] In reacting to paradigm shifts in politics, the literary genre of dystopia has served as a traditional lens for assessing changing sociopolitical climates. As Fátima Vieira points out, often in dystopian fiction, "images of the future are put forward as real possibilities because the utopist wants to frighten the reader and to make him realize that things may go either right or wrong, depending on the moral, social and civic responsibility of the citizens."[5] In fact, forebodings in literature regarding fascism abounded during the 1930s and 1940s in response the rise of Italian fascism and the National Socialist German Workers' Party. Authors cautioned against hysterias and hard-lined chauvinism wreaking havoc on marginalized populations and homogenizing civic structures into antiquated, amberized relics that actively served as the arms to foment widespread discrimination and oppression. These books ranged from Olaf Stapledon's *Last and First Men* (1930) and Sinclair Lewis's *It Can't Happen Here* (1935) to Karel Čapek's *War with the Newts* (1936), but more apropos to the political climate of Trumpism, where its supporters applaud misogyny and advance hypermasculinity, is Katherine Burdekin's anti-fascist dystopia *Swastika Night* (1937). Feminist dystopian literature has been invoked already as a means of resisting Trump and the

Republicans' agenda. Media outlets recently covered reactionary protests against anti-choice legislation in Texas where women donned white hoods and red gowns, evoking Margaret Atwood's *The Handmaid's Tale* (1985) and its timely television series adaptation (2017). Although Atwood's novel is certainly apt, the expansion of the alt-right, which is simply a euphemism for white nationalism and similar nativist hate groups, would be better critiqued using Burdekin's novel, which arrestingly approaches fascism from a feminist perspective, as opposed to a radical Christian theocracy, to illustrate the excessive reach of belligerent men desiccating the lives and abilities of females. Burdekin's novel suitably captures and magnifies the commandeering force of fascism and can be useful in assessing Trumpism, or what political scientist Richard Falk terms a "pre-fascist movement."[6]

There is something of the fable embedded into dystopian narratives and in the twentieth century, the morals of the most recognized fictions admonished against the optimism of scientific and social engineering. Yevgeny Zamyatin's *We* (1924), Aldous Huxley's *Brave New World* (1932), and Kurt Vonnegut's *Player Piano* (1952) all cast a wary eye on technological advancement as degrading human dignity and passion while corrupting political structures. Gregory Claeys categorizes this dystopian motif as featuring "a monolithic, totalitarian state demanding and normally exacting complete obedience from its citizens, challenged occasionally but usually ineffectually by vestigial individualism or systematic flaws, and relying upon scientific and technological advances to ensure social control."[7] The fears of a monolithic state certainly have not subsided early in the twenty-first century as similar leaders have risen to power (e.g., Putin, Erdoğan, and Duterte), and technologically, an effective contributor to Trump's rise took the form of the cyberwarfare orchestrated by Putin's Russia. There is a notable difference of dystopia, though, as it relates to political spikes in ultraconservativism. Like fascism's expansion leading up to and during World War II, the fallout of Trump's ascendancy once more drags the themes of dystopia away from a fear of technology and futurism and directs the orientation toward one of repressive anti-intellectualism and dogmatic totalitarianism. Writers such as Burdekin adopt the double-negative platform of dispensing with the Frankenstein myth of a civilization developing technologies beyond its control and emphasizing the fear of stunted progress and reversion, where societies retain the status quo of suppressive weaponry but reverse sociocultural values to a level that matches more closely the standard of a medieval persuasion. Fascism fosters a regressive utopia, a return to a place preoccupied with how things are believed to have been, and for those who dissent (i.e., those who celebrate or welcome variables and difference), this utopia serves as a dystopia. In fact, Sargent avers that "[m]any utopias are nostalgic in that they look back to an idealized past which is then moved into the future, with the utopia found in living the cleaned-up version rather than the way people had actually lived."[8] In the context of Trump and discourse on fascism, Samir Akin blames capitalism for paving the way for leaders to arrest the aims of democracies and stifle the maturation of material relations. He writes:

> This reversal of values is then always accompanied by a return of backward-looking ideas. . . . The proclamation of the supposed necessity of returning to the ("medieval") past, of submitting to the state religion or some supposed characteristic of the "race" or the (ethnic) "nation" make up the panoply of ideological discourses deployed by the fascist powers.[9]

In Burdekin's novel, the dystopia reverts all subjects under Hitlerdom, Nazis included, to a serfdom that crystallizes the prestige of a gentry class that centers and sustains its power through a worship of masculinity. Ideology, not technology, nourishes the totalitarian nightmare of fascist rule, where the mythos of Hitler and the fictions surrounding the history of Germany's victory in war lull people into a discriminatory complacency where the theocracy of maleness keeps them in a psychic trance of aggression. Burdekin's depiction finds kinship with the worldview of Italian fascist Julius Evola. John Bellamy Foster discusses Evola's postwar writings as encouraging fascists "to emphasize only their 'positive' characteristics, allying themselves with the 'aristocratic' values of the European tradition. The goal was the creation of a new, spiritual 'European *Imperium*. . . . We must create a unity of fighters.' The ultimate intent was the resurrection of traditional sovereignty understood as the spiritual power of a nation, or *patria* (i.e. fatherland)."[10] The method of pledging allegiance to a "fatherland" and encouraging manic anger can be seen in Trump's policies and attacks on government officials, celebrities, and the media as a whole. Whether he targets Lebron James, Snoop Dogg, Robert Mueller, or John McCain, Trump points his finger and waits for his supporters to lash out like unquestioning sons as they displace their collective frustrations onto indirect targets, vitalizing Trump's claim at a campaign rally that he "could stand in the middle of 5th Avenue and shoot somebody and [he] wouldn't lose voters."[11] The unity of Trump followers is palpable as Trump's doublespeak allows him to promise to "drain the swamp," while also appointing billionaires and Wall Street executives to positions in his administration that will ensure the protection of elite capitalism.

Although Burdekin's "Reduction of Women" fuels comparisons between Trump's and his followers' misogynistic tendencies, the fascist elements of the author's Hitlerian society draws striking parallels to the structure forming under the Trump administration. The direction of both societies tends toward a celebrated regression, enlisting a paradise-lost motif and propagandizing policies that peddle a utopian image predicated on the eradication of progress, inclusivity, and plurality. John Gray writes that twentieth-century "fascists wanted to roll back the modern world—a project that appealed to figures such as T S Eliot and G K Chesterton, who hankered after the cultural homogeneity of medieval Christendom."[12] For Trump and his associates, regressing toward the establishment of an archaic hegemony relies on peddling outmoded fictions that prey upon populist fears of a rigged economy and using racial minorities as scapegoats for the market's failure to reward "forgotten Americans." Bessner and Sparke describe the strategy in remarking that "Trumpism itself traded on a mix of nationalistic nostalgia and willful political-economic amnesia."[13] They further state that "[global right wing campaigns such as Trump's] tap into popular resentment emanating from and about market-led globalization. . . . [T]hey take advantage of the mismatch between neoliberalism's utopian promises about the benefits of a borderless free market and the realities of a global market economy defined by increasing inequalities, austerities, and dispossession."[14] Job creation in the United States grew under policies of the Obama administration, but the power of wages remains a slave to monopsony and escalating inflation as the government fails to modernize regulations for compensation of US labor. Scapegoating this lack under Trump is as manifest as the camps for women in Burdekin's novel as well as the very real concentration camps of Nazi Germany, and his blame game has garnered him support. Trump's governance has not yet led to the genocide of a mass ethnic group, but his leadership incites hatred toward minorities with an energy similar to that of the Nazis. Trump's analogous black shirts take the form of neo-fascist protestors and his camps bear the name of detention centers where US Immigration and Customs Enforcement have separated children from their parents and their abuse of detainees has remained largely unchecked. He has even gone as far as to praise Filipino President Rodrigo Duterte's drug war, which has included summary executions of mere suspects.[15] This institutionalized aggression propagated by insecure white males such as Stephen Miller, Jeff Sessions, Tom Cotton, and President Trump has been labeled by liberals as a nativist attempt to prevent "the browning of America." The Trump administration's maneuvers evoke a sense of racial primacy, and Burdekin's novel traces the roots of these kinds of aggressions, personality cults, and sense of racial purity to the simple principle of an insensate male hunger to dominate and consume the fabric of all cultures.

The fearful aspect of fascist and authoritarian regimes is that marginalized populations are more than excluded but are systematically corralled from their residences into enclaves designed to eject their presence, which themselves function as locales of displaced and misplaced aggression. Even today as elected officials have tried to survey the environment of immigrant detention centers, the personnel manning these facilities prevent their inspection. Enzo Traverso critiques these maneuvers as orchestrated to misdirect conservative voters from the root problems facing the country. He writes:

> [Trump] pretends to defend the popular classes that have been deeply affected by the economic crises of 2008 and the deindustrialization of the country—not by denouncing the main culprit, financial capitalism, but by offering them a scapegoat. His campaign reproduced features of old anti-Semitism, which defined a mythical, ethnically homogenous national community against its enemies: the Jews. Trump took this model and enlarged the spectrum to include African Americans, Latinos, Muslims, and non-white immigrants.[16]

To similar ends, Burdekin's primary theme indicts patriarchal chauvinism to its core in imagining a society where women, not Jews, become the scapegoats for inadequacy, condemned to be a collection of ghostly, enclosed outliers whose presence and bodies only terrifies men with their ugliness and function as depository objects of rape that remotely issue offspring for the glory of the empire. Carlo Pagetti et al. note that "woman is of such a low social status that she is not even allowed to rise to the dignity of being a character in [Burdekin's] fiction."[17] When the Nazi Hermann observes the Women's Worship, the effect communicates a detestation beyond human esteem: "He was terrified. The mere sight of so many women all in a static herd and close by him . . . with their small shaven ugly head and ugly soft bulgy bodies . . . women have no souls and therefore are not human."[18] Burdekin underscores her feminism in presenting the complete inverse of feminism's goals of equal rights. In the nightmare world where Hitlerism prevails, men more than deprive women of their personhood, they purloin it entirely, confiscating the traits that patriarchal tradition had celebrated as becoming a woman and adopting them as if the traits were always theirs from the beginning of time. The hope for women's condition in the novel is bleak because the two most progressive men who are interested in rehumanizing women and rebuffing Hitlerian culture laugh at various points at the idea of a woman holding a value that can equal that of a 1930s' man. The status quo for Burdekin and other contemporaries of hers was already overbearingly disproportionate to males, and she noted in fascism a chauvinism with the potential to render the female's substandard position into no position at all.

In Burdekin's novel, the diminution of women integrally ties into the propaganda and ignorance transmitted by the Inner Ring of Ten regarding the superiority of the race and Hitler's mythological status as a deity. The fascism of the Nazi Empire is a digestive chasm that coopts culture and reconstitutes it as its own innovation. Not only are the traits of womanhood hijacked, but the Nazis seek to requisition all corners of the past in a never-changing present to sustain a façade that rightness and power have been inherently theirs since civilization's dawning. The mirage of always being right correlates with Trump's denying and revising easily verifiable historical occurrences in his tenure. In the novel, the rescripting is beyond overreaching plausibility. On the first page, there is a hodgepodge of Norse, Christian, and Greek mythology combined into a metanarrative that sanctifies an essential maleness: "*in God the Thunderer . . . in His Son our Holy Adolf Hitler, the Only Man. Who was, not begotten, not born of woman, but Exploded!*"[19] The passage proceeds to allude to Hitler as an embodiment of the Nietzschean *Übermensch*, and the most important aspects in Burdekin's exposition highlight that Hitler manifests as a new Christ figure in the culture minus the need for immaculate conception and any veneration of a Virgin Mary figure. Instead, Hitler all at once becomes Thor, Christ, and the Greek Goddess Athena, who burst from Zeus's head; the deity of Hitler is Alpha and Omega, and all things, including feminine beauty and ingenuity. All things of culture derive from Lord Hitler's masculine potency. He is the organizing principle upon which the dystopian society of German male privilege is based.

In describing anti-Utopian fiction as a genre, Frederic Jameson writes, "much of the force . . . [of the] genre derives from this essentially narrative fear, in which the name of Big Brother or Zamyatin's Benefactor can only itself be figured as an absence or an actantial fiction which has real and baleful results . . . the mythic founder must be without all human frailties in order to be able to stand outside a corrupt society and to reform it."[20] The regression highlights the attempt to make chauvinism an omnipresent and transhistorical eventuality, supplying a mysticism that interdicts questioning, doubt, and reform.

Trump's administration appears to share affinities with Burdekin's Nazi Empire in their impulse to color over their pageantry with strokes of a superlative machismo that ostracizes and antagonizes women and their rights. Days into Trump's presidency, he issued an executive order that reinstated the Mexico City Policy, preventing the United States from funding organizations that voice support for abortion, and he signed the legislation in the Oval Office, straddled by a line of white men. The posturing continued in March 2017 when Vice President Mike Pence met with the Freedom Caucus to deliberate over the future of the Affordable Care Act, and among the features being discussed was maternity benefits. Once again, the administration populated the room with a retinue of men, entirely devoid of female representation. The staging methods convey the idea that the power to preside over future decisions regarding women's rights and bodies will lie in the hands of men like these. Despite these oppressive gestures, Trump supporters have sanctioned his affront to women, as well as minorities, as a step to correct a political landscape that has molded a climate they see as overly threatening traditional values. William E. Connolly describes the phenomenon:

> Critics spouting objections to a particular item can now be lumped together under the rubric of political correctness, a stopgap phrase designed to halt receptive communication with suspects outside the core movement.
>
> That line of negative associations is then treated as if it can *only* be defeated by a positive between alpha-masculinity, ultra-self-assertion, compliant

> women, violent gestures, impermeable territorial walls, an aggressive unitary nation, and police and military ruthlessness.[21]

Far-right conservative politicians willingly inflate the problems of plurality and change, directing their constituents toward an insular and outdated nationalism that promises a return to a chimerical sphere of a simpler, less-threatening era where sameness is comfortable and maintained through a shared reverence for virility. Tim Prentki avers that "Trump won a sufficient number of hearts, if not minds, of the US electorate, in no small part through swamping (anti-) social media with his mix of myth, selective truth and lies. In essence, he told people what they wanted to hear in return for their votes."[22] Supporters of Trumpism's neo-fascist tendencies genuinely believe that the current political disruption serves to bridle progressive, socialist proclivities and espouses a dialogue that disqualifies oversensitivity as being worthy of attention. However, the lamentable reality is that the cavalier dismissal of political normalcy functions as a smokescreen for Trump and his own inner-circle's own self-aggrandizement and cupidity. As Giroux observes, "With this regime change will come the suppression of civil liberties and dissent at home through the expansion of a punishing state that will criminalize a wider range of everyday behaviors, expand mass incarceration, and all the while enrich the coffers of the ultra-rich and corporate predators."[23] Trump and his cronies have fashioned a system that hoodwinks its base into demonizing those who champion equality and fair rights (i.e., the opponents of Trump's thrift, cheating, and white preference), so that the administration may squander funds from taxpayers (e.g., Trump's excessive and unnecessary employment of the secret service and Scott Pruitt's lavish travel and office accommodations) and endorse corporations' exploitation of the citizens they fraudulently represent.

A common intersection between the portrayal of government in *Swastika Night* and the course of Trump's tenure revolves around fictions of superlative citizenship that act as a ruse for a small cadre to consolidate wealth and power through plutocratic means. A pattern has emerged in that when extremes on either side of the political spectrum (e.g., Hitler, Mussolini, Franco, Erdoğan, and Putin on the right; Stalin, Zedong, Castro, and Jong-Un on the left) embrace intolerant stances regarding their opposition during their rises to power, the scales tip to the extent that governments establish a system of oppression on a massive scale while a select few, or inner circles, siphon the country's lucre like parasites. Trump's agenda appears to be a new riff on this classic song of history. Many scholars underscore the accumulative aims of Trump and the favors he bestows on members of the wealthy class. Foster writes:

> Trump's initial seventeen cabinet picks . . . had a combined wealth that exceeded that of a third of the population of the country. This does not include Trump's own wealth, reputedly $10 billion. Never before has there been so pure a plutocracy, so extreme an example of crony capitalism, in any U.S. administration.[24]

Trump and his associates abuse the grassroots appeal to traditional values and xenophobia as a grifting tactic that permits them to embezzle or misuse government resources for lining their own pockets. Trump has not only foregone the placement of his assets into a blind trust to at least create the semblance of upholding the emoluments clause, but his recent tweet in May 2018 calling for legal sanctions to be rolled back to aid the Chinese telecommunications company, ZTE, in salvaging jobs brazenly shows a disinterest in not appearing avaricious. Helaine Olen quickly identified his motive for supporting ZTE: "As it turns out, the S*outh China Morning Post* reported last week that a real estate development project in Indonesia, containing a number of hotels, homes—and let's not forget the golf course—bearing the Trump name, received $500 million in loans from the Chinese government."[25] The transaction is an unequivocal instance of a quid pro quo infraction. Yet, rather than react with ire toward Trump's leveraging of his office for personal gain, those who approve of him defend his conflict of interest as simply a dexterous business move that shows a rugged US individual staking claim to a market opportunity. As Bessner and Sparke point out, "Trumpism is presently being pursued as a national political project in ways that remain closely tied to the economic interests of business elites, ties that in turn promise to deepen the very same inequalities and resentments which Trump translated so successfully into votes."[26] Trump's misuse of power essentially scaffolds the fictional aura emanating from the American Dream, and lower- and middle-class Americans are stuck in a dystopic limbo, reaping no benefits from the Republican Party's guidance.

In *Swastika Night*, the knights likewise lead their Nazi underlings by the nose, simultaneously stifling their opportunities for growth while peddling the supremacy of the Aryan race among the masses. The illusory mirage of myth and natural hierarchy grapples the Nazis subjects' discernment into a rigidity where they lack consciousness as to the state of their condition and position within the state. The laws of feudal hierarchy dictate placement without mutability, and although the senses of characters like Hermann lean toward heterodoxy when encountering variables that contradict their ideology, such as formidable foreign men like Alfred, whom Hermann admires and views as bearing qualities equaling that of a Knight, the Evolan racism readjusts their internarrative back to a homogenous line of thought, which itself parallels the cognitive dissonance of Trumpists.[27] Alfred even confronts Hermann with the truth of his nation's fallacy: "as long as Blood is a Mystery none of you will ever be men. You hide behind the Blood because you don't really like yourselves, and you don't like yourselves because you can't be men."[28] The salient identifier in the abuse and dominance resides in the definition of masculinity. The foundations of the Hitlerian empire celebrate reaching the zenith of masculine expression, but Alfred in confronting Hermann suggests an ironic opposite, and the fact that Hermann reacts with a temper tantrum that directs him toward thoughts of murdering Alfred shows the effectiveness of Nazi indoctrination on its subjects. The adult men are impulsive, boyish, and callow. Alfred's criticism of the Nazi order is even more poignant given the fact that his dialogue with von Hess shows that he, too, is formed by Nazi ideals of masculinity while he ironically opposes them. When the Reduction of Women is described to Alfred, he sees female submission as natural and is surprised to learn that women can read.[29] Pagetti et al. write that, "[n]either the knight von Hess, nor the obtuse Hermann, nor the shrewd Alfred can embody the ideological response that Burdekin gives to all this. Each of them takes part, with some glimpses of awareness, in the redefinition of a language and of a behavior which they will never be able to interpret directly, or put into practice themselves."[30] Like many flawed protagonist men in dystopias (e.g., Winston Smith and John the Savage), even the rebels Alfred and von Hess are not immune from breathing in the air of German chauvinism and are fortunate to think of objecting to it. Their insistence on male greatness is the result of Nazi interpellation, and it ultimately limits their ability to fully conceive and even endorse the personhood of women.

Like the worldview held by Trump's voters, the Nazis living under the German empire project and impose a fantasy of how the world should be shaped based upon a past age, which hinges on static, intractable categories of stature and command. Such is the reason why Hermann readily doubts the veracity of his own account regarding his horrific encounter with the chorister. In hearing Hermann's charge regarding a German boy raping a Christian, von Hess laces his inquiries with a gravity intended to steer his subordinate toward doubting his memory, so Hermann may disbelieve the course of his experience and save the Knight the hassle of adjudicating the offense. The rewriting and erasure of history stands as a prevalent trope in dystopian fiction (e.g., the burning and "rectifying" of artifacts to fit the government's narrative in *Nineteen Eighty-Four*), and the dialogue between von Hess and Hermann lucidly depicts the effect dissonance has on subduing the masses into blind submission:

> "It's a serious accusation . . . There must be *absolute certainty*. Do you still want to make a deposition against this boy?"

> Hermann hesitated. The will of the Knight was now set in its full force against the young Nazi's. He even began for the first time to be a shade doubtful of what he *had* seen.[31]

The indubitable reverence due to hierarchy fosters an intractability that defies actuality and traps followers, like Hermann, in the fictional bubble of myth. The insular walls obstruct expressions of truths that reflect diverse experiences in that von Hess's codes of speech and attire override Hermann's attempts to signify his reality, even though his deposition fully accords with Nazi ideology. Burdekin uses the interaction to belie the basis of Nazism as a dystopian framework where the knights issue dictums regarding race and religion but selectively enforce them to serve their own interests. Thus, the effect of language becomes a tool exclusively at the disposal of an elite few. In this vein, Trump manipulates language and ideology to suit his purposes similarly to the Knights, contradicting state apparatuses such as the FBI and the CIA, as well as market apparatuses such as media outlets, and he dupes his own constituents, preaching the return of manufacturing to the United States while having outsourced jobs within his own business overseas.[32] Giroux describes the manipulation as a weapon.

> Under Trump, ignorance has been weaponized and will continue to be used to produce a profoundly disturbing anti-intellectualism that leaves little room for critical reflection. It is important to remember that in his various pre-election speeches, Trump's endless lies emptied language of any meaning, giving credence to the charge that he was producing a kind of post-truth in which words did not count for anything anymore, especially when informed judgements and facts could no longer be distinguished from opinion and falsehoods.[33]

Like Hermann, the contrarian's constituents excuse him based upon the false ethos of him being an immensely successful businessman as his image as an entrepreneur grants him immunity from accountability in their eyes. Trump's shaping of narrative bears a dystopic effect on Americans' ability to counter and protest his claims as his invention of facts and his schoolyard bravado mythologize his success as granting him the license to deflect responsibility. Despite flying the banner of democracy and representation, like Hermann, the majority of Americans are rebuffed by gerrymandering, representatives who refuse to check and balance the unethical behavior demonstrated by agents in other branches of government, and the passing of legislation, such as Tax Cuts and Jobs Act, that has further put underprivileged citizens at a disadvantage.

The result of any government seeking to control and direct the output of culture toward a sense of perfection carries the obverse effect of stifling and murdering the factors that historically allow art, philosophy, and science to bloom in diverse directions. The unwavering demand for perpetual obedience and reverence stunts reflection and the elevation of thought and expression. In a dystopian gesture particular to twentieth-century fiction, von Hess confides to Alfred the fate of a civilization that operates under the pretense of immutable perfection.

> [O]ne culture seems to grow out of another, one will go rotten, and another spring up on its grave, with a little bit of the old one in it, like manure. . . . Now we have nothing in the ground. . . . We are stagnant . . . in the rich mental and emotional life men live when they are *going somewhere*, aiming at something beyond them, however foolish, we have no part. We can create nothing, we can invent nothing—we have no use for creation, we do not need to invent. We are Germans. We are holy. We are perfect, and we are dead.[34]

Von Hess's analogy suggests that the old must die to give birth to the new, that cultures naturally expire and lead to a yield of new cultures that grow from it. However, Burdekin's Nazis with their feudalism and the Trump administration with their insistence on returning to a past mode of culture disrupt the pattern of progress and barrel its citizen subjects toward creative sterility and innovative dereliction. President Barack Obama may not have helmed the most progressive administration in the United States. By many standards, his policies may be adjudged to align more with moderate conservatism in his expansion of the Troubled Asset Relief Program and his part in renewing the Patriot Act. However, the image conservatives have painted of him as a radical progressive who took the nation in a direction toward socialism has been hyperbolized enough to rouse members of fringe groups and sway moderate voters into curbing a government straying too far from the old. Conservatives see their votes as dutifully preserving elements of a past culture from being completely overwritten. On the other hand, liberals see Trump's policies as inhibiting the rise of better social values and technologies. In Burdekin's fiction, the radical regression rallies around the former sentiment but spirals beyond it as the face of past cultures undergo a symbolic annihilation through the destruction of cultural artifacts and institutions: book burnings; the splintering of families to promote a nationalist agenda; and the men's purloining of femininity and transferring these qualities onto boys. The fear of losing the past to cosmopolitanism manifests as a hypercorrection that commandeers ideology, artifacts, and gender roles, subjugating peoples and the freedom of thought to Fascist dominance. Despite the insistence on German supremacy in the novel, von Hess recognizes that the empire's trajectory of falsehood and repressed discontent may culminate in a restive predicament that fosters civil war and a rejection of Nazi superiority. Like a corpse unearthed by the flood waters of a collapsed levee, the omnipresent lie of Hitlerism cannot maintain its façade and perpetually conceal its farce among the German multitude. Von Hess claims as much stating that their civilization "*is* a stinking corpse, and its smell is coming through."[35] In her novel, Burdekin foresees the debilitating force a pervasive Nazism can have on rewriting rich histories and undoing a tradition of liberalism, but she propagandistically sees the permanence of power built upon falsehood as unsustainable.

As I write in September 2018 with congressional midterm elections approaching, Democrats anticipate a similar dismantling to occur against Trumpists and his Neo-Nazi supporters as they encourage their base to react in force against Trump's flouting of conventional mores. Even the media has seized upon the second Unite the Right rally as a symbol of the alt-right's waning influence. On August 12, 2018, reporters noted that the number of white supremacists rallying in Washington, DC, decreased significantly to dozens from the hundreds who participated the previous year at the first Unite the Right Rally in Charlottesville, Virginia, where in 2017, a Neo-Nazi murdered a counterprotestor with his automobile. Both Burdekin and the constituents of the political left view the movements of their opposition as sputtering out, but there is a difference between perceiving these views as either hubris or resistance, and the attitude affiliates more closely with the latter. Burdekin's novel and the media's reporting function to prompt their audiences to resist oppression, hate, and the denial of reality.

Within the novel, the seminal expression of barren growth comes through the plight of women and the lack of females being born as Burdekin suggests that the hypermasculinity of the Nazis dehumanizes women and its hegemonic manhood overrides the yield of girls to a destabilizing degree. Rather than celebrate women as integral members of the empire, whom the Nazis could at the very least keep as pets like the remnants of Christians in the novel, they instead erect a dictum that lifts worms above women in stature. The opening scene at the chapel underscores the hijacking as Hermann looks longingly on a chorister with flowing blonde hair while the women are begrudged to even breathe the same air lest it putrefies the dogma of male sanctity.[36] Therein lies a deep-seeded flaw in all essences of divinity. In many religions, sanctity lies so easily susceptible to profanation that it belies its own superiority, and such a philosophical problem plagues the foundations of Burdekin's Nazi empire as the stores of emotional energy incorporated into von Wied's cultural program are in limited supply.[37] The rituals may persist in reinforcing ideas of supremacy, but the fear of women and their ability to ruin their own perfection reveals a weakness in the Nazi ideology of maleness.

The misogyny and chauvinism in Burdekin's dystopia echo too clearly in Trump's conduct. In her Hitlerian world of overwrought virility, the law demands that women submit to rape and sexual assault without any objections or recourse. There is no word for rape, and in the Hitlerian empire, "[t]he most important thing was to get it firmly in the heads of the younger women that they must not mind being raped. . . . rape implies will and choice and a spirit of rejection on the part of women, there could be no such crime."[38] Similar attitudes have been held by the President. Trump's 2005 recording with *Access Hollywood* host Billy Bush amplifies and promotes a culture of erasing consent with regards to sexual contact. Trump explicitly comments to Bush when eyeing another woman: "Yeah, that's her. With the gold. I better use some Tic Tacs just in case I start kissing her. You know, I'm automatically attracted to beautiful—I just start kissing them. It's like a magnet. Just kiss. I don't even wait. And when you're a star, they let you do it. You can do anything . . . Grab 'em by the pussy. You can do anything."[39] Like the Germany Burdekin foresees, a country where the future pivots on the abjection of women who lack any sustainable agency to protect their own interests or make decisions, the leader of the free world's misogynistic disregard of women's volition in regard to consent cultivates a message that sanctions impudent men to sexually assault females as if they are objects that serve to pacify men's egos. His behavior is galvanized by the words of Pagetti et al., who write about sexual abuse in *Swastika Night* and its reflection of fascism. They state, "A sick universe engenders the madness of a nightmare, which nonetheless is used to strip away the political fictions of the present in much the same way that, behind the noble face of the charismatic leader, the brutal sneer of the rapist is revealed."[40] Under modern political standards, endorsing a candidate that gives approbation to abusive misconduct would typically disqualify their candidacy as untenable and undesirable. In the twenty-first century, however, these standards of morality act as a mere smokescreen for political opportunity and are selectively evoked. Republicans may have spearheaded impeachment proceedings in accusing President Bill Clinton of obstructing justice during his tenure, but they actively provide special dispensation for the numerous allegations that President Trump faces: harassing women, paying women hush money to keep his encounters with prostitutes quiet, and obstructing justice.

Trump excuses his recorded comments as mere "locker-room banter," but the words disclose a lust for power over women's bodies and features.[41] In Burdekin's novel, the angle of violation carries the same weight as Trump's rhetoric of disregard, and the effects on ideology are far from the suggested innocence of boys being boys. Although the political right dismisses objections to Trump's comportment as a slippery slope of unchecked political correctness, a leader who nonchalantly encourages sexual assault without consequence licenses his or her followers to view the comments as a permissible and appropriate endorsement for the reckless release of testosteronal energies.

Burdekin's erasure of consent parallels Trump's audacity in that she fittingly depicts how the demand for compliance and violation leads to an erosion of identity through theft, through the taking of what one desires. When von Hess shows Alfred and Hermann a picture of the human Hitler next to a blonde teenage girl, the pair mistake the teenager for a boy, disbelieving that women could exhibit a delicate physical beauty.[42] The book itself promises a rediscovery of a stolen identity. It supplies a new sense of literacy and the presentation of the truer history has a varying effect on the novel's characters. George McKay writes that Alfred "is physically transformed. He moves 'lightly,' like a triumphant man,' and speaks 'excitedly'" while Hermann "'stumble[s] back . . . like a drunkard' . . . The book functions to destabilize subjectivity. Both men's worlds are turned upside-down."[43] Learning the content of von Hess's book carries the potential to alter the course of identification and agency. Of course, in the novel, the exposure is understandably limited as such deviation is illegal. Yet, even as the best advocates for truth and resistance, von Hess and Alfred are severely shortsighted in their views, which underscores the subliminal influence hegemonic chauvinism can effect in the worldview of its opponents. Von Hess claims that women will conform to the image men carve out for them, and Alfred echoes the sentiment, claiming that he cannot imagine women defying the will of men.[44] The closest the pair come to recognizing women as creatures capable of autonomy and respect arrives in Alfred's conjecture that women should value themselves as a superior sex.[45] Although a small step for man, the progress is later undone when Burdekin shows Alfred expressing jealousy over Ethel's nursing of his daughter in the women's camp, a nourishment outside of his abilities.[46] Burdekin populates her future with bleak possibilities for women, and while Trump spouts rhetoric of a return to conservative values, his actions and words compare to the Nazis in the novel who stoke the fires of ignoring dialogue in favor of surrendering to destructive impulses.

The cultural milieus of both the Trump administration and Burdekin's Thousand-Year Reich are those of stasis and decline. The ultimate transgression of fascism and alt-right orientations rests in the belief of racial and gendered perfection that leads to a static death that results from socioeconomic immobility. As ideology conquers nature in Burdekin's world, women give birth to fewer girls, and despite the passage of around a thousand years, the state of technology has stagnated to that of a twentieth-century level. Trump's insistence on an aggressive patriotism, even proposing to hold a military parade in his honor, and his desire to preserve industries such as coal, coupled with his denial of climate science, threatens to lead the United States to its own stasis, which, in an ever-changing, mutlinational world, equals culture death. In recent history, there have been men who serve as megaphonic heralds for these hyperactive, uncompromising platforms: Julius Evola, Stephen Miller, Sean Hannity, Joseph Goebbels, and Stephen Bannon. In Burdekin's novel, the engineer of normalized misogyny and the character responsible for apotheosizing Hitler is Von Wied who, anticipating Trumpist tactics, formalizes the obliteration of memory through the rewriting of history and burning of cultural artifacts. As Giroux contests:

> [H]istory, as Marx observed, sometimes repeats itself with farcical vengeance. When it does, it signals a crisis of memory, politics, and civic literacy. This is particularly true in the current moment [i.e., 2017], as the return of menacing ghosts of the past has been abetted by a comforting silence that the culture of consumption, privatization, and individualization produces in the space that politics once occupied.[47]

Fictional or nonfictional, the totality of dominance in the United States strangles art, science, and life as a form of compensation for the racial and sexual inadequacies of white men. Although readers of dystopias commonly see these cautionary tales as championing the preservation of bourgeois individuality as the key to liberation from oppressive governments and institutions, the message most useful to twenty-first–century readers of dystopias will revolve around collective individuality, a paradoxical mix of individual value stitched into the fabric of collaborative forces. These groups ought to mobilize to disapprove of criminality and dislodge those from power who threaten the foundations of plurality, diversity, and the assertion of respect beyond capitalistic norms. Burdekin's novel underlines how a collective culture organized under a tapered sense of supremacy threatens to sprout like an unweeded garden, dispersing its rotten seeds across all corners and disallowing the flowering of forward thought and cultural actualization. Trump is spreading seeds of his own.

NOTES

1. David Leonhardt, "Is Trump's Support Slipping?" *New York Times*, September 4, 2018. Accessed https://www.nytimes.com/2018/09/04/opinion/trump-approval-ratings.html on September 16, 2018.
2. Daniel Bessner and Matthew Sparke, "Nazism, neoliberalism, and the Trumpist challenge to democracy," *Environment and Planning A* 49, no. 6 (2017): 1218.
3. Henry A. Giroux, "Trump's America: Rethinking 1984 and Brave New World," *Monthly Review* 69 (2017): 20.
4. Giroux, "Trump's America," 21.
5. Fátima Vieira, "The concept of utopia," in *The Cambridge Companion to Utopian Literature*, ed. Gregory Claeys (Cambridge: Cambridge University Press, 2010), 17.
6. Richard Falk, "The Dismal Cartography of Trump's Pre-Fascist State (and Opportunities for Progressive Populism)," *Mondoweiss*, January 26, 2017.
7. Gregory Claeys, "The origins of dystopia," in *The Cambridge Companion to Utopian Literature*, ed. Gregory Claeys (Cambridge: Cambridge University Press, 2010), 109.
8. Lyman Tower Sargent, *Utopianism: A Very Short Introduction* (Oxford: Oxford University Press, 2010), 21–22.
9. Samir Amin, "The Return of Fascism in Contemporary Capitalism," *Monthly Review*, September 1, 2014. Accessed https://monthlyreview.org/2014/09/01/the-return-of-fascism-in-contemporary-capitalism/ on September 16, 2018.
10. John Bellamy Foster, "Neofascism in the White House," *Monthly Review*, April 2017, 11–12.
11. Jeremy Diamond, "Trump: I could 'shoot somebody and I wouldn't lose voters;'" *CNN*, January 24, 2016. Accessed https://www.cnn.com/2016/01/23/politics/donald-trump-shoot-somebody-support/index.html on September 16, 2018.

12. John Gray, "Fictions of Fascism," *New Statesman*, March 3–9, 2017.

13. Bessner and Sparke, "Nazism, neoliberalism, and the Trumpist challenge to democracy," 1221.

14. Bessner and Sparke, "Nazism, neoliberalism, and the Trumpist challenge to democracy," 1219.

15. David E. Sanger and Maggie Haberman, "Trump Praises Duterte for Philippine Drug Crackdown in Call Transcript," *New York Times*, May 23, 2017. Accessed https://www.nytimes.com/2017/05/23/us/politics/trump-duterte-phone-transcript-philippine-drug-crackdown.html on September 16, 2018.

16. Enzo Traverso, "Trump's Savage Capitalism: The Nightmare is Real," *World Policy Journal* 34 (2017): 14.

17. Carlo Pagetti et al., "In the Year of Our Lord Hitler 720: Katharine Burdekin's 'Swastika Night' (*L'Ann é e de Notre Seigneur Hitler 720: 'Swastika Night' de Katharine Burdekin*)," *Science Fiction Studies* 17, no. 3 (1990): 361.

18. Katherine Burdekin, *Swastika Night* (New York: The Feminist Press, 1985), 9.

19. Burdekin, *Swastika Night*, 5.

20. Frederic Jameson, *Archaeologies of the Future* (London: Verso, 2005), 86.

21. William E. Connolly, "Trump, the Working Class, and Fascist Rhetoric," in *Theory & Event* 20 (2017): 23–37.

22. Tim Prentki, "Hearts are Trump's: Post-truth as intervention," *Social Alternatives* 3, no. 2 (2017): 41.

23. Henry Giroux, "White nationalism, armed culture and state violence in the age of Donald Trump," *Philosophy and Social Criticism* 43, no. 9 (2017): 891.

24. Foster, "Neofascism in the White House," 20.

25. Helaine Olen, "Trump's latest violation of the emoluments clause," *The Washington Post*, May 15, 2018. Accessed https://www.washingtonpost.com/blogs/plum-line/wp/2018/05/15/trumps-latest-violation-of-the-emoluments-clause/?noredirect=on&utm_term=.a6e7c96b5dca on September 16, 2018.

26. Bessner and Sparke, "Nazism, neoliberalism, and the Trumpist challenge to democracy," 1218.

27. Burdekin, *Swastika Night*, 21.

28. Burdekin, *Swastika Night*, 28.

29. Burdekin, *Swastika Night*, 70, 109.

30. Pagetti et al., "In the Year of Our Lord Hitler," 365.

31. Burdekin, *Swastika Night*, 42.

32. Rosalind S. Helderman and Tom Hamburger, "Trump has profited from foreign labor he says is killing U.S. jobs," *The Washington Post*, March 13, 2016. Accessed https://www.washingtonpost.com/politics/trump-decries-outsourced-labor-yet-he-didnt-seek-made-in-america-in-2004-deal/2016/03/13/4d65a43c-e63a-11e5-b0fd-073d5930a7b7_story.html?noredirect=on&utm_term=.7468249f4e2a on September 16, 2018.

33. Giroux, "White nationalism," 890.

34. Burdekin, *Swastika Night*, 121.

35. Burdekin, *Swastika Night*, 130.

36. Burdekin, *Swastika Night*, 5, 9.

37. Burdekin, *Swastika Night*, 5.

38. Burdekin, *Swastika Night*, 12–13.

39. "Transcript: Donald Trump's Taped Comments About Women," *New York Times*, October 8, 2016. Accessed https://www.nytimes.com/2016/10/08/us/donald-trump-tape-transcript.html on September 16, 2018.

40. Pagetti et al., "In the Year of Our Lord Hitler," 362

41. Fahrenthold, David A, "Trump Recorded Having Extremely Lewd Conversation about Women in 2005," *The Washington Post*, October 7, 2016. Accessed https://www.washingtonpost.com/politics/trump-recorded-having-extremely-lewd-conversation-about-women-in-2005/2016/10/07/3b9ce776-8cb4-11e6-bf8a-3d26847eeed4_story.html?utm_term=.3e167764166f September 16, 2018.

42. Burdekin, *Swastika Night*, 67–68.

43. George McKay, "Metapropaganda: Self-reading Dystopian Fiction: Burdekin's *Swastika Night* and Orwell's *Nineteen Eighty-Four*," *Science Fiction Studies* 21, no. 3 (1994): 306.
44. Burdekin, *Swastika Night*, 70.
45. Burdekin, *Swastika Night*, 109.
46. Burdekin, *Swastika Night*, 163.
47. Giroux, "Trump's America," 21.

Chapter Fourteen

Diverse New World

David L. McNaron

Albert Camus's novel, *The Plague*, and Jean Raspail's *The Camp of the Saints* seem to have wildly opposed themes: human solidarity in the former versus pathological altruism in the latter. There are striking similarities, however, between them. Both novels feature dual-threat scenarios: external threats combined with inner moral complicity. Both were prompted by large-scale disasters; in *The Plague*, World War II and the German occupation of France; in *The Camp of the Saints*, mass immigration to Europe. Camus wrote in retrospect; Raspail in prophetic dread. In keeping with dystopian works such as *Brave New World*, *Darkness at Noon*, and *1984*, *Plague* and *Camp* issue warnings. Both works identify evil that lies coiled within human nature as the main enemy and threat: the plague is *within* us. The novels differ in their conceptions of that internal form of plague. For Camus, plague is indifference to human suffering; for Raspail, it is Europeans' weakened inner defenses.

This chapter will develop the plague metaphor and determine whether the novels' themes might be compatible after all. *The Plague* and *The Camp* speak to our political predicament. Their viewpoints, or variants thereof, represent those held by combatants engaged in a *mostly* cold cultural and political war that shows no signs of abatement or peaceful resolution.[1] This conflict came to the fore with Brexit and the election of Donald Trump. What if our chances of reconciling these two novels approximate those of resolving our political differences?

A number of nonfictions deal with the same subjects. Camus himself wrote companion books of essays for his most influential novels, *The Stranger* and *The Plague*: *The Myth of Sisyphus* and *The Rebel*, respectively. Works that reinforce the preoccupations of *The Camp* include Douglas Murray's *The Strange Death of Europe: Immigration, Identity, Islam*; Peter Brimelow's *Alien Nation: Common Sense about America's Immigration Disaster*; and Ann Coulter's *¡Adios, America! The Left's Plan to Turn Our Country into a Third World Hellhole.* If Raspail is right, such titles bespeak the pathetic downfall of European civilization that we have been witnessing: a *Camp-of-the-Saints* scenario unfolding in slow motion.

THE PLAGUE

The Plague, like *The Stranger*, is set in French Algeria, in the prosperous but featureless city of Oran. Although Oran is a seaside town, it does not open to the water. According to the narrator, Dr. Rieux, its most prominent feature is ugliness. Oran would not likely inspire a coffee-table book. The business of Oran is business, its pace of life routine. But life anywhere has a certain monotony; such ennui forms the very texture of *The Stranger*. There is precious little, however, to offset the boredom in Oran. Life is not bad there, though. People make enough money to go out evenings, and they spend occasional days off at the beach.

The crisis begins when a rat staggers down a hallway, pirouettes, and dies, to a resident's disgust. As the sight of dead and dying rats increases the matter is brought to the attention of Dr. Rieux who, in turn, alerts the mayor and director of public health. These authorities downplay the situation and warn against frightening the public. They seem more afraid of identifying the disease than the disease itself. The situation resembles the one in *Jaws*[2] when the mayor of Amity refuses to close the beaches after a deadly shark attack for fear of scaring off tourists. The exasperated shark expert says the mayor would not know a Great White if one bit him on the ass. Here we see one typical response to disaster: denial born of venality. Those in charge had rather cloak a threat than meet it.

As people become sick and die, the disease is confirmed as bubonic plague. Nothing to do now but quarantine the city. Some residents flee or attempt to do so, unconcerned about the risk they pose. The narrator stresses the state of *exile* of those who remain, their estrangement in the once-familiar place they called home. There are no consolations; letters exchanged with loved ones on the outside, initially full of news, hope, or passion, turn cliché with the passage of time. There is not much to say; life goes drearily on and no one knows how long the epidemic will last. Sweet memories become a torment. As the plague cuts a swath through town, district by district, we are presented with grisly scenes of its ravages. The pace of the novel is slow, like the tedium of life in "occupied" Oran.

Although human weakness is on display, the novel treats neither the townspeople nor officials as villains. Oran is no Hadleyville in *High Noon.*[3] The novel is not misanthropic, despite some characters' shortcomings and foibles. A municipal employee, Grand, spends the entire novel working to perfect the "first" (read: *only*) sentence of a novel he is writing. He imagines the publisher's response upon receiving it: "Hats off, gentlemen, hats off!" Even the sneaky Cottard, who profiteers on the black market, inspires more amusement than contempt (compare Harry Lime in *The Third Man*[4]). Cottard, wanted for an unnamed offense committed elsewhere, evades detection during the crisis. On the whole, the narrator states, there is more to admire in people than despise.

One character does seem tainted with a plague-like moral condition: the fire-and-brimstone priest, Father Paneloux. The moral center of the novel concerns the death of a child. The novel graphically charts the final stages of plague over the course of a night as the doctor, parents, and priest helplessly stand vigil. Early in the epidemic, during his Week of Prayer, Father Paneloux blamed his congregation for the outbreak: "Calamity has come on you, my brethren, and, my brethren, you deserved it."[5] Their only recourse is to repent for their sins.

After the boy dies, Dr. Rieux follows Father Paneloux outside and lets him have it for his sermon, which, in effect, justifies the death of an innocent child. For Rieux, there is no scourge of sin, original or otherwise. The sanctimonious priest promotes an ideology that blames innocent victims.

The "telling-off" scene is reminiscent of one in *The Stranger*. The protagonist Mersault lambasts the chaplain who comes to his cell to offer consolation and save his soul. Mersault uncharacteristically loses his temper, grabs the priest by the collar, and unleashes a tirade about the priest's life-slandering views. Mersault remarks, "He seemed so cocksure, you see. And yet none of his certainties were worth one strand of a woman's hair."[6]

The Stranger and *The Plague* criticize "abstractions." Mersault cannot understand "love" or "guilt." The goal of an authentic life, Camus argues in *The Myth of Sisyphus*, is to live "without appeal" or illusions—to refuse, as Mersault did, to lie. In *The Plague*, Rieux and Rambert make sure they do not become ensnared by abstractions; their resolute stand against the plague arises solely from a sense of decency. For Rieux, "[I]t's a matter of common decency" to remain and fight, to risk oneself for the sake of others.[7] Rambert, a visiting journalist who's trapped in town, misses his wife and arranges an escape. Rieux declines to blame anyone who opts for happiness. But Rambert has a change of heart; he remains and joins the sanitation squads. It seems we do not need ethical theory to discover the right thing to do; one "just knows." In this respect Dr. Rieux resembles the beleaguered hero, Marshal Will Kane, in *High Noon*.

The malefactors in *The Plague*, though mild and few, receive their comeuppances. Father Paneloux contracts plague, refusing medical assistance to the end. He maintained his "strict logic," insisting that, "it's illogical for a priest to call in a physician."[8] Cottard, found out at last, is dragged off screaming by the police.

The novel's famous closing paragraph secures the plague's status as metaphor. It deserves quoting in full.

> And, indeed, as he listened to the cries of joy rising from the town, Rieux remembered that such joy is always imperiled. He knew what those jubilant crowds did not know but could have learned from books: that the plague bacillus never dies or disappears for good; that it can lie dormant for years and years in furniture and linen-chests; that it bides its time in bedrooms, cellars, trunks, and bookshelves; and that perhaps the day would come when, for the bane and the enlightenment of men, it would rouse up its rats again and send them forth to die in a happy city.[9]

The Plague and *The Rebel* mark a turn from Camus's nihilistic early period to one of solidarity. In *The Rebel* Camus argues that all nonhuman absolutes justify murder. These include God and the notion of history in classical Marxism (hence, his break with Jean-Paul Sartre). Camus advocates this credo for his solidarity-ethic: "I rebel—therefore we exist."[10] Camus has in this formula tried to subvert the solipsism of René Descartes's *cogito*: "I think; therefore, I am." That solipsism applies to *The Stranger*: Mersault has no emotional connection to others, even his own mother. He seems locked inside his own consciousness. Camus's inference provides a bridge from self to others. Compare this snatch of dialogue from *The Plague*. Tarrou: "Who taught you all this, doctor?" Rieux: "Suffering."[11] *The Rebel*'s appeal to solidarity invites comparison to Stoicism. Stoicism stresses universal brotherhood and citizenship, based on a common human nature and capacity for suffering, in the cosmopolis or universal political order. For the Stoics, nature supersedes convention. That which is permanent and universal in human nature establishes our identity, not particularities such as country, tribe, language, or religion.

Camus varied his position in the short story "The Artist at Work." A painter after long seclusion finally reveals his masterpiece: a canvas on which he has written a single ambiguous word, which could be read as either "Solitary" or "Solidary."[12] Thus, there is no final resolution to the problems of self or community, egoism or altruism. Any viable ethics must balance the two.

Camus received the Nobel Prize for Literature in 1957, according to *The Plague*'s editor, for bringing to light "the problems of the human conscience in our time."[13] He continues: "France, and for that matter most of Europe, was sunk in a kind of nihilistic stupor that many American GIs found more depressing than the physical ruins of war."[14] The editor thus locates Camus's concerns in the previous war-torn years. The novel's *translator*, however, links plague to "racism, colonialism" and claims that we are all infected by it.[15] Yet he refers uncritically to Arab nationalism. (More on double standards later.)

The editor's comments square with Raspail's diagnosis of French attitudes in later years. But the translator's comments show how Leftist "interpreters" seized upon Camus's theme for their own purposes. Here we see the expression of an outlook that constitutes the internal plague in *The Camp of the Saints*. Europeans' overwrought sense of guilt renders them defenseless against nonstandard forms of warfare. They are made to feel guilty over "racism," a sin that can never be expiated except by committing civilizational suicide.

The Plague and *The Rebel* raise several questions. First, was Camus right to endorse *universal* solidarity, if indeed that was his view? Second, can a *human* absolute, "humanity," or an abstraction such as "universal brotherhood" also justify murder? Third, suppose that in the name of humanity and universal brotherhood an entire civilization allows itself to be destroyed: is that fair and just? *The Camp of the Saints*, in effect, answers No, Yes, and No to those questions.

Plague as a metaphor for dual threats works well: unlike a menace such as a shark, disease is a condition of the *person* caused by pathogens from the environment. Plague thus straddles the internal–external distinction. But the plague metaphor is rich with interpretive possibilities. Either side, Left or Right, globalist or nationalist, can employ it to good effect.

THE CAMP OF THE SAINTS

Although *The Plague* subtly implies a diseased moral condition, *The Camp of the Saints* (hereafter, *The Camp*) endorses such a notion explicitly. *The Camp* is about a demographic plague that threatens Europe: an armada, one million strong and only the first wave, set sail from the Third World. The inner disease in *The Camp* is loss of a people's identity and belief in itself. An outlook is associated with this disease: a "complex" of multiculturalism, egalitarianism, and pathological altruism. Some would call it cultural Marxism. This view constantly identifies new categories of victims and blames Europeans as the sole oppressors. The "priests" in *The Camp* wield a rigid orthodoxy of their own, which they use as a cudgel against anyone who balks at anti-European rhetoric. The minute someone questions "diversity" these defenders of the faith label them "racists and fascists" and thereby prevent discussion and stifle dissent. Does this sound familiar?

The dual aim of white Leftists and their nonwhite clients in *The Camp* is to promote racial diversity and suppress viewpoint diversity. The Leftists, with a religious fervor, charge others with racism and support measures ruinous to their own people. But will their complicity as "allies" of nonwhites help their standing once the invasion begins? As in *The Plague*, the authorities in *The Camp* resist calling the threat by name.

The armada is quite a sight—and has quite a smell. It trails thousands of floating corpses in its wake: the remains of those who have died from starvation or disease. The galleys use human feces for cooking fuel, rolled by hand and dried by the sun, the wood supply having been exhausted in cremations. The fleet hails from India, the rusty freighters *India Star* and *Calcutta Star* leading hundreds of past-service commercial vessels.

Here is what is truly exasperating: the French pretend the armada's arrival is *inevitable*, as if it were a meteor hurtling toward Earth, instead of easily stopping it. A failure of nerve stands in their way. Why will the French not act on their own behalf? Because of taboos against whites speaking out about their own interests. The whites in *The Camp* are allowed no collective interests or solidarity, whereas other groups loudly proclaim theirs. *The Camp* reveals the entrenched double standard: Raspail has tapped into the vein of anti-white-identity politics.

The farther in time we move from slavery, segregation, and colonialism, the more virulent the charges of "racism." One wonders why *so many people* would wish to move to such wicked, racist countries. When no evidence exists, racism takes invisible forms: "institutional racism" and "white privilege." The secular religion of egalitarianism allows no other explanation for nonwhites' failures. Thus, innocent people—like Father Paneloux's congregation—are blamed. In the end, *The Camp* argues, after its centuries of alleged oppression Western civilization ends by succumbing to flimsy moral arguments. It dies with a whimper.

The Belgian Consul in Calcutta tried to stop the armada from sailing. The narrator's gloss on the event bears an uncanny resemblance to Camus's aforementioned short story, "The Artist at Work." The Consul, having made fruitless pleas to a local official, went down to the docks with his "army," a Sikh guard, to oppose the boarding of the *Calcutta Star*. Ordered to "Fire!" the guard tossed the Consul his rifle and ran. The Consul fired one shot before he was beaten to death. "In its outward appearance, at least, the Consul's heroic gesture was something of a prototype after the fact [of the decline of the Western powers] . . . as perfect and pure as the final creation of some terribly famous artist, who paints a single line on his canvas, or dabs one dot, and calls it his crowning achievement."[16] The Consul's act was futile, but he was no coward.

Australia and South Africa turned the flotilla away with mere words. A shot fired across the bow by an Egyptian torpedo boat induced the captain to change course. The Middle Eastern countries—like Saudi Arabia today—do not want the migrants either. Fewer people would die in the long run if the French Navy were to sink a ship. The Western world would be spared. But this will not happen because of the good work of the sophists and priests of the Left.

Among these are partisan media personalities—the Rachel Maddows and Don Lemons!—and celebrities who trumpet their support for the migrants. Then there are race hustlers of the Al Sharpton school. Clémont Dio (Ben Suad) typifies the prima-donna reporter and purveyor of political correctness. After children contract gonorrhea from swimming at a public pool frequented by infected Arabs, city officials required Arabs to show medical papers if they wished to swim. Dio ran a story with the headline, "Anti-Arab Racism Alive and Well!"

Dio's headline could easily appear in today's *Washington Post* or *New York Times*, the operative word, "Islamophobia." In the runup to the 2016 election, Hillary Clinton's *initial response* to an act of terrorism was to rebuke anyone who might think of blaming Muslims or Islam, not to decry the heinous act itself. In our "film," the expert would tell Clinton that she would not know a terrorist if one grabbed her by the pantsuit. She labeled Americans who opposed Muslim immigration "deplorables." Of course, Clinton's attitudes had nothing to do with her election loss: that was the work of space aliens.

Constantly telling nonwhites that racism is to blame for all their problems encourages them to *hate* whites. This would help explain the glaring disparity in interracial crime statistics.[17] We see the results of this hatred in *The Camp* once the invasion starts: black workers at one slaughterhouse murder a white foreman and send his body down the production line, to end up in a can of *pâté*. The nonwhites assume that with the disappearance of white majorities and white norms, harmony and justice will ensue.

As officials bloviate, the armada makes its shaky but inexorable progress. Human rights' committees convene, Ganges support organizations form. Much ado, but no action. Compare Iris's words in *The Iliad* as the Achaean armies advance on Troy: "Old Priam, / words, endless words—that is your passion, always, / as once in the days of peace. But ceaseless war's upon us!"[18]

Government spokesmen hold press conferences. At one, Dio speaks: "[M]ay I ask if the government has any plans to ease the plight of these poor, suffering souls? It's reaching a point where we can't sit idly by."[19] His question assumes what should be proven, that the government *should* help the migrants. The narrator remarks on such tactics: "[t]hey aim for the head. Those remote lobes of the brain where remorse, self-reproach, and self-hate, pricked by thousands of barbs, come bursting out, spreading their leukemia cells through a once healthy body."[20] Here we find the disease metaphor vividly stated.

At another presser the skeptical newspaper publisher, Machefer, challenges the government spokesman, human rights' crusader Jean Orelle, to explain how the government plans to repel the armada. Dio knew, when he "launched the debate on a lofty, altruistic note, that any other point of view would be seen as revolting."[21] Dissenting views were overruled on the spot. The Arab appeals to a universal ethic when dealing with Europeans while he subscribes to a tribal one. The French are thus playing a rigged game.

Orelle states that Machefer's question "is revolting! Do you ask a drowning man where he was going and why, before you pull him out of the water? Do you throw him back in if, assuming the worst, he admits he was swimming to your private residence to break into your cottage?"[22] Machefer replies that you hand him over to the police, but with a million such people there will not be enough police to do the job. *Touché!* Machefer has refuted Orelle's analogy. Of course, his good point has no effect. The moral imperative to promote "diversity" trumps all else.

Why think the migrants were not peaceful? The Belgian Consul's death was widely publicized. The South Africans intercepted the armada and delivered vast medical and food supplies. As they sailed away, the migrants formed lines and threw the cargo overboard. The message *should have* been clear. European papers were awash in fake news: "Was Poison Their Real Motive?"; "Blackmail in Human Despair"; "Charity South African Style: A Slap in the Face."[23] A delegation that included the World Council of Churches, the Pope (a Brazilian), the Red Cross, the Knights of Malta, high-profile celebrities, and pop music groups attempted a new mission. Delegation barges sailed out to meet the armada, but the ships had no intention of stopping. The *India Star* tried to ram a French barge. When the papal barge pulled alongside the *Calcutta Star*, that ship dumped the murdered cadaver of a once-famous white Buddhist writer onto the barge's deck. News of the murder was never made public.

As the armada approaches France, the president decides to meet the invasion with force. Then he does an about-face in his address to the nation. He cannot bring himself to order his troops to shoot. The French government will *welcome* the migrants. Meanwhile Colonel Degrasès, already dispatched, marches toward the sea. His army suffers mass desertion. The non-white soldiers celebrate the invasion. The white soldiers are split: some are cowards and others sympathize with the migrants. Supporters pour from the north of the country. At the same time, an exodus of Frenchmen from the south clogs highways heading north. *The Camp* uncannily predicts what occurred during the 2015 migrant arrival in Germany. Douglas Murray writes: "At the borders and at the train stations like Munich and Frankfurt crowds of hundreds of people gathered to welcome the arriving migrants. . . . Here were crowds of Germans not merely offering assistance to the migrants as they arrived, but giving them what often looked like a welcome party."[24]

Until this point in the novel, the one thing Raspail gets *wrong* about the future is the *peaceful* character of Leftist protest. For example, he describes orderly rallies in DC. Even Raspail did not foresee the violent tactics of groups such as Antifa in the Age of Trump. Even so, peaceful protest soon gives way to armed conflict.

Among the well-wishers rushing southward is Panama Ranger, a 1960s' type anarchist who wants to bring down the system, and his band of followers, the "Rhodio-Chemical People's Strike Force." They acquire Army deserters and party on supplies left behind by Frenchmen. Ranger celebrates "the revolution" and wishes to embrace the migrants as his brothers, naïvely assuming they will reciprocate his sentiments. He calls those who oppose him "fascists" and the police "pigs."

Ranger enjoys the support of media figures. Along the road he meets with Dio. Ranger points to his group's "Last Will and Testament"—a banner they have spread across a toll gate:

> "WORKERS, SOLDIERS, GANGES REFUGEES
> UNITED AGAINST OPPRESSION"

Dio exclaims, "Beautiful!"[25] Shortly thereafter Col. Dragasès' tanks arrive and blast the toll gate to bits.

The Camp opens with a jarring episode on the eve of the invasion. We find a retired professor of French literature, Monsieur Calgués, who has decided to remain, enjoying a beautiful day at his ancestral home in southern France. His home is located atop a rocky slope overlooking the sea. He sits on a covered terrace gazing at the fleet through his telescope. He has seen this day coming for a long time.

Suddenly a barefoot young man climbs the steps to Calgués' house. The young man is overjoyed by the flotilla's arrival. He says the migrants are his real family. France is finished, its days of privilege over. The country will now take in the oppressed and needy of the world; the old man's home, too, will go to the migrants. "Twenty generations without a conscience, without a heart. What a family tree! And now here you are, the last, perfect branch. Because you are, you're perfect. And that's why I hate you. That's why I'm going to bring them here, tomorrow. The grubbiest ones in the bunch. Here, to your house."[26] The migrants will use Calgués' fancy things then burn down his house. He orders Calgués to clear out. Calgués tries to reason with him, to no avail. Calgués says there's no point in staying and asks the man to wait a minute while he gets his hat. Calgués returns carrying a shotgun. "What are you going to do with that?" "I'm going to kill you, of course!"[27] After making a little speech of his own, Calgués shoots him. Afterward, he prepared a sumptuous meal, something of a Last Supper. As he sipped wine and listened to the radio by candlelight—the power having gone off hours earlier—he beheld his cherished belongings: books, linens folded in the linen chest, left by his mother, furniture, etc. The radio alternates between Mozart's *Eine kleine Nachtmusik* and status reports on the president's speech. After much bluster, the president announces the landing will not be opposed.

Meanwhile Colonel Degrasès, accompanied by a handful of loyalists, advances. Degrasès lost his tanks to Ranger's Molotov cocktails. On the beach, Degrasès and his men cremated bodies of migrants washed ashore, then made their way up to "The Village." Calgués welcomes them with a feast he prepared in their honor. The men spend their final day shooting migrants and French turncoats then celebrate in style. The French government sends in an air strike, not to support Colonel Degrasès' operation, but to kill the "racists," that is, the patriots. The planes bomb their position atop the hill, killing all.

We glimpse the new regime. "All that was missing were the black crosses that, in ages past, marked out the houses where the plague had struck."[28] French homes are forcibly integrated. Frenchmen and migrants worked out informal arrangements through bribery: half the house to people of color, the other side white. But the government cracked down and banned these "racist" practices. It could not outlaw discrimination in public only to permit it in private. Migrants debate whether or not they will accept assistance from the defeated enemy and set up a multiracial state.

Equality had finally triumphed. Western civilization had come to an end: "The thousand years are over" went the refrain of a migrant song. Elites would now have to live with the consequences of policies they formerly visited on others. An academic in Manhattan sipped scotch as the tide of migrants rose, floor by floor, in his building. The multicultural "utopia" signaled not the destruction of the West, but "the world reborn." Douglas Murray identifies our two forms of plague, the external and internal, as the chief reasons for Europe's fall: mass immigration and Europe's loss of confidence in itself.[29]

What a film this novel would make. Think of the images. Open with Calgués's lovely deserted village. Cut to the rusty armada seen through the lens of his telescope—its closeness—darkening the *Côte d'Azur*. Cross-bearing monks on the beach are swamped by the tide of migrants: an image that could leap off a Dalí canvas. Who would play Panama Ranger? This film could gross $1 billion. What are the chances Hollywood would make it?

RAPPROCHEMENT?

Are *The Plague* and *The Camp*'s themes compatible? There is reason to think so. Solidarity among the French is precisely what is missing in *The Camp*. Most people have stronger attachments to their own group than to others.[30] *The Camp*'s narrator states: "Man never has really loved humanity all of a piece—all its races, its peoples, its religions—but only those creatures he feels are his kin, a part of his clan, no matter how vast."[31] From *The Camp*'s perspective, there is nothing irrational about in-group preference; what is irrational is to *lose* it. After all, in *The Plague*, those who joined Dr. Rieux were fellow Frenchmen. To see a chilling documentary-style film about what happened *between* Algerians and Frenchmen, watch *The Battle of Algiers*.[32]

Elevating solidarity to a universal desideratum is folly. The bonds that bind us are mostly natural, innate. So the Stoics, in extoling nature over convention, should recognize this fact too. But particularities such as culture and religion also matter because they sometimes separate genetically close ethnic groups: Irish and English, Czechs and Slovaks, Serbs, Croats and Slovenians, etc. The absolutes and abstractions that *The Stranger* and *The Plague* deride make their appearance in *The Camp* as empty appeals to humanity and universal brotherhood. The morality from *Plague* has been stood on its head and turned into pathological altruism: the practice of promoting those who undermine one's own interests. A virtue has become a vice. Calgués thought to himself, as he watched a young soldier turn and run, that the traditional pride in his own people was wholly absent in him: "[t]he monstrous cancer implanted in the Western conscience had quashed it in no time at all."[33]

Europeans have unilaterally disarmed, whereas others have developed an intense and belligerent racial consciousness. Speaking of the common man, *The Camp*'s narrator says: "They've gelded his will of the instinct of self-preservation."[34] The result is that: "[i]n this curious war taking shape, those who loved themselves best were the ones who would triumph."[35] Europeans fear being called racists more than they do rape and murder. Officials crack down on those who sound the alarm rather than addressing the threat itself. What a strange lot to befall a brilliant and heroic people. Murray writes that Europe is finally lost because it "has little desire to reproduce itself, fight for itself or even take its own side in an argument."[36] He pronounces Europe's condition as terminal.

Where does *The Camp* leave cosmopolitanism?[37] We should reject the following in that view. (1) Universal human nature: the world is populated by distinct peoples that have different natures and interests. (2) "No borders": no one feels equally at home everywhere. Borders allow space where distinct peoples can fulfill their destinies. (3) Radical egalitarianism: people are not equal.[38] They have different capacities and they build different societies. What remains? (1) An egalitarianism of advocacy: all peoples have a right to advocate for their legitimate interests. (2) Common interests: everyone has an interest in certain things (e.g., preserving the integrity of the natural environment).

Westerners face a demographic plague that is reducing them to minorities in countries their ancestors founded and built. They have been led to think they are not a distinct people with collective interests having the same right as others to advocate for their legitimate interests. One of those interests is to remain majorities in their own countries. Europeans are not replaceable: no one else can carry their culture and institutions forward. Murray despairs: Europe is committing suicide and "neither Britain nor any other Western European country can avoid that fate because we all appear to suffer from the same symptoms and maladies."[39]

Murray notes an exception: *Eastern* Europe. Countries there have developed a *resistance* to plague. Murray thinks that part of the explanation is that Eastern Europeans have retained their tragic sense of life (a most unprogressive notion). Yet he fails to appreciate that citizens in plague-stricken countries everywhere are waking up from their nihilistic stupor. Many people have been taught by suffering—and their numbers are on the rise. The death of Europe is *not* inevitable.

MÉDECINS AVEC FRONTIÈRES?

Based on the message conveyed in *The Camp*, I hold that an ounce of prevention is worth a pound of cure. The most effective measure at the disposal of today's Dr. Rieuxs who wish to prevent demographic plague is *strong borders*. *Solidarity with one's own people* inoculates against moral plague. Fellow feeling protects against toxic rhetoric that poisons a people's self-confidence.

What is needed in this struggle, therefore, are doctors *with* borders. Doctors should remain free to cross borders and engage in humanitarian missions—but not to bring infected persons home. After all, one must have a healthy country before one can venture forth to help others. Flight attendants instruct passengers that, in the event of pressure loss, they should fix their own oxygen masks first. Likewise, doctors should address disease conditions at home. Sanitary measures should be taken against "sanctuary cities" that breed crime, filth, and disease, undermine the rule of law, and consign their citizens to exile.

Interestingly, Leftists believe that moral plague is an affliction of the *Right*. This is why they refuse to debate their opponents and instead seek to silence them. Greg Johnson writes that Leftists think those who advocate for whites do not present facts or arguments; they *spew*. And what they spew is *hate*. To stop the spread of this psychological virus, quarantine is necessary (i.e., censorship). Johnson turns the metaphor around:

> It is increasingly clear that the establishment does not have the capacity to refute the intellectual case of the rising tide of populist nationalism. . . . Academia is the establishment's intellectual immune system. Its function is to fend off the nationalist-populist virus, or the system will succumb. But the system has AIDS. Its immune system is gone. Hence the establishment retreat into the plastic bubble of censorship, brainwashing, paywalls, and general academic autism.[40]

Johnson has increased our stock of metaphors for intellectual insularity by adding "plastic bubble" to "ideological echo chamber," the latter made famous by James Damore, formerly of Google. Damore dared question egalitarian orthodoxy's assumption that the only explanation for unequal outcomes in the workplace was white male oppression and was fired as a result.[41]

WAYS FORWARD

The plague, once again, has roused up its rats and sent them forth to die in happy cities. This time, if they succeed, they will never have to be summoned again. There will *be* no more happy cities to infect. Although the plague can come from different directions, today it is borne on winds of the Left. Compare Raspail: "The Left is a conflagration. It devours and consumes in deadly dull earnest."[42] But wishing one's own people to survive does not make one "Right-wing," let alone, an "extremist."

Europeans, wherever they live, are undergoing dispossession and loss of homelands. As a consequence, oblivion looms on the horizon as surely as a million-person armada. Such a plight befalls no other peoples. No black, Hispanic, or Asian countries are admonished to practice diversity and become less of what they are. The direction of moral invective is *the same as* the flow of migration: from nonwhite to white countries.[43]

We should fight common threats to human welfare: that is the perspective of *The Plague*. Europeans must overcome taboos and insist on their own collective interests: that is the lesson of *The Camp*. On a recent trip to Europe, President Trump stated that European countries are losing their cultures because of mass immigration and they had better act soon. The goals of *The Plague* and *The Camp* can be realized by recognizing the right of all peoples to homelands.

Ways forward involve language, logic, and empathy. A good start to framing issues properly is to avoid emotive expressions. Then we can debate facts. Attorney General Jeff Sessions has instructed his staff to refrain from using the euphemism "undocumented workers" and instead use the accurate term, "illegal aliens." Leftists will howl, "No human being is illegal!" That is an uncharitable attribution: no one is saying that *human beings* are illegal. But entry without permission *is* illegal, whether it is entry into a woman's body or a nation. Likewise, because "diversity" means the reduction of whites, there is no reason for whites to *celebrate* it.

Sarah Jones writes: "Raspail's enemy is the entire non-white world."[44] Here is another egregious violation of the principle of charity. Raspail opposes the destruction of the white world. Love of one's own does not entail hatred of others. A 2017 eighteen-country Ipsos-Mori survey revealed crucial information about political differences.[45] Most liberals drew no distinction between racial self-interest and racism: wishing to limit immigration to protect the integrity of one's own group was for them racist. In contrast, majorities in all countries surveyed saw nothing racist in wanting to maintain their own demographic share. These attitudes reflected voting trends.

Empathy requires that we acknowledge others' points of view. To treat others as persons, we must take account of what philosopher Charles Taylor calls their "self-ascriptions."[46] Thus, we should refer to others as they self-identify instead of, for example, branding them "white supremacists." We should state others' positions in ways *they* would accept, without distortion. *Labeling* does not advance dialogue or refute arguments. A statement is true or false, an argument sound or unsound, independent of facts about the person who makes it. When someone presents an argument, they have met the burden of proof. If others disagree, it is incumbent on them to show why the argument is incorrect.

National policy must be built on a sound understanding of human nature, not wishful thinking. Humans are tribal: most prefer the company and culture of people like themselves.[47] Trying to force everyone into the Procrustean bed of equality is doomed to failure; one size does not fit all. A people cannot be replaced by others and its culture and institutions survive. The replaceability of peoples is a perverse notion: a symptom of moral plague.

Solidarity is a good thing. But universal brotherhood and multiculturalism are utopian delusions. Dystopias result from misconceived utopian schemes. Diverse New World is one such dystopia. Diversity is not a strength at all, let alone our greatest strength.[48] It is a source of tension and conflict. Throwing different peoples together without regard to civilizational differences is a prescription for disaster that no competent doctor would endorse. No one is satisfied; everyone lives in exile. Diversity has undermined trust.[49] Not all divisions can be overcome by peace, love, and understanding. Moreover, one *ought not* to make peace with the prospect of extinction.

Permitting all distinct peoples homelands allows for true diversity. Homelands promote the harmony and trust that make human flourishing possible. Thus, there is a place for solidarity, within limits prescribed by nature, culture, and common sense. Why should anyone think otherwise? In times of plague, the world needs more doctors and fewer priests. What is dystopic for the Left may, in the Age of Trump, signify a new Utopian vison.

NOTES

1. But *see* Anti-Trump Hate Map and Hate Hoax Map at American Renaissance at www.amren.com.
2. *Jaws*, directed by Stephen Spielberg (Hollywood, CA: Universal Pictures, 1975).
3. *High Noon*, directed by Fred Zinnemann (Hollywood, CA: United Artists, 1952).
4. *The Third Man*, directed by Carol Reed (London: London Film Productions, Ltd., 1948).
5. Albert Camus, *The Plague*, trans. Stuart Gilbert (New York: Alfred A. Knopf, 1948), 81.

6. Albert Camus, *The Stranger*, trans. Stuart Gilbert (New York: Alfred A. Knopf, 1946), 151.
7. Camus, *The Plague*, 137.
8. Camus, *The Plague*, 198.
9. Camus, *The Plague*, 269.
10. Albert Camus, *The Rebel*, trans. Anthony Bower (New York: Vintage Books, 1956), 22.
11. Camus, *The Plague*, 112.
12. Albert Camus, trans. Justin O'Brien, "The Artist at Work" in *Exile and the Kingdom* (New York: Alfred A. Knopf, 1958).
13. Camus, *The Plague*, Editor's Preface, v.
14. Camus, *The Plague*, Editor's Preface, vii.
15. Camus, *The Plague*, Introduction, x.
16. Jean Raspail, *The Camp of the Saints*, trans. Norman Shapiro (Petosky, MI: The Social Contract Press, 2018), 46.
17. See Edwin S. Rubenstein, *The Color of Crime: Race, Crime, and Justice in America* (Oakton, VA: New Century Foundation, 2016). Rev. ed. In black-on-white crimes, blacks were the perpetrators 85 percent of the time.
18. Homer, *The Iliad*, trans. Robert Eagle (New York: Penguin Books, 1990), Book 2: sec. 900.
19. Raspail, *The Camp of the Saints*, 72.
20. Raspail, *The Camp of the Saints*, 92.
21. Raspail, *The Camp of the Saints*, 75.
22. Raspail, *The Camp of the Saints*, 76.
23. Raspail, *The Camp of the Saints*, 131.
24. Douglas Murray, *The Strange Death of Europe: Immigration, Identity, Islam* (London: Bloomsbury Publishing, 2018), 160.
25. Raspail, *The Camp of the Saints*, 180.
26. Raspail, *The Camp of the Saints*, 11.
27. Raspail, *The Camp of the Saints*, 11–12.
28. Raspail, *The Camp of the Saints*, 280.
29. Murray, *Strange Death*, 2.
30. See J. Phillippe Rushton, "Genetic Similarity Theory, Ethnocentrism, and Group Selection" in *Indoctrinability, Warfare, and Ideology: Evolutionary Perspectives*, eds. I. Eibl-Eibesfeldt and F. K. Salter (Oxford: Berghahn Books, 1998), 369–88.
31. Raspail, *The Camp of the Saints*, 7.
32. *The Battle of Algiers*, directed by Gillo Pontecorvo (Italy: Stella Productions; production, Igor Film, 1966).
33. Raspail, *The Camp of the Saints*, 7.
34. Raspail, *The Camp of the Saints*, 86.
35. Raspail, *The Camp of the Saints*, 7.
36. Murray, *Strange Death*, 2.
37. For a critique of cosmopolitanism, see Greg Johnson, "What's Wrong with Cosmopolitanism?" in his book, *In Defense of Prejudice* (San Francisco: Counter-Currents Publishing Ltd., 2017), 143–53.
38. For a thorough review and interpretation of the scientific literature on racial differences, see Michael E. Levin, *Why Race Matters: Race Differences and What They Mean* (Westport, CT: Praeger, 1997).
39. Murray, *Strange Death*, 1.
40. Greg Johnson, "Bubble Boys." Accessed www.counter-currents.com on July 29, 2018.
41. James Damore, "Google's Ideological Echo Chamber: How Bias Clouds Our Thinking about Diversity and Inclusion." Accessed https://assets.documentcloud.org/documents/3914586/Googles-Ideological-Echo-Chamber.pdf on August 7, 2017. See also "GOOGLE Memo: Four Scientists Respond." Accessed http://quillette.com/2017/08/07google-memo-four-scientists-respond/ on August 7, 2017. The Damore incident gave rise to the "GOOLAG" meme.
42. Raspail, *The Camp of the Saints*, 215.

43. See Jared Taylor's interview with Jorge Ramos, YouTube. Accessed https://www.youtube.com/watch?v=2f8q71hzd_Q on August 22, 2018.

44. Sarah Jones, "The Notorious Book that Ties the Right to the Far Right." Accessed https://newrepublic.com/article/146925/notorious-book-ties-right-far-right on February 6, 2018,

45. Eric Kaufmann, "Is Tribalism Racist? Antiracism Norms and Immigration." Accessed http://blogs.lse.ac.uk/politicsandpolicy/antiracism-norms-and-immigration on January 23, 2018.

46. See my discussion of Taylor in "Social Science and the *Verstehen* Thesis" in *From Kant to Weber: Freedom and Culture in Classical German Social Thought*, eds. Thomas M. Powers and Paul Kamolnick (Melbourne, FL: Krieger Press, 1999), 113–16.

47. See Jared Taylor, *White Identity: Racial Consciousness in the 21st Century* (Oakton, VA: New Century Books, 2010). People overwhelmingly opt for the company of their own race whenever possible, as evidenced, for example, by church congregations and housing patterns. Forced diversity causes conflict in the workplace, schools, neighborhoods, and prisons.

48. See Barbara Oakley, *Pathological Altruism* (Oxford: Oxford University Press, 2012). See also Jared Taylor's application of the central concept to racial issues in his "Pathological Altruism," in *If We Do Nothing: Essays and Reviews from 25 Years of White Advocacy* (Oakton, VA: New Century Foundation, 2017), 49–58.

49. Robert Putnam, "*E Pluribus Unum*: Diversity and Community in the Twenty-first Century: The 2006 Johan Skytte Prize Lecture," *Scandinavian Political Studies* 30 (2007), 134–74, cited in Jared Taylor, "Diversity Destroys Trust," in *If We Do Nothing*: *Essays and Reviews from 25 Years of White Advocacy* (Oakton, VA: New Century Books, 2017), 43–48.

Selected Bibliography

Arendt, Hannah. *The Origins of Totalitarianism*. Cleveland: Meridian Books, (1952) 1962.

Atwood, Margaret. *Dire Cartographies: The Roads to Ustopia and the Handmaid's Tale.* New York: Anchor/Penguin Random House, 2015.

———. *The Handmaid's Tale*. Toronto: McClelland & Stewart, 1986.

Baccolini, Raffaella, and Tom Moylan. *Dark Horizons: Science Fiction and the Dystopian Imagination*. New York: Routledge, 2003.

Beaudrillard, Jean. *Selected Writings*, edited by Mark Poster. Stanford, CA: Stanford University Press, 1988.

Burdekin, Katherine. *Swastika Night.* New York: The Feminist Press, 1985.

Camus, Albert. *The Plague*. Translated by Stuart Gilbert. New York: Alfred A. Knopf, 1948.

Claeys, Gregorye, ed. *The Cambridge Companion to Utopian Literature.* Cambridge: Cambridge University Press, 2010.

Coogan, Peter. *Superhero: The Secret Origin of a Genre*. Austin, TX: MonkeyBrain Books, 2006.

Daly, Herman E., and John B. Cobb, Jr.. *For the Common Good: Redirecting the Economy Toward Community, the Environment and a Sustainable Future*. Boston: Beacon Press, 1989.

Edel, Leon. *The Treacherous Years.* Philadelphia: J. B. Lippincott Co., 1969.

Ellis, Bret Easton. *American Psycho.* New York: Picador, 1991.

Fawaz, Ramzi. *The New Mutants: Superheroes and the Radical Imagination of American Comics*. New York: New York University Press, 2016.

Ferreira, Rachel Haywood. *The Emergence of Latin American Science Fiction.* Middletown, CT: Wesleyan University Press, 2011.

Foucault, Michel. *Discipline and Punish: The Birth of the Prison*. New York: Vintage Books, (1975) 1995.

Giroux, Henry. *The Public in Peril: Trump and the Menace of American Authoritarianism*. New York: Routledge, 2017.

Gordin, Michael D., Helen Tilley, and Gyan Prakash. Introduction to *Utopia/Dystopia: Conditions of Historical Possibility.* Princeton, NJ: Princeton University Press, 2010.

Housel, Rebecca, and J. Jeremy Wisnewski, eds. *X-Men and Philosophy: Astonishing Insight and Uncanny Argument in the Mutant X-verse.* Hoboken, NJ: John Wiley & Sons, Inc., 2009.

Huxley, Aldous. *Brave New World*. New York: Harper & Brothers, 1932.

James, Edward, and Farah Mendlesohn, eds. *The Cambridge Companion to Science Fiction.* Cambridge, UK: Cambridge University Press, 2003.

Jameson, Frederic. *Archaeologies of the Future*. London: Verso, 2005.

Jenkins, Henry. *Fans, Bloggers, and Gamers: Exploring Participatory Culture.* New York: New York University Press, 2006.

Kavadlo, Jesse. *American Popular Culture in the Era of Terror: Falling Skies, Dark Knights Rising, and Collapsing Cultures*. Santa Barbara, CA: Praeger, 2015.

Ketterer, David. *New Worlds for Old: The Apocalyptic Imagination, Science Fiction, and American Literature.* Bloomington: Indiana University Press, 1974.

Le Guin, Ursula. *The Dispossessed: An Ambiguous Utopia.* New York: Harper and Row, 1974.

———. *No Time to Spare: Thinking About What Matters*. New York: Houghton, Mifflin, Harcourt, 2017

L'Engle, Madeleine. *A Wrinkle in Time*. New York: Square Fish, 2007.

McCarthy, Cormac. *The Road*. London: Picador, 2007.

Meachem, John. *The Soul of America: The Battle for Our Better Angels*. New York: Random House, 2018.

Meehan, Paul. *Tech Noir: The Fusion of Science Fiction and Film Noir.* Jefferson, NC: McFarland, 2008.

Mohr, Dunja M. *Worlds Apart? Dualism and Transgression in Contemporary Female Dystopias.* Jefferson, NC: McFarland and Company, 2005.

Murray, Douglas. *The Strange Death of Europe: Immigration, Identity, Islam.* London: Bloomsbury Publishing, 2018.

Orwell, George. *Nineteen Eighty-Four: A novel* (*1984*). New York: Harcourt, Brace & Co, 1949.

Otto, Eric C. *Green Speculations: Science Fiction and Transformative Environmentalism*, Columbus: Ohio State University Press, 2012.

Raspail, Jean. *The Camp of the Saints.* Translated by Norman Shapiro. Petosky, MI: The Social Contract Press, 2018.

Shapiro, Jerome F. *Atomic Bomb Cinema: The Apocalyptic Imagination on Film*. London: Routledge, 2002.

Sharp, Patrick. *Savage Perils: Racial Frontiers and Nuclear Apocalypse in American Culture.* Norman: University of Oklahoma Press, 2007.

Vonnegut, Kurt. *Player Piano*. New York: Charles Scribern's Sons, 1952.

Weiner, Mark S. *The Rule of the Clan: What an Ancient Form of Social Organization Reveals about The Future of Individual Freedom.* New York: Farrar, Strauss, and Giroux, 2013.

Wolff, Michael. *Fire and Fury*. New York: Henry Holt, 2018.

Woodward, Bob. *Fear: Trump in the White House*. New York: Simon & Schuster, 2018.

Index

About the Contributors

Daniel M. R. Abitz is the associate director of the South Atlantic Modern Language Association as well as a PhD candidate at Georgia State University in Atlanta. His current project focuses on women's utopian novels from the nineteenth and early twentieth centuries and that body of literature's various approaches to gender, sexuality, race, and colonialism. His scholarly work appears in *Women's Studies: An Interdisciplinary Journal*, *Henry James Review*, and *Victorians: A Journal of Literature and Culture*, and his poetry can be found in *Literary Laundry*. He lives with a brilliant Derridean, a precocious kitten, and a dangerously silly beagle.

Daniel Adleman is an assistant professor of Writing and Rhetoric at the University of Toronto, where he teaches Digital Rhetoric and Writing for Social Change. He holds a PhD in English Language and Literature from the University of British Columbia. From 2012 to 2017, he was the codirector of the Vancouver Institute for Social Research (VISR), a critical theory free school project held at Vancouver's Or Gallery. His most recent work explores an array of encounters between new-rhetorical thought and media ecology in contemporary dystopian fiction. Adleman lives in Toronto's Little Portugal neighborhood with a photographer, a drummer, and two cats.

Jeffrey Barber, president of Integrative Strategies Forum, has engaged in public-interest advocacy and organizing efforts, locally, nationally, and internationally, focusing especially on the importance of strategic collaboration among environmentalists, consumer, health, and social justice advocates, trade unions, and other members of civil society. He is cofounder of the Global Research Forum on Sustainable Production and Consumption and has worked over the years with a range of research, education, and advocacy networks promoting public participation and engagement in sustainability policy making at the United Nations and other international processes. His research background is in media and audience research.

Elisabetta Di Minico works on fictional dystopias and on historical dystopian aspects of sociopolitical and cultural control, focusing her studies on violence, power, and embodiment. She provocatively uses science fiction novels, comics, graphic novels, and films to unveil the dystopian realities of our world. She has a BA (Italian Laurea Triennale) in Literature and an MA (Italian Laurea Specialistica) in Contemporary History from University of Rome "Sapienza." She obtained her PhD (Cum Laude) in History at the University of Barcelona and is currently part of the Project HISTOPIA at the Autonomous University of Madrid.

Ryan Farrar is an adjunct professor of Literature at Nova Southeastern University. He has worked across the southern United States, teaching in Texas, Louisiana, Arizona, and Florida, and he also serves as an assistant editor at CRC Press, a division of Taylor & Francis Group. He earned a PhD in English literature in 2014 from the University of Louisiana at Lafayette, and his work has appeared in *The Journal of Utopian Studies*.

Christine Jackson, PhD, is a professor at Nova Southeastern University in Fort Lauderdale, Florida, where she teaches detective and science fiction. She has published numerous critical essays on popular culture, including a contribution to the previous volume in this series, *Apocalyptic Chic*. Dr. Jackson's most recent book is *The Tell-Tale Art: Poe in Modern Popular Culture* (2012).

Sue Matheson is an associate professor of English at the University College of the North in Manitoba, Canada. She specializes in writing about American popular culture and film. Her articles have appeared in numerous periodicals, including *The Journal of Popular Film and Television* and *The Journal of Popular Culture*. She is the editor of four collections of essays and the author of *The Westerns and War Films of John Ford* (2016).

David L. McNaron is professor emeritus at Nova Southeastern University in Fort Lauderdale, Florida, where he taught philosophy for thirty-three years. He was educated at the University of Alabama at Birmingham and received a PhD from the University of Miami. He received an MFA in Writing from Vermont College of Fine Arts. McNaron's philosophy publications are in the areas of philosophy of science, ethics, and philosophy and popular culture. He has also published a number of poems in literary magazines.

Kibiriti Majuto is an undergraduate in sociology at Piedmont Virginia Community College. He has innumerable interests in the field, including race and ethnicity, social movements, and class and inequality. He is a first-generation college student from the Democratic Republic of the Congo and plans to attain a PhD.

Emily A. O'Dell is a PhD candidate and teaching assistant in the Comparative Literature program at Louisiana State University in Baton Rouge, Louisiana. Her research interests include children's and young adult literature, literature of the Caribbean, folklore, cultural studies, festival studies, postcolonial studies, world literature, and digital humanities.

Todd K. Platts is associate professor of sociology at Piedmont Virginia Community College. He has published numerous journal articles and book chapters on horror and zombie cinema. His recent publications include: "Scary Business: Horror at the North American Box Office, 2006–2016" (with Mathias Clasen), "A Comparative Analysis of the Factors Driving Film Cycles: Italian and American Zombie Film Production, 1978–82," and "From White Zombies to Night Zombies and Beyond: The Evolution of the Zombie in Western Popular Culture." He has numerous projects in development, including a coedited volume on Blumhouse Productions with Mathias Clasen and Victoria McCollum.

Matthew Paproth is an associate professor of English at Georgia Gwinnett College. He received his PhD from Southern Illinois University–Carbondale in contemporary British and Irish literature; he currently studies modernist and postmodernist literature, as well as digital media. He has published essays on Samuel Beckett, Zadie Smith, *Veronica Mar*s, and *Friday Night Lights*.

Raúl Rodríguez-Hernández teaches Latin American literature and film, comparative literature, and cinema studies at the University of Rochester, New York. His publications focus on European intellectual influences on Mexican thought, the ambiguities of modernity, films of the Mexican Golden Age and New Wave, Frankenstein and the legacy of the Gothic, the Frankfurt School, and Critical Theory's impact in the Americas. He co-authored with Claudia Schaefer *The Supernatural Sublime* (2019).

Claudia Schaefer, Rush Rhees Chair, teaches Hispanic literatures, film, and comparative literature at the University of Rochester, New York. She has published numerous articles and six books on literature, the visual arts, Gothic films, and gender studies. Her seventh book, *The Supernatural Sublime* (2019), on supernatural films in Spain and Spanish America is co-authored with Raúl Rodríguez-Hernández. She is currently working on the cultural impact of Walter Benjamin's travels to Spain.

Tom Shapira is a PhD candidate at the Tel-Aviv University School of Cultural Studies. He is the author of *Curing the Postmodern Blues: Reading Grant Morrison and Chris Weston's The Filth in the 21st Century* (2013). He writes about comics for such sites as Sequart.org, Alilon.net, and Multiversity.com.

Kate Waites, PhD, is a professor at Nova Southeastern University, where she teaches courses in literature, women's and gender studies, and film studies. Her scholarly work focuses on the representation of gender in popular culture and in the visual media, and it has appeared in a variety of scholarly journals as well as edited texts. Most recently, "Hollywood's Warrior Woman for the New Millennium" appeared in *Bad Girls and Transgressive Women in Popular Television, Fiction, and Film*.

About the Editors

Barbara Brodman is professor emerita in the Department of History and Political Science at Nova Southeastern University, where she taught courses in history, economic development, global issues, and literature. She holds graduate degrees in Hispanic languages and literature, Latin American Studies, and International Business; she has been awarded an honorary doctoral degree, two Fulbright awards, and she has published a variety of scholarly works that deal with global cultures and affairs, including *The Mexican Cult of Death in Myth, Art and Literature*, *Looking for Mr. Guevara: A Journey through South America*, and *Around the World in 70 Days . . . at 70*. She presently devotes her time to writing projects and to managing the nongovernmental organization she founded in 1997 and the Amazon research center it protects and supports.

James E. Doan is a professor in the Department of Literature and Modern Languages at Nova Southeastern University (NSU), where he teach courses in literature, the arts, folklore, mythology, and world religions. He holds degrees in Literature, Folklore and Mythology, and Celtic Studies and has published numerous works dealing with Irish and other Celtic myth, folklore, literature, and history. He has taught a course at NSU on the vampire in myth, literature, art, and film for almost thirty years and authored the play, *The Irish Dracula: A Melodrama in Five Acts*, performed by the Irish Theatre of Florida and at the International Acting Irish Theatre Festival in 2014 and published in *Images of the Modern Vampire*. He and colleague Barbara Brodman coedited *The Universal Vampire: Origins and Evolution of a Legend* and *Images of the Modern Vampire: The Hip and the Atavistic*, both published in 2013, *The Supernatural Revamped: From Timeworn Legends to Twenty-First-Century Chic* (2016), and *Apocalyptic Chic: Visions of the Apocalypse and Post-Apocalypse in Literature and Visual Arts* (2017).